THEY REMAINED UNKNOWN

THEY REMAINED UNKNOWN

By

SAVITRY DUBEY

Translated by

Rajeev Dubey

YATRA BOOKS

An imprint of Vani Prakashan Group

Hardback First Edition : 2023

vaniprakashan.com

Yatra Books is an imprint of Vani Prakashan Group

Head Office

4695, 21-A, Daryaganj, New Delhi-110 002, India
Phone : +91 11 23273167, 23275710

Registered Bookstores and Offices

Ashok Rajpath, Patna-800 004, Bihar
Coffee House Campus, Mahatma Gandhi Marg, Allahabad-211 001, Uttar Pradesh
Mahatma Gandhi International Hindi University, Wardha-442 001, Maharashtra
36-A, Shakespeare Sarani, Near Rani Birla Girls College, Kolkata-700017, West Bengal

sales@vaniprakashan.in
vaniprakashan@gmail.com

They Remained Unknown
by **Savitry Dubey**
Translated **by Rajeev Dubey**

ISBN : 978-93-5775-271-8
History/Autobiography

Price : ₹ 850

Printed and bound in India at Thomson Press (India) Ltd.

Preface

It was Mahatma Gandhi who said that India's soul resides in her villages, and it is the villagers who nurture and nourish Mother India.

If the Mahatma had not awakened India's soul by reaching out to her villages, the nation's life-force would have remained inert and lifeless, and freedom would have remained a mirage, a destination never reached.

This is the story of one such rural family caught up in the social and political upheaval of the freedom struggle in the Mithilanchal area of Bihar, as seen through the eyes of the now eighty-six year old Kaushalya Devi.

No political movement can succeed without a visionary leader who inspires the masses and leads them into action, a leader who knows and understands his followers, gives voice to their aspirations and leads from the front even in the most difficult and trying of circumstances. While Gandhi and Nehru provided such leadership at the national level, regional and local leaders were required. The late Pandit Suresh Chandra Mishra was one such leader who worked tirelessly and ceaselessly from 1920 to 1942 in his constituency, the district of Munger. A staunch Congressman, he was as committed to the party principles and ideals as he was wedded to the iron discipline of ashram-life.

In his days, his influence was so powerful that thousands of youth would respond to his call and come forward to join him in anti-government activities that would inevitably land them in jail.

Many political observers have commented that in Bihar, the district of Munger contributed the largest number of volunteers for both the non-cooperation movement and the salt satyagraha. No matter what the revolutionary activity, large numbers of youth stood by his side ready to suffer any punishment meted out by the British administration. His favourite song* was

The desire to sacrifice our lives
Now occupies our heart.
Let us see how much strength
The hands of the killer have.*

Suresh Chandra Mishra was my uncle, and in 1975 I asked him if he would be willing to share his reminiscences with me for a book I was planning to write about his life. He was silent, and said neither yes nor no -- it seemed as if he was suddenly lost deep in thoughts and memories of times and events long gone by.Meanwhile my three sons --his grandnephews Pradeep, Rajeev and Ravi – appeared there with a taperecorder and mike. After being lost in reverie for some time, he looked up at the four of us and burst out laughing, one uproarious laugh after another.

When his laughter subsided, he said, "Where should I start? I suggest at the very beginning, with my birth on the 1st of April 1901 -- which I guess makes me a permanent April Fool!!

I will share one more dark and hidden secret.There was a raging smallpox epidemic at the time of my birth, and in those days it was widely believed that drinking donkey's milk gave you immunity from

---

*Sarfaroshi ki tamanna,
Ab hamare dil mein hai,
Dekhna hai zor kitna,
Bazu-e-katil mein hai...

small pox . So my mother fed me donkey's milk, and that is how a donkey was born and grew inside me and from time to time raises its head and makes its presence felt!"

Saying this, he again burst into laughter and added, "So, my dear grandchildren, your Nana (maternal grandfather) remained a stupid and obstinate donkey all his life!"

And then he narrated the "stupidities' of his life, which in fact were the selfless actions of a simple and sincere human being. On my pointing out that these were admirable acts of a person who thought not about himself but about the welfare of others, his answer was prompt: "In today's context, my actions can only be termed foolishness of the highest order. Let me share with you a recent experience. I came to Delhi and went to meet a senior Cabinet Minister who I know well. After the initial pleasantries, this eminent personality tells me, 'Why did you help so-and-so despite my telling you not to?' I got up immediately. 'I carried Gandhiji's bag for him, but that does not mean I will carry yours too'. Saying this, I walked out of his room."

The grandchildren clapped in applause "Well done, Barka Nana: you are truly great!"

With much reluctance, and on my persistent prodding, over the next few days he shared only those parts of his life that were connected with the freedom struggle. These recollections had great clarity and detail, and shed light on many major events of that epochal period. But each time I suggested that I was ready to start writing, he would say, "Do it later".

Perhaps he was hinting that I should write only after his death, and reluctantly I shelved my project. Many years later, after he and his younger brother had both passed away, the question of writing a book on that period came up again. The only living family member from that generation, who had lived through the seminal events of that era and was witness to them, was my mother Kaushalya Devi. It was after a friend remarked that she was a living and talking history book, that the thought of writing about it took birth once again in my mind. But the real credit for getting me started must go to my erudite sister-in-law Kalpana Dasgupta, who told me, "Sabo di, you must write your mother's memoirs".

Getting started is difficult, but once started the momentum gathers pace and becomes self-sustaining. So it was with my book.

Memories and recollections of my grandparents Anoop Devi and Mohit Mishra, have always fascinated and mesmerized me. Nani (maternal grandmother) died young, but Nana lived to see three generations of his family. He was a great story-teller and I used to listen spell-bound to his stories from the Ramayana, Mahabharata and the Panchatantra. Equally fascinating were his tales of events from his own exciting and colourful life, including the 'Sati Mai' incident that was to change his life forever. Not surprisingly, my book starts with that incident.

The framework of my narrative grew out of the recollections of my two uncles Suresh Chandra and Shiva Kant, while the intricate colours in that framework came from my mother. Much like the legendary Ved Vyasa of Mahabharat fame, Ma (mother) controlled the narrative of this book with her rendering of the story of her slife. My younger sister Nalini sat with me through the large number of sessions with Ma, which often saw her become excited and animated as emotions came flooding through the windows of her mind. I often had to ask her to stop because I could not keep pace with her speed of talking. It was as if a dam had burst and hidden memories came pouring out, overwhelming her with all kinds of emotions.

Both of us sisters felt that we would use Ma's everyday colloquial Bihari Hindi in the text, as that would sound more natural. But, as we listened in dumbfounded amazement, instead of her normal everyday language Ma would switch to chaste Hindi as soon as she started talking -- it was as if her personality would transform during those sessions!! All efforts to persuade her to talk in her normal dialect failed!!!

She would insist that we read back what we had written in each session, and would correct the smallest deviations from what she wanted to convey, often spending hours on a particular sentence or phrase.

While I did consult some books to double-check dates and places of events referred to, the book is based purely on what family members saw, heard and experienced.

I am very grateful to the renowned historian Dr. Bimala Prasad for taking time out from his busy schedule to read and give suggestions on the text.

Savitry Dubey
August, 2022

Contents

Chapter 1

THE CLAN TRADITION

Village Shirnia on the banks of the mighty Ganga River in the Munger District of Bihar circa 1880, a village inhabited primarily by Maithil Brahmins. A village famous for being located right opposite the site of the ancient Jahnu Ashram, home of Rishi Jahnu who had stopped the flow of the rampaging Ganga by drinking up all its water.

Legend has it that in a fit of uncontrollable rage, Kapil Muni had burnt to ashes the sixty thousand sons of Raja Sagar, and the *shraddha* ceremony could not be performed for these unfortunate souls. But when Kapil Muni learnt that these were the sons of the pious and virtuous (*dharmatma*) King Sagar, he was full of remorse and declared that if the river Ganga descended from the heavens on this spot, the dead sons of the good king would attain salvation. King Sagar's descendant, King Bhagirath managed to get Ganga to descend from the heavens by dint of long and severe penance and prayer. The swift-flowing waters of the Ganga submerged the Ashram and destroyed everything in it. It was then that the angry Jahnu drank up all the waters of the river.

On King Bhagirath praying and explaining the circumstances, Jahnu relented and released the waters of the Ganga through his thighs, and the mighty river started flowing again. That is why Ganga is also called Jahnvi.

The Maithil Brahmins used to speculate that they were descendants of the disciples of Jahnu Rishi, and despite Shirnia being devastated every year by floods, used to return to the site once the waters had receded. They believed that the rich silt deposited by the flood waters was a boon to them from the River Goddess, for it would beget gold from the bountiful harvest that was bound to follow. The Maithil Brahmins were very proud of their ancient lineage and traditions.

It was a young man from this village who fell ill, and his fever refused to subside. There were no roads connecting this village to the nearby towns, and no doctor could be found who would agree to come to this remote and isolated village. The family turned to the local medicine man, the vaid, who tried all his cures but the burning fever persisted, and in a few days the young man died.

His young newly-married wife, who had tended to him day and night, went into a state of deep despair and despondency. She had seen the pitiable condition of the village widows, and knew that would be her lot too. She cried and prayed that God may lift her up, what sins had she committed that she should suffer the living death of a widow in that lonely and isolated hamlet by the River Ganga? The village women cried with her to show their solidarity and support, but in their heart of hearts they were sure she would soon accept the situation and would calm down.

She did calm down, but with it emerged a steely resolve to obey an inner voice that told her that she should follow her husband from this mortal life by committing Sati. Her crying stopped, her inner turbulence gave way to a strange energy which radiated strongly from every pore of her being. She called the males of the family and declared her intention of becoming a Sati Mai by immolating herself on her husband's funeral pyre.

This sensational news spread like wildfire throughout the village. People starting talking of how her face was glowing like that of a Goddess, and crowds thronged from the nearby villages to get a glimpse of the heavenly Sati Mai.

The village elders discussed the matter among themselves and came to the conclusion that she could not possibly mean what she said. They were sure she had made this proclamation in the throes of her grief, but would change her mind once she had calmed down from this heightened state of emotion.

But to their surprise the young woman kept insisting that she really wanted to commit Sati. So they decided to test the strength of her intention. The men went to the room where the woman sat by the side of her husband's corpse, and said it was time to take the dead body for cremation. She said she would accompany the corpse, for she wanted to burn along with her dead husband. They tried to dissuade her, explained the enormity of the situation, the horrors of being burnt alive.

But to no avail. She just said, "I know all this, but my mind is made up."

So then they said she would have to prove her intention by going through a test.

"I am ready", she said. "Tell me what I have to do to prove my intention?"

The elders got her a ghee-fed flame and asked her to burn a finger in that flame, which she did, sitting next to her husband's corpse without any outward show of pain. At this, the onlooking spectators burst into cries of "Sati Mai ki jai (Victory be to Sati Mai)". The whole village resounded with cries of "Jai! Jai!", and people readied themselves for the amazing spectacle that was to follow. The corpse was readied for the funeral by ceremonially bathing it, and the young widow was adorned in her bridal finery--yellow sari, bangles, necklace and other intricate jewels and finally *sindoor* (vermilion) in the parting of her hair, a total of sixteen adornments prepared meticulously by the women of the household. Then grains of rice, *doob* grass, areca nut and coins were put in her lap, after which she sat on the funeral bier with her dead husband's head in her lap. The bier was lifted amidst cries of "Sati Mai ki Jai", and the funeral procession made its way on foot to the burning ghat on the banks of the river to the beating of drums and the playing of pipes. The entire male population of the village joined in, the elders carrying the wood, ghee and *chandan* wood for the cremation, with the children in tow. All along the way, Sati Mai kept throwing coins and rice grains to the accompanying folk, who eagerly kept them as a blessing from the goddess Sati Mai whose incarnation they were fortunate enough to see in their own village.

The funeral pyre was readied and to the accompaniment of the drums and pipes, the young widow sat on it with her husband's head in her lap. But when the pyre was lit, the young woman panicked and tried to get up and jump out of the flames that were now engulfing the pyre. The surrounding elders pushed her back into the flames with bamboo sticks and staffs, her hideous shrieks of pain drowned out by the deafening noise of the drums, pipes and cries of "Sati Mai ki Jai". Within moments the intense flames consumed everything in the funeral pyre, signalling another glorious event in the annals of village history and tradition. The family was blessed, the fame and glory of Sati Mai would spread to all the surrounding areas and people would remember the events for ages to come.

This entire spectacle was witnessed by an eleven-year old boy, who was watching the unfolding of the gory events with shock and horror. This boy was my father Mohit Mishra, who was distantly related to the young widow. He had witnessed the attempts made by the young woman to flee from the flames that were engulfing her, heard her shrieks of pain, seen the horror in her eyes and how the spectators forced her back to her fiery death. This gruesome sight left an enduring wound on his psyche and its memories would haunt and torture him for a long, long time.

He was just an eleven year old boy and while he could do nothing immediately, he was possessed by a burning desire to do something which would prevent the recurrence of such an incident. After completing his Middle School studies locally, he went to the town of Munger with his cousins Pyarelal, Tejnath and Kesho Mishra for further studies. He completed his Intermediate course, but could not take the exam. Pyarelal became a lawyer and Tejnath a Court Clerk. Mohit could have opted for many professions, but he had other plans.

Kali Puja had great significance for Shirnia. Influenced by the traditions of neighbouring Bengal, Diwali was celebrated here as Kali Puja. Idols of Kali would be made in the village, the priests would perform the rituals, prayers would be offered to the Goddess, goats would be sacrificed in her honour and the meat distributed to each household as "prasad". The meat would then be cooked with great reverence before being consumed in a household feast. Earthenware lamps would be lit and then the males would take part in the time-honored game of "hukka pati", where a log fire would be ceremoniously lit and the participants would leap over the flames one by one shouting "Sati Mai ki Jai"as they did so.

Mohit Mishra stood to one side, quietly observing the festivities.

He was now twenty years old, married to the sixteen year old Anoop Devi of Sahoda village. Anoop Devi was a short and petite beauty, with fair complexion, sharp chiselled nose and long hair falling in dense tresses down to her knees. Mohit was tall and good-looking, with a wheatish complexion. His years as a student in Munger had enhanced his self-confidence, and he stood apart from the other village youth. The worship and praise of Sati Mai evoked anger and rebellion in him, in sharp contrast to the reverence and devotion shown to the Goddess by the others, who considered her blessings necessary for success in any venture, be it an exam or a court case.

This belief in Sati Mai had been passed on from one generation to the next, and was rooted in local folk-lore. Shirnia was an important place for Maithil Brahmins, and the reason was its location on the ancient and important pilgrimage route from Darbhanga to Deoghar. A short distance to the east of Shirnia on this route was Aguanighat on the banks of the Ganga, where devotees would take the boat to the Ajgaibee Temple. This was a Shiva temple on a hilltop in an island located in the middle of the river, and the locals addressed Shiva as "Ajgaibinath". Devotees would offer holy Ganga water at the shrine and cross over to Sultanganj, from where they would proceed on foot to Baidyanath Dham, carrying with them water from the Ganga. Thousands undertook this pilgrimage on foot twice every year, carrying colourful 'kavars' with them and chanting "Bhole Bam, Bhole Bam...' as they walked to the Baidyanath Dham temple in Deoghar. The villagers of Shirnia would join the pilgrims as the latter wound past the village. This also meant that the villagers got all the news from Darbhanga to Deoghar, and all the happenings of Shirnia would travel to the Maithil Brahmins on this route, often with a lot of spice added!

All this did not attract or interest Mohit Mishra. He was being inexorably drawn to some other path less trodden, away from the blind superstition and external trappings of the ritual-dominated society he lived in. Without being able to articulate it so, he was being drawn to Shiva not through idol-worship and blind rituals, but something more raw and elemental -- Shiva as Truth and Cosmic Energy, forces which benefit the common man.

Swami Dayanand Saraswati was born in the tiny hamlet of Tankara in Gujarat. His given name was Moolshankar, and his father Krishnaji Lalji Tiwary was a conservative, traditional and orthodox Brahmin. Given to study and reflection from early childhood, by the age of fourteen Moolshankar had memorized the entire Yajur Veda and had studied many other religious scriptures.

In keeping with the time-honoured tradition, the entire family would fast on Shivratri, and stay up all night to worship the Shiva Linga. It was during one such all-night vigil, when everything was quiet, that Moolshankar saw a rat climb atop the Shiv Linga and fearlessly eat the food that had been offered to the Lord Shiva.

This was a moment of epiphany for the young man. If the Linga cannot protect even itself from a rat, he wondered, how will it protect me, leave alone the world?

After this incident, he intensified his study of the Vedas. Sometime later, he left home because his parents wanted him to get married. After visiting many religious sites and interacting with numerous religious scholars, he reached Mathura where he embraced Swami Virjanand as his guru, and took Sanyas. From that time onwards he was known as Swami Dayanand Saraswati.

Swami Dayanand Saraswati is acknowledged as one of the leading lights of the Indian Social Reform movement, and as one of the architects of modern Indian society. He considered the Vedas to be the root-source of all knowledge and wisdom, and laid great emphasis on the study of these ancient scriptures. He stressed that there was a Supreme Force that was the Creator of the Cosmos and which governed whatever happened in the Universe, and we should worship this Supreme Force. This Supreme Force does not take physical form in this world as an Avatar and we should not worship it in the form of idols.

By tirelessly traversing the length and breadth of the country, Swami ji waged a relentless war against blind superstition, idol worship, the caste system, child marriage, the purdah system and the practice of sati. He campaigned for educating all children, especially the girl child and was a strong supporter of widow remarriage. To articulate his thoughts clearly and codify them so that they could be disseminated easily, he wrote a book called "Satyarth Prakash".

A landmark event was the establishment of the Arya Samaj in Lahore and the subsequent expansion of its branches across India. Co-educational gurukuls were opened in many places, where in addition to Vedic education, social skills were also imparted. The Arya Samaj played a leading role in the fight against superstition, lack of education and the evils of the caste system.

Swami Dayanand was a nationalist social reformer, and was the one who coined the term 'Swaraj' (self-rule) and brought it to national consciousness. He wrote against the imposition of tax on salt and against the impostion of English as a medium of instruction. It is no wonder that the Arya Samaj movement gave the nation two outstanding nationalists, Lala Lajpat Rai and Swami Shradhanand.

His magnum opus *Sanskar Vidhi* documented Vedic practices and principles from birth to death.

Swami ji came to Bihar in 1872 and reached Munger via Patna and Bhagalpur, and stayed there for 15 days giving lectures and organizing get-togethers. It was in Munger that as a student Mohit Mishra first met adherents of the Arya Samaj and started taking part in their activities. In 1913-14 he became a firm and committed member of the Arya Samaj. Every Sunday he would go to the Arya Samaj temple and participate in the *havan* and subsequent discussions. He would then do his chores as a full-time preacher of the Samaj.

In the Samaj and its teachings, Mohit found resolution and closure of the restlessness, doubts and worries that had assailed him from an early age, and discovered direction and purpose in his life. He gave up stitched clothes and shoes, wearing only dhotis and a simple sheet to cover the upper part of his body. In winter he would keep himself warm with a rough woollen shawl called "*loee*".

Mohit's preaching strongly opposed entrenched orthodoxy in religious and social practices, raising the banner of revolt against them. Arya Samaj branches were established in Khagaria and Jamalpur, though they were small establishments. Vedic fire rituals and discussions were regular features.

In Bihar the early adherents of the Arya Samaj were largely from the *baniya, sonar, teli* and related castes. They were economically well-off but had low social status, and many were not allowed to drink water from the same source as the higher castes. The Brahmins used to laugh at them when they talked of the anti-caste ideals and logic of the Samaj, but when a Brahmin like Mohit Mishra talked, his words carried weight. Calling himself a Dayanandi or a Vedic pundit, he showed how the Vedas never advocated caste divisions, idol worship, child marriage or the untouchability of food and water handled by the lower castes -- these were inventions of the post-Vedic era.

This caused immense consternation and outrage in the Maithil Brahmin community of Shirnia. The news spread like wildfire from Darbhanga to Deoghar. The ancient scriptures were consulted, but they could not better Mohit Mishra on scriptural logic. So the Shirnia residents hatched a cunning plot. They asked Mohit if, in line with his preachings against caste, he would be willing to drink water from the hands of a person from one of these proscribed castes. Mohit replied he would.

On a summer's day in 1915 in Jamalpur market, the day of the crowded weekly *haat* when people poured in from the surrounding villages, a group of Maithil Brahmins from Shirnia reached the centre of the marketplace. There was a well in the centre of the *haat*, surrounded by a raised circular platform. A large crowd had gathered, because they had heard a Maithil Brahmin was going to publicly accept and drink water from the hands of a person of lower caste, something they had never seen and could never imagine they would see in their life-time. "Will he lose his caste status as a Brahmin, what will happen to his children, will his daughters ever be able to marry....?" -- these were the questions in their mind that summer's afternoon in Jamalpur bazaar.

At 4 pm Mohit Mishra, who had stared calling himself Mohit Sharma after becoming an Arya Samaji, stepped on to the circular platform. A murmur went through the thronging crowds which surrounded the platform. Mohit folded his hands in Namaskar to the crowd in each direction. A small group of Arya Samaj volunteers stood in front of him, pride glowing in their eyes as witnesses to such an act of courage and defiance. Or will Mohit falter and back out at the last moment? Sundar Choudhry, Gokulprasad and the other Arya Samaj volunteers waited in hushed silence for Mohit's next move.

Then one of the Shirnia Brahmins spoke out: "Mohit Pundit, if you drink water today from the hands of a person from a proscribed caste, we will ex-communicate you from our society and no amount of repentance will make us rescind this decision."

Mohit stood rock-firm on the raised platform and turning to one of the volunteers, who was from a lower proscribed caste, requested him to draw water from the well and offer it to him. No one moved, for who had the courage to break a time-honoured taboo in front of such a large crowd? If indeed someone dared to do so, would the crowd not lynch him there and then? The women-folk watched this unfolding drama from a distance, from behind half-open doors and windows, wondering what calamity would occur if such an outrageous defiance of religion and custom actually took place -- will there be an earthquake, will an epidemic break out or will the earth split open and swallow all present that afternoon in the bazaar?

Mohit broke this hushed and tense silence by saying he was determined to do what he had come here to do. Stepping off the platform, he marched to the huddled group of Arya Samaj volunteers and pulled one of them by the arm toward the well. The frightened young man wriggled out of his grasp and ran for his life. But Shyamal Sah Teli and two of the other volunteers took their lives in their hands and stepped onto to the platform. But they could not proceed further to actually draw the water out from the well, they just stood there silently.

"Brothers, we came here to challenge and take on these tradition-bound Brahmins" Mohit said loudly so that all could hear. "They say that the touch of your hands will sully the drinking water and make it unfit for human consumption. I want to test the validity of their claim in front of this huge audience, who are all witnesses today. Brother, please draw water from the well and let me taste it to see how it gets transformed by the touch of your hands."

With trembling hands, Sundar Choudhry stepped forward and drew water from the well. In full view of that large hostile crowd, the brave and resolute young man, my father Mohit, poured the water into his mouth. There was pin-drop silence, not a soul stirred. Mohit spoke again; "Brothers, you have just seen how I drank the water drawn and handled by my friends from the proscribed castes. Believe me, there was no change in the water, neither its taste nor its colour has changed. If any of you have any doubt, there is still some water left, come and check it out. Let the

Brahmins come and taste the water. If there is in fact any change, I will give up the Arya Samaj and become their disciple for life. If not, they should become my disciples for life."

No one moved. The Arya Samaj volunteers, long used to being insulted and humiliated in public, clapped their hands in joy and admiration, and the Maithil Brahmins started slinking away quietly.

This incident won Mohit Sharma many admirers and disciples, and the Arya Samaj movement started gathering momentum in Jamalpur, Khagaria and other areas.

While the Shirnia Brahmins had to accept defeat thet day, they seethed with inner anger and started plotting revenge. All the Brahmins who were present that day started talking in their villages about how Mohit Mishra drank unclean water from the hands of the proscribed castes, and therefore had made himself 'untouchable". The news reached the pandas of Deoghar, and the scribes of Sourath who kept the list of all Maithil Brahmins of the area. Emergency meetings were held in every village to discuss how the sacrilegious behaviour of one young man had brought disgrace to, and threatened the purity of, the entire Maithil Brahmin community. Action was required to restore the honour and prestige of the community.

One rich family of Shirnia was particularly enraged with Mohit Mishra. As we know, every year the village would be inundated and destroyed in the floods, and houses would be rebuilt. After the 1913 floods, instead of rebuilding his house on its earlier site in the centre of the village, Mohit Mishra relocated to a site on the western outskirts, away from the villagers opposed to his Samaj activities, since he knew they would indulge in acts of reprisal sooner than later. The plot he moved to had emerged from the river when it had changed its course (which it frequently did) and was one which many families had their eyes on. His getting it in the auction of the Srinagar Principality with the help of its Chief Manager Raibahadur Lakshmiprasad Singh, earned him the anger and enmity of many families. They were relatives, and there was one more reason for their anger. They were among the richer families of the village and used to lend money on usurious rates of interest, a practice Mohit abhorred. He would often lend money interest-free to the really needy, and this was the other reason the rich families wanted to punish him. The village Council of Elders (panchayat) met and decided to "outcaste" him which also meant that neither would Mohit be invited to their feasts nor would anyone eat food in his house.

In 1915, the Mohit Mishra household comprised his two sons, two daughters, wife Anoop Devi, father Pandit Yagyadutt Mishra and his mother. In addition, his widowed sister Dharmadaya and her son Ramanugraha Jha, and his widowed sister-in-law with her son. His elder son Suresh Chandra and nephew Ramnugraha were studying in Munger, and the latter had also joined the Arya Samaj under the influence of his uncle Mohit Mishra.

In 1916 there was another upheaval in the Maithil community of Shirnia. Villagers who went looking for bridegrooms for their daughters, came back with many stories. People had refused to talk about any marriage prospects the moment they came to know they were from Shirnia, the village of the "impure" Mohit Mishra. They jeered at them, saying their village was home to "Dayalingis" (the local corrupted version of "Dayanandi", which was the term often used for Arya Samajis). The humiliated and insulted villagers returned to Shirnia seething with anger. The whole region was abuzz with talk of the Maithil Brahmin Pandit who had brought disgrace and destroyed the religious purity of the entire community by the sacrilegious act of drinking water from the hands of an outcaste in front of thousands of people in a crowded marketplace.

On the auspicious date of Shuklapaksh in the month of Falgun, a "Marriage Council" of Maithil Brahmins would meet annually in the Sourath village of Madhubani. Special scribes known as Panjikars would be there with detailed family-tree records of each family, along with the names and other details of marriageable bridegrooms. The aspiring bridegrooms would be there with their male elders, as would the male elders of potential brides, and the latter would chose grooms for their girls. The Panjikars would then consult their records to ensure there were no blood relations for seven generations on either side, and only after fully satisfying themselves would they give the clearance for the next step in the process. Then the marriage negotiations would take place between the two sides. Many times grooms would be taken straight from Sourath to the girl's home and the marriage ceremony performed!

In the Sourath annual event that year there was much discussion of the renegade pandit from Shirnia, and from there the news spread to similar Marriage Councils in other parts of the region.

The villagers of Shirnia held a panchayat meeting and summoned Mohit, his father Yagyadutt Mishra and the few other village youth who had joined the Samaj. This was the spring of 1916. The elders demanded that Yagyadutt answer the charge that because of Mohit Mishra's nefarious activities, the young girls of the village would not be able to find grooms for themselves and would remain single all their lives.

The old man was silent. He himself was deeply troubled and concerned about his son's irresponsible behaviour and wondered what evil spirits had possessed his son. He had pleaded with Mohit that even now, after having disgraced everyone in the marketplace, he should express remorse and tell the panchayat that he was sorry for his irresponsible behaviour and would mend his ways going forward. But Mohit had refused to budge. "I went through the test in front of everyone, the water did not change in any way. All our village elders and relatives were there, why did no one come forward to check the water? To me it is proof that they inwardly know that the Vedic way is the true way. I refuse to get ensnared in their tradition-bound falsehoods and superstitions."

Thus silenced by his son, the old man remained quiet.

Seeing his silence, one of the villagers asked him, "Do you know that Arya Samajis do not believe in performing the shraddha ceremony after death? When you die your only son Mohit will have to light the funeral pyre, but he will not perform the *shraddha*. As a consequence, your soul will never attain salvation and will be condemned to linger indefinitely among the demons of the dark nether world. All subsequent generations after you will face misfortunes of the highest order. Your young grandson is standing in front of you, at least think of him -- this worthless son of yours will ruin you and the entire family."

The mention of the nether world and the demons that inhabit it, sent a shiver down the old man's spine..... add to that, the prospect of future generations suffering untold miseries. Was there no way out of this calamity?

One of the Brahmins said, "It is not enough to just ex-communicate the family. There is only one way out, and that is to remove Mohit Mishra from our lives forever. He must die!"

Another added, "Yagyadutt, your grandchildren will never be able to marry in the Brahmin community, not even the shudras will marry them. Will you then marry them to the chandals, the lowest of the low?"

His world collapsed on the old man, he could see no way out. His response was to sink into deeper silence.

The villagers did not stop there. An elaborate plan was hatched and waiting for the opportune moment, a few days later, a crowd of roughly two hundred people was assembled. Around 9 pm, armed with staffs and spears, this motley crowd started moving towards Mohit Mishra's house. His house was located just outside the village, and they had to cross an orchard to reach it.

Mohit had gone to Jamalpur that morning, had come back bone-tired after walking for hours on end, and had gone off to sleep after an early meal. The ladies of the household had retired to bed after completing all their chores and extinguishing the earthenware lamps which had been lit after sunset. There were no other grown-up males in the house that evening, and Mohit's three young children were fast asleep --son Shiva Kant, and daughters Vidyadhari and Kaushalya. The elder son Suresh lived in Munger, where he was studying.

In total silence, the armed mob reached the orchard separating Mohit Mishra's house from the village. Suddenly there were cries of "Kill the snake, use your stick". A large snake had crossed their path, and it was these cries that woke Mohit up from his deep sleep. Meanwhile something else was happening--the young men leading the mob stepped aside, unwilling to proceed further. They were silent admirers of Mohit and did not want to take any further part in the planned killing. Seeing them, several others followed suit. By then, Mohit's wife Anoop Devi too was awakened by the cries of "Kill, kill...". She rushed to the front door, where Mohit had been sleeping on his wooden bed. She had heard rumours of plots to kill her husband, and quickly sized up the situation. "Leave immediately by the back entrance" she whispered to her husband, "I will handle the mob".

Mohit hesitated. It went against his grain to slip away in the darkness like a thief, leaving his wife and children at the mercy of the approaching mob. Seeing her husband's hesitation, she said firmly "What are you waiting for? Run, these people are coming to kill you. They have no enmity with your wife and children".

Mohit reluctantly agreed, slipped out of the back door and started his long and lonely walk to Jamalpur in pitch darkness.

The approaching crowd was still in the orchard, recasting their plans after this unexpected interruption because of the snake. They then forged ahead brandishing their lathis and spears, the plot leaders urging them on with exhortations to move swiftly and kill the heretic who had brought shame and dishonour to the village and the entire Brahmin community.

But what they saw was just an empty cot outside the main door. "He is hiding in the courtyard, the coward," was the next command. "Enter the house".

How could they? A young woman stood in their way, arms extended sideways, blocking the entrance door. Used to dealing with women whose head and face were veiled, the unexpected sight of this young woman unnerved them, and the mob stood still, not knowing what to do. Mohit Mishra's relatives in the mob recognized her. She was the village beauty, standing proud and fearless in their path, head raised in defiance. "What do you think you think you are doing, entering someone's house in the dead of night? What and who are you after? Do you intend to kill us all? I will not let you enter my house. "Thus spoke the small and petite Anoop Devi, like the Goddess Durga confronting the army of Demons.

The mob did not stir. Then whisperings started. The elder relatives could not dream of laying hands on the young woman. After all, they were Protectors of the Faith come to punish a heretic, not harass the women of their own clan. It was decided that the younger relatives would move her aside and clear the entrance.

Thus they entered the inner courtyard, convinced that Mohit Mishra was hiding there. Anoop Devi, burning with righteous indignation, kept blocking their every step. 'Why are you going into that corner? This is my kitchen, I will not let anyone enter that sacred space.....'. She kept up this charade for as long as she could, giving precious moments to her husband to put as much distance as possible between himself and his would-be-murderers.

With no sign of Mohit anywhere, the disappointed and angry crowd slowly drifted away and silence returned to the Mishra household.

Such an exceptional person was my father Mohit Mishra, and such a fearless and strong person was my mother Anoop Devi.

While the mob was entering our house to kill my father, I, Kaushalya Devi and my elder sister Vidyadhari, were fast asleep in one of the rooms. My brother Shiva Kant too slept soundly through it all in the next room. This was the family I was born into, and these were the circumstances I grew up in.

My elder brother Suresh Chandra was born in 1901, my sister Vidyadhari in 1904, my brother Shiva Kant in 1909 and I was born in 1912. All of us were born in Shirnia.

There was not a single non-Brahmin house in the village, and the villagers took great pride in the "purity"of their village. Most households were dependent on agriculture, but Brahmins would not plough the land themselves and all the manual work on the land was done by labourers from the lower castes. Cows and bulls were bred, and they required vast quantities of fodder. Those who had large landholdings were prosperous, but most familes had small land parcels and struggled economically since they were dependent on others to farm the land.

My grandfather Yagyadutt Mishra was also a farmer. Of tall frame, strong physique and radiant health, he always wore a dhoti with a linen shawl thrown over his shoulders, and whenever he ventured out of the house he would carry a stout staff seasoned in oil. In those days young men would put much emphasis on building a strong and robust physique. My father (Babuji) was so absorbed in the Arya Samaj that he could not pay much attention to the family lands and this was a sore point with my grandfather. However, since Babuji had bought some extra land, it somewhat compensated for his neglect of the family farms and brought a little cheer to grandfather. But giving up the Sanatan Dharma tradition of his ancestors to embrace the newly-founded ways and practices of the Arya Samaj, was a major act of rebellion in that tradition-bound society. The Brahmin society looked on it as an act of arrogance and he was targeted in many ways, with the consequent huge impact on the financial and mental well-being of the entire family, which literally had to be on the run to save itself.

In keeping with the Samaj view of the world, Ma had given up the practice of purdah and wearing jewellery. The village girls and brides all wore elaborate clothes and jewellery, for which the region of Mithila was famous. From *kajal* in the eyes, *bindi* on the forehead, vermillion in the centre parting of the hair, to all manner of ornaments in their nose, earlobes, neck, arms, wrists, waist, feet -- from top to toe the Maithil Brahmin women revelled in adorning themselves for the innumerable festivals and auspicious events that occurred with great regularity throughout the year. Of these, the major events were Holi, Dussehra and Diwali (Kali Puja).

Our family stayed away from all this and followed the Vedic way of life espoused by the Arya Samaj. As a young girl I was inwardly envious of the colourful clothes, ornaments and manner of hair-styling which pre-occupied the village girls of my age. But the one thing I had which they did not, was education.

Babuji campaigned ceaselessly and tirelessly for the cause of education, for he believed that lack of education was the root cause of blind superstition. He had made a thatched platform in front of his house, and that became the meeting point for the village youth to read and discuss with great interest and enthusiasm, news and views from the newspaper that he would regularly get from nearby Jamalpur. Those were the days of the British Raj, but the demand for Independence was slowly becoming stronger and stronger. My elder brother Suresh was away studying in Munger, but Shiva Kant and Vidyadhari used to go to school in Jamalpur. One other Shirnia girl, Annapoorna, used to go with Vidyadhari to school in Jamalpur. She was a regular visitor to our home, and was greatly influenced by all the talk of education and its importance, that she heard in our family conversations. My mother's simple way of life and high principles also left a huge impression on her. Babuji meanwhile encouraged Ma, who was illiterate but very intelligent, to start reading and writing. She had in any case understood and internalized much of the Arya Samaj teachings and would talk about them to the women of the village.

Of major importance were the Samaj views against child-marriage and the ill treatment of widows in Hindu society. Ignorance also led to lack of social and personal hygiene, resulting in disease and infection. These were the things Ma spoke about, as if in preparation for her life to come. Of course, no one had an inkling of the drama that was to unfold and engulf the family.

The village women had a long tradition of having designs tattooed on their skin, and it was considered compulsory for women to get themselves tattooed after marriage. It might even have been a sign of belonging to the Hindu faith. My father's sister (Bua) was heavily tattooed, but Babuji forbade his wife from following this tradition, much to Bua's chagrin and disappointment. "When you die, you take nothing with you, neither jewellery nor other ornaments, only the tattoos go with you."

The tattoo artists came around in the winter months, they were mostly male. A basket on their head, they would wend their way through the village lanes shouting "Tattoos, get yourself tattooed, tattoo s...". Prospective clients would call them into their homes, where typically a group of women would be assembled, each a customer. The tattoo artist would use needles of various sizes and thickness, tied together to carve intricate patterns and motifs on the skin. They were mostly forms of jewellery, with different shapes and sizes for different parts of the body: the neck, the arms, wrists, ankles... Many would get their husband's names engraved. After the needle work, a lotion would be spread over the tattoos, which would turn blackish in colour and would never fade. It was a very painful process, and many women would develop swelling and fever.

Much later, when she became an active participant in the freedom struggle, Ma would often say, "How lucky I am that I did not get myself tattooed. I gave up so many things, I would never have been able to give up this part of my past, and it would have been a constant source of shame and embarrassment for me."

Ma was her husband's partner and fellow-traveller in the true sense. With a great sense of equanimity, she had embraced and internalized her husband's outlook on life and his religious views and practices. The consequences of this started taking shape that fateful night of the murderous mob attack, when she had taken on the role of the Warrior Goddess and protected her husband and the family. This made a huge impression on the villagers in the entire region. People started saying and believing that because the mob had set out to kill a member of Sati Mai's family (remember, it was a distant relative who had taken to the pyre with her dead husband's body and become Sati, when Mohit was just a young boy), the Snake God had himself appeared to save the family. Many members of the mob had turned back on seeing the snake cross their path, and the story spread that it was only because the Goddess entered Anoop Devi's body that she was able to single-handed defeat the 200-strong mob. It was the Goddess too who ensured Mohit's disappearance into thin air, without a trace.

Mohit Mishra and his wife became objects of reverence and awe for many.

In fact, that night Mohit Mishra reached Jamalpur and quickly continued onwards to Munger, where he discovered that the hostel inmates had ostracized his son Suresh and would not allow him to have his meals with them. "Why are you doing all this?" his young son asked him. "I have been humiliated so badly." Saying this, Suresh burst into tears.

"If you think like this, who am I doing all this for and why?" Babuji replied.

One of Babuji's friends was Yahiya, a young Muslim barrister practising in the Munger Court. Babuji went to him for advice, and Yahiya advised him not to stay quiet but to lodge a complaint with the Government authorities. This advice was accepted and a complaint was lodged against the villagers of Shirnia -- for religious persecution.

An Englishman was the Sub- Divisional Officer (SDO) in Khagaria.In those days the first posting of entrants into the Indian Civil Service (ICS) was as an SDO, and ninety per cent of ICS officers were Englishmen. That young Englishman in Khagaria ruled that he would personally go to Shirnia to investigate the case. This news spread down the ranks, and the local police swung into action in preparation for this visit.

The news reached Shirnia also. Babuji felt that for some time at least there would be no further violence and returned home. He even supervised the sowing of maize in his lands. Meanwhile the leaders of the plot started closing ranks. An edict was issued that no villager would give evidence in favour of Mohit Mishra. If anyone did, it would be at his own peril, for there had been at least one member of each village household in that mob. Moreover, these folks were familiar with and experienced in litigation, and knew enough intricacies of the law to be able to twist them to their own advantage.

Meanwhile, another act of revenge was enacted. They uprooted the entire crop on Mohit's lands and then let loose cattle to trample and graze on the remaining stumps, so that the land bore a barren look.

The SDO Sahib arrived, the villagers gathered and in one voice swore that no one had done anything to harm Mohit Mishra. Babuji had reported the damage done to his standing crop, to which charge the reply was that this was in fact barren common land, used traditionally for the grazing of livestock. However the young Englishman insisted that the villagers give a written assurance that they would allow Mohit Mishra to live peacefully in the village. They replied that it was he who roamed all over the countryside preaching the ways of the Samaj, but he was most welcome to live in the village. Of course, because he had accepted drinking water from the hands of an untouchable, the villagers would not accept food or drink from his household. Surely the SDO Sahib would not punish them for that?

The young SDO had no choice but to return to Khagaria. Babuji was now convinced that staying on in the village was fraught with danger, and for their safety the children should study elsewhere. By now, my elder brother Suresh had left Munger due to the harassment he was being subjected to in the hostel, and was studying in the Patna Collegiate. He had jointly rented a place to reside in along with his cousin brother Ramanugrah Jha. He was already the recipient of a scholarship, in addition an Arya Samaji lawyer engaged him to help in drafting of legal petitions, for which he paid him a monthly stipend of five rupees. This ensured enough money to comfortably take care of food and other essentials. This was the year 1917, and my brother was seventeen years old.

That same year Mohit Mishra reached Patna with his son Shiva Kant and daughter Vidyadhari. In consultation with his elder son Suresh, it was agreed that my sister would be admitted to the Jalandhar Girls Gurukul, while my younger brother would go to the Mustafapur Gurukul. Both were Arya Samaj institutions.

When they reached Mustafapur, they found that the Gurukul was in a dilapidated state. There were cattle roaming in the premises, and the students looked underfed and unhappy. Shiva Kant whispered in his sister's ear that he would not be able to stay in this place. However, Babuji and elder brother Suresh somehow manged to persuade my younger brother to agree to stay on, and then Babuji left for Jalandhar in Punjab to enrol my sister in the Gurukul there. Having done that, he returned home to Shirnia.

Shiva Kant, who I called Bhai ji, ran away from Mustafapur in less than a month.

There were terrible floods in 1919 and Shirnia was completely wiped out by the swirling waters of the Ganga in spate. My family took shelter in one room of the Middle School building, but Yagya Dutt Mishra came down with a bad attack of dysentery and died. Mohit Mishra was not at home, but elder brother Suresh was visiting from Patna when this tragedy struck.

Almost all the villagers came for the funeral ceremony held on the banks of the river, and Bhaiya (elder brother Suresh) offered the sacred fire to his grandfather's body. On the advice of the elders, my brother performed all the traditional Sanatan Dharma rituals. The villagers insisted that Mohit Mishra be present during the Shraddha ceremony, which was duly performed by Bhaiya. Babuji was present, but remained a silent spectator. A proposal was now mooted that he make peace with the villagers and live peacefully with his family in the village of his ancestors. The family livelihood and sustenance depended on farming, to which Mohit was unable to pay much attention, resulting in severe economic hardship for the family. Till now it was my grandfather who had managed the family land and the running of the household.

The villagers again took a hard line. "Go to Gaya to complete the *shraddha* ceremony, and only then will we talk further."

Bhaiya had already returned to Patna, and Babuji told the village elders that the journey to and from Gaya would take quite some time. On the pretext of making the journey to Gaya to complete the *shraddh* rituals, Babuji quietly loaded essential household belongings onto a bullock cart and left Shirnia with his wife and family. Their house was already submerged in the flood waters, and the family reached the crossing point on the river with their remaining meagre worldly possessions. A boat was hired and the first stop on the other bank was Jamalpur Bazaar. Since we were ravenously hungry, we stopped there for enough time to go to the house of Babuji's fellow Arya Samaji and friend Hiralal, who owned a sweetmeat shop in the main market. He welcomed us profusely, gave us a tasty and hearty meal and then insisted that we take packed food for the journey ahead. "Where are you headed Sharma ji (the Arya Samaj epithet for addressing each other instead of using the traditional caste name)?" he asked.

"I don't know," replied Babuji. "Wherever the boat takes us..."

The boat reached Khagaria via Maheshkhunt, and we disembarked with our meagre belongings. For two days we stayed with Kartik Lal, another Arya Samaji, and then moved on to the village of Mathurapur. We camped in a *bagicha* (fruit orchard) owned by Pulkit Thakur, who allowed us to use the tiny thatch hut there. Some kind soul from the village sent us food for dinner, and that night itself we were joined by Bhaiya who had got news of our whereabouts in Patna and had immediately left to be with us in this difficult hour. We spread our bedding on the floor of the hut and were soon fast asleep. Suddenly Bhai ji got up with a shout, "Ma, ma, I can feel something moving under my bed!"

It was a poisonous snake, which we killed immediately. No one could sleep a wink thereafter on that wild, dark and rain-swept night in the lonely *bagicha* outside the village of Mathurapur.

After much discussion the next day, it was agreed that Babuji would accept the job which had been offered to him in Munger by the Arya Samaj as a Preacher, which he had not accepted earlier. Ma, Bhai ji and I accompanied Bhaiya to Patna, while Babuji left for Munger.

In Patna, we joined our cousin brother Ramanugrah Jha, who I called "Nunu Bhai", and his mother Dharma Didi who I called 'Nunu Bhai Mai', who used to live with Bhaiya in a rented house. My grandmother had stayed behind in Shirnia in a relative's house and she now joined us. But the city air did not suit her and she returned to Shirnia after a month.

A few months later Babuji came visiting from Munger. He gave Bhai ji some pocket money, which he promptly spent on eating in the marketplace. That night he came down with dysentery, and we had to call the well-known *vaid* Brijbihari Choubey. He examined Bhai ji and gave him some ayurvedic medication with the assurance that he would be fine by next morning. His eyes fell on Mother, and he immediately commented that the patient's mother was looking very unwell, and it was actually she who needed extensive treatment.

Ma took the *vaid's* medication for some days, but there was little improvement in her condition. There was economic hardship, but in addition she was also by nature someone who worried a lot. Cooking and doing household chores for so many people was becoming increasingly difficult, and the *vaid* suggested a change of location, away from the city. So within seven to eight months of living in the city, we moved out of Patna and went back to the rural countryside. There was no question of returning to Shirnia, and so we moved to Patharghat on the banks of the Ganga, where Babuji owned some land. We erected a thatched hut on that plot and started living there.

To our pleasant surprise, within a few days Ma became completely normal. The fresh air and home-grown vegetables, combined with total silence and peace, had worked wonders for her health and mental well-being.

Babujee sent Bhai ji to a Gurukul in Kashi. Gurukul rules allowed parents to visit their children only once a year during the annual Utsav. The annual fee was fifty rupees, and this took full care of board and lodging, clothes and study material. The brahmchari (as students were called) could return home only after becoming a "Snatak" on completion of studies, a process which took many years.

Hence Sister Vidyadhari and Bhai ji would be away from home for many years at a stretch.

Bhaiya entered college after completing his Matriculation. He was a brilliant student and came first in the Board in the Matriculation Examination. At that time there was a combined Board for Bihar, Bengal and Orissa. Bhaiya was awarded a scholarship to pursue college studies.

It was in college that he met Jayprakash Narayan and Singheshwar Babu, who were both Science students. Bhaiya was more inclined to take up an Arts curriculum, but took up Science because of his friends.

Shortly afterwards, Nunu Bhai left Patna on completion of his ISC degree, and Bhaiya had to leave the house they had stayed in for several years because he could not singly afford the rent. After trying out several places, moving from one room to another, he finally found one which suited him. This became the meeting place of passionate and driven young men, including of course Jayprakash Narayan and Singheshwar Babu, who would discuss and debate various aspects of the nascent freedom struggle that was slowly but surely gaining momentum. They had contacted the revolutionaries in Bengal, but could not reach their inner circle.

Plots and plans for achieving independence from British rule were made and discussed threadbare. Bhaiya told me he had gone as a delegate to the conference called by Annie Besant's Home Rule League in Patna in September-October of 1917.

Handloom dhotis were being produced in Bihar Sharif, and when on outlet was opened in Patna, Bhaiya bought handloom dhotis for himself. These were coarser and thicker than today's khadi garments. He had taken a solemn pledge not to use any foreign goods. Jayprakash Narayan used to refer to Bhaiya's house as "Ashram Padam."

Bhaiya later told us, "What Subhash Chandra Bose did in 1942, we had planned to do in 1919 itself. We had dreams and plans of finding our way to Germany via Afghanistan, and once there, invent weapons that would frighten the British so much that they would leave India. But all these remained pipe dreams, and not only did we remain in Patna, we even took our college exams."

Then came the infamous Rowlatt Act. The British had told Gandhi ji that if he helped in the enlistment of large numbers of Indians in the armed forces of the British Empire, they would in return ensure the right of Indians to join Government service. Gandhi ji had devoted himself to this initiative after the Kheda Satyagraha. In Bihar, Rajendra Prasad took up this mantle. But after the World War was over, the British saw the rise of revolutionaries demanding freedom from British rule. This revolutionary fervour started spreading across the length and breadth of the country, and instead of the promised right for Indians to join Government, the British gave us the despicable Rowlatt Act. This gave the Government the legal right to arrest and detain indefinitely anyone they wanted to without due legal process. Armed with these draconian powers, the government machinery had the legal right to act ruthlessly and mercilessly against the populace.

Gandhi declared: "Instead of giving us the promised rights, the Government has given us a 'Black Law' through the Rowlatt Act. If the Bill passes in the Council and becomes an Act, we have no alternative but to protest through Satyagraha".

The government introduced this Act through two Bills in the Delhi Council. One Bill was passed. Protest meetings erupted across the country. Every corner of India, every religious community, every strata of society, took part in these nation-wide protests. Sensing the pulse of the people, on 6th April 1919 Gandhi asked for a nation-wide lockdown. Patna too observed this lockdown and all shops remained shut. A massive procession was taken out, led by Rajendra Prasad and Hasan Imam walking bare-feet. Bhaiya was part of this procession, enthusiastically raising anti-government slogans. The number of people who joined the procession became so large, that the meeting could not be held in the originally proposed venue. The crowd moved to the banks of the Ganga river, and it was here that an orderly and peaceful protest meeting was held against the Rowlatt Act.

The success of this massive and peaceful protest converted Bhaiya into an ardent disciple of Gandhi ji. He told us that he was the man who could steer the nation successfully towards the achievement of independence from British rule.

Immediately after this event, Bhaiya went to Shirnia and started regular daily sessions with the young men of the village, where they would sit in the covered platform (choupal) outside the house, read aloud from the newspaper and discuss all the news about the freedom struggle. He would use these interactions to also talk about Gandhi and his teachings.

Returning home to Patharghat one evening, he found Ma crying while Babuji stood quietly next to her. He handed Bhaiya the telegram in his hand. I sat next to Ma on the ground, clutching one end of her sari, bewildered and fearful about what I was going to see and hear. Seeing the contents of the telegram, Bhaiya burst out "This telegram is from the Arya Kanya School in Jalandhar, informing us that sister Vidyadhari is dead!"

"No, no, it cannot be true" Ma cried, bursting into loud and wrenching sobs. I too started crying. Babuji was too stunned to even cry, for only a few days ago he had received a letter from the school inviting the family for the annual get-together to meet their daughter, and preparations had begun for the trip to Jalandhar.

What had happened so suddenly, and how?

The telegram mentioned that sister had died of cholera, but we found it impossible to accept the news that our beloved Vidyadhari was no more. Babuji left immediately for Jalandhar. A couple of days later we got another letter informing us that the Arya Samaj Society which ran the school had performed the cremation and death rites.

Babuji gave us all the details on his return, but Ma was still unable to accept the fact that her daughter was no more.

Bhaiya put all the blame on the British Rule, and ranted and raved for many days, swearing that one day he would ensure that the British left the country and returned home. They had created only misery and suffering for Indians, had forced us to send our beloved sister far away to study, where she died hundreds of miles from home and family and we could not even see her body. Mother genuinely believed that someone had kidnapped her daughter, and she would turn up at home one of these days. She had already lost two daughters and two sons in infancy, she could not comprehend how her beautiful and healthy daughter could suddenly die. This death was a grievous blow to her and she was never fully able to reconcile with this fact all her life.

Now she started worrying about Bhai ji. Her daughter died while in a far-away hostel, would her son too meet with the same fate? She repeatedly implored her husband to go to Kashi and confirm that Shiva Kant was all right, but the tight financial position of the family led to a delay in his being able to undertake the trip.

Meanwhile, Mother's only brother also died of cholera. Her parents had died when she was very young, and it was the grandparents who had brought up the three sisters and one brother. Her brother had come to Shirnia to visit their other sister, my aunt who was married into a family from that village, and came down with the early signs of cholera that very evening. Aunt's husband was a Priest and all night long he prayed and tried local cures to control the fast developing symptoms. By morning his condition was critical. By then news had reached my parents in Patharghat, and while Father rushed to Jamalpur to get a doctor, Mother rushed to Shirnia. But the poor man died before Mother could reach the village, and the doctor from Jamalpur never made it to Shirnia.

This incident occurred a few days after the news of Vidyadhari's death, and Mother was very badly affected by these twin incidents. She sank into a depression and was ridden with anxiety about everything and everyone. She stopped eating and had premonitions of something terrible happening to Bhai ji in the Kashi Gurukul. Communication and travel was a big problem those days, and every passing day increased her sense of helplessness and despair.

Mother was a firm adherent to the principles and practices of the Arya Samaj, and did not perform any of the Sanatan Dharma rituals. The village women would tell her that as a wife and mother it was incumbent on her to pray for the health and welfare of her husband and children, she must observe the auspicious festivals and prescribed prayers and fasts. The male folk had far more degrees of freedom and laxity to depart from religious norms and mores, but it was the women who were the guardians and keepers of the Faith, it was they who kept families together and ensured their happiness. Mother would listen to all this in silence.

An incident had occurred when we were living in Patna with Nunu Bhai. His mother, Nunu Bhai Mai, was a staunch Sanatani who had been widowed very young. She had been married into a "Kuleen" Maithil Brahmin family, who were traditionally allowed many wives. I am aware of Maithil Brahmins with more than twenty wives, in fact Dharma Didi (Nunu Bhai Mai) had told me her father-in-law had twenty two wives!! It was impossible for so many wives to be under one roof, so they would stay on in their parent's home. Their husband would visit them once in a while and extract all husbandly rights, including having children. Such wives who stayed on in their parent's home were called "Savasin", would be accorded a lot of respect and honour and be given the full rights of a daughter-in-law. Their children were considered holy and blessed, and would be fed first in marriages and other auspicious occasions.

Dharma Didi's husband had three wives, and she herself had three daughters and a son (Ramanugrah Jha). The husband died when her son was less than a month old and her brother, my Grandfather Yagya Dutt Mishra, brought her back to Shirnia. While the three daughters got married and went away, Ramanugrah became an integral part of our household. The young widow spent a lot of time in prayer and ritual, and was often critical of Ma for not doing so.

In the village, Dharma Didi had her separate kitchen and living quarters, so interaction was limited. But in the small house in Patna there was no question of separate kitchens and prayer room or keeping to oneself, and hence there would be plenty of interaction and sharing. On one occasion, the ritual fast for "Chand Chautha", Dharma Didi prepared a basket of offerings to the deity, and hung it on a hook on the wall. Bhaiya came, and being hungry, ate some of the food from that basket.

Dharma Didi could not believe her eyes when she came to collect the basket for prayers and saw the food missing. Fear gripped her at the thought of the sacrilege that had been committed and folding her hands in fervent prayer she beseeched the deity to forgive her for she had not committed the sin, and urged Him to punish he who had done so!

Ma was listening to her, and a shiver of fear ran down her spine. As a mother, how could she not be aghast listening to such ill-wishes being directed towards her son? But she could say nothing, since Dharma Didi was not only an elder relation but also a Savasin with special privileges. As a Savasin, in the household she had all the rights that a mother-in-law had in their relationship with their daughters-in-law. There was no way Ma, as a dutiful daughter-in-law, could say anything to Dharma Didi, and her fear and uneasiness festered internally for many days. She told us that God was Almighty, and in her mind she must have reasoned that the deity who Dharma Didi had beseeched to punish her son Suresh, was less powerful than the cosmic Brahman. As long as the Almighty was not displeased, no harm would come to her son, and this led her to perform the ancient Vedic fire – ritual of *havan* morning and evening. This practice of performing *havan* twice a day continued for long in our family.

Village life abounds in fasts and festivals, and one such festival observed widely in Bihar is "Chattha", which is devoted to the Sun God. Prayers are offered to the setting and rising sun, and both women and men seek fulfilment of their wishes, for which they observe "Manyata". On fulfilment of their wishes, offerings of fruit and sweetmeats are made to the Sun God. Standing in the running waters of a river, or on the river bank, these offerings are made to the accompaniment of songs in the local dialect. Women who have sons must compulsorily perform the Chattha Puja. But Babuji had forbidden Ma from participating in this traditionally very important event since it went against the tenets of the Arya Samaj. In fact, he had gone one step further and committed another act of great courage a year ago. The village women had gathered on the banks of the Ganga to make offerings to the setting sun on the occasion of the Chattha Puja. They were dressed in their festive finery, bedecked with jewels and were singing songs. Babuji strode through the gathering and picking up sweets and fruits from the baskets that were ready to be offered to the Sun God, started eating them in full public view. Mayhem broke loose, with women crying and pouring curses on him. Nonplussed by all the commotion, Babuji calmly strolled back to the village.

He narrated this incident to his wife in graphic detail. "There is nothing to be worried about", he assured Ma. "God is not so petty-minded as to take offence at such trivial matters."

Ma's own belief in her husband's views grew stronger with the passage of time. I grew up surrounded by such incidents and discussions. Right from childhood, Ma instilled in us the importance of compassion, duty, truth, etc, and ensured that she lived these values in her daily life.

But Vidyadhari's death had really shaken her up, and her worry about Bhai ji kept increasing. She kept remembering all the incidents in which the family had not shown respect and reverence for various deities. Premonitions of bad luck and doom haunted her, and she kept praying for Shiva Kant's safety and well-being. One evening she was sitting in the courtyard lost in thought, when in the distance she saw two figures walking down the narrow path to the house. As they came nearer she recognized them-it was Bhai ji and a friend who had accompanied him to the Kashi Gurukul.

Bhai ji had lost so much weight that she could hardly recognize him at first, but when she did, she clutched him and sobbed and sobbed till she could cry no more. Then she helped them wash up and sat them down to eat.

Bhai ji narrated in detail his experiences at the Gurukul. Discipline was brutal and funds were always scarce since most of the boys came from families that were unable to pay the fees regularly, leaving it to the local Samaj chapter to fund the upkeep of the Gurukul. Breakfast was tulsi leaves and black pepper, which they were told to chew properly and slowly, followed by a glass of water. The boys were assured this was the elixir of life and would keep them healthy forever.

Lunch was at eleven o'clock and consisted of small portions of dal and roti or dal and rice, never enough to fill the young and hungry stomachs. Bhai ji was used to his mother's lovingly prepared nutritious and filling meals at home, supplemented by large quantities of milk, curd and ghee. He starting losing weight, and lack of nutrition soon led to the early stages of night blindness. He decided that if he was going to lose his eye-sight, it would not be possible to study.

Babuji's Arya Samaj friend Adhiklal Mandal's son had accompanied him to the Gurukul. The two boys started planning their escape from the Gurukul. They had not a penny between them, and wondered how they would buy the train tickets to get back home. Bhai ji picked up one of the Gurukul utensils, a *lota* and the two boys ran all the way to the railway station. They wanted to sell the lota and use that money for the rail tickets, but were too scared to go the market to do that since they may get caught trying to sell the stolen utensil.

As luck would have it, within minutes of their reaching the station, a train steamed in. Hasty enquiries revealed that this train was bound for Munger and would also pass through Khagaria.

Lota in hand, the two got on to the train without tickets. A short while later the Ticket Collector (TC) came by and asked them for their tickets upon which the two young boys burst into tears. It was their good fortune that he was a kind and compassionate man, and he allowed them to continue on their journey home.

This is how Bhai ji returned home, where good food and motherly care ensured he was back to good health very soon. But his faith in Ayurveda and Sanskrit was destroyed forever, and he made up his mind to learn English. Ma put her foot down as far as my education was concerned--I could study at home or in school in the nearby town of Jamalpur, but would not go away from home to a hostel. And so it was.

Chapter 2

Non-Cooperation Movement

My elder brother Suresh Chandra Mishra was now twenty years old, tall and fair and considered very handsome. He was an extraordinarily brilliant student, and was the recipient of government scholarships from the Middle School onwards. It was now almost time for his I.S.C exams, and he came home for money to pay his fees.

Babuji was totally caught up with his Arya Samaj duties and could not pay much attention to the financial situation at home. It was left to Ma to manage the farming activities and somehow make both ends meet at home. She had great hopes from her elder son, everyone would tell that he was so brilliant that he could easily make it into the much-vaunted and sought-after I.C.S (Indian Civil Service). She was told how that would ensure wealth, power and prestige as a "Burra Sahib" in the British Government.

She was surprised when he came back home from Patna after a few days. She wondered why he had come back before the exams and was worried that he might be unwell.

Bhaiya announced in no uncertain terms "I have decided to give up studies."

"What do you mean--give up studies?" she queried.

"I will not study any further, it is as simple as that," Bhaiya replied.

'How can you do that? What has gone wrong with you? Do you have any idea how I have managed all these years to scrape enough money for you to pursue your education and make a man of yourself? I had pinned all my hopes on you to turn around the fortunes of the family, and is this how you repay me? Do you realize what you have done?"

Ma burst into tears, while Bhaiya stood quietly in front of her. I was standing silently in a corner, watching this drama unfold in front of my eyes. Bhaiya put his hands on her heaving shoulders and gently sat her down. He then sat in front of her and said ,"Ma, let me explain, this is nothing to get worried and anxious about. You too know how the British are looting this country. The produce of the toiling masses of India are being drained to England. Mahatma Gandhi has started a movement to force the British out of India".

"So you are starting a revolution, is that it?"

"Please listen to me first, Ma."

"Why should I listen to you, "replied my distraught mother." First your father wants to reform society, and now you want to drive the British out of the country. Who will look after home and hearth?"

This was the first time I ever heard Ma say a word against her husband. All her pent up emotions, the anger and sorrow accumulated over the years, came pouring out.

Bhaiya went on calmly. "Gandhi ji says the British rule this country with the help and support of Indians. We must not co-operate with them in any sphere, non-cooperation is the way to freedom and Independence. Therefore no one must study in government schools and colleges, we must boycott all studies in government run institutions."

"Is this why you have left college? What good will it do? You will ruin your life and the family. I beseech you, son, finish your exams and then do what you will, I will not stand in your way."

"No, Ma, I have to leave college now, there is no point in leaving it later. Gandhi ji has announced a four-point programme: leave schools and colleges, give up legal practice and other jobs in government courts, give up all titles given by the British administration like Sir Rai Bahadur etc. and finally do not stand for election to government Councils. I can only do one of these four and I am doing that by leaving college studies. In addition, we have to boycott all imported goods."

"So what will you do now?"

"There are lakhs of mothers and sons in this country who are mired in poverty and suffering. Whatever I do, it will be for the upliftment of these suffering millions. A highly successful lawyer like Rajendra Prasad has given up his profession along with countless other lawyers in Bihar, who have joined him and taken up the mantle of the fight for freedom from British Rule. From his base in Patna, Rajendra Prasad has given the clarion call to all students to boycott their colleges. Jawaharlal Nehru, scion of the illustrious family of the renowned barrister Motilal Nehru and himself a trained lawyer from England, has joined Gandhi ji's movement. If a family like ours does not join the movement, who will? You have always supported Babuji's work to reform society, why are you stopping me?"

"Son, I am bearing the burden of your father's idealism, it is on my strength that he goes around being a Dayanandi. He does nothing but give lectures and engage in ideological debates day and night, and now you want to abandon your college studies just before your final exams!!"

"You are a brave and fearless mother, the country needs women like you. Give me your blessings, Ma."

Ma knew she had lost, and had no choice but to silently watch what her son did in the days ahead.

Gathering a band of committed and passionate youth, Bhaiya started spreading the message of non-cooperation. The freedom struggle had had a nascent beginning in 1906 when foreign garments and goods were publicly burnt. Bhaiya had heard about this and even though this was not one of the four points in Gandhi's non-cooperation manifesto, it was included by the young revolutionaries. Foreign garments were collected and consigned to the flames in a huge bonfire lit in the main square of Jamalpur bazaar.

What was to happen to the education of the large number of children who pulled out of government-run schools? Many of the lawyers who had given up their profession now opened nationalist schools and even started teaching in them.

Gandhi ji advocated spinning yarn on the traditional Indian spinning wheel, the charkha, and making garments out of the resultant linen. This became famous as 'khadi' and its usage became the dress code for those who joined the nationalist movement. The kind of cap he wore came to be known as the 'Gandhi topi'.

Bhaiya laid the foundation for a nationalist school in Jamalpur. He was helped in this venture by his Shirnia relatives Pandit Dashrath Jha, Chakradhar Jha and Chandrakumar Jha who were joined by Awadhnarayan Singh of village Madhepur. Nunu Bhai also left college and joined Bhaiya in his anti-government activities.

While the school building was being constructed, a large house was taken on hire and teaching started there with ten students who had left government schools. Of course, spinning yarn on the charkha was a compulsory activity, and a centre was created for that.

On the repeated and persistent pleas of her son that the movement needed women like her if it was to succeed, Ma slowly started participating in her son's work.

She would go from village to village to preach about the adoption of khadi and usage of the charkha. I was eight years old and since she could not leave me alone I too moved with her. All travel was on foot, and that was no easy task. We had hired a house near the school. Of course, the charkha and khadi had become an integral part of our daily lives, and that helped Ma in her role of encouraging people to do so too.

We were now far removed from Shirnia.

The khadi of those days was much coarser and heavier than present-day khadi, and wearing a khadi sari was not very comfortable. Wearing such a heavy and uncomfortable sari, wooden staff in hand, Ma would go from village to village to mobilize women and enlist them into the Movement. This was not an easy task, for there was a lot of mistrust and resistance from male members of the family, who were afraid their women would be led astray, and often Ma would be turned away from the door itself without being able to meet the women of the house. She would often be the subject of taunts and verbal abuse. I observed all this as her constant 'tail'.

Younger brother, Bhai ji, started studying in the Jamalpur National School, while I was enrolled in the Jamalpur Upper Primary Model Girls School. Our headmistress was Mrs. Ambika Devi, a child widow from a Bengali family settled in Ranchi. She had done her Teachers Training after finishing Middle School and was the first female teacher of the area. She was formally 'Adhyapika ji' but most of the girls and parents called her "Dhapka ji', and it was only after some time that I realized that this was not her real name!

Kanhaiyachak was about ten miles from Jamalpur Gogri and was inhabited only by high caste Bhumihars. They were informed and resolute folk and joined the Movement en masse - Suryanarayan Sharma, Bhubhaneshwar babu, Ramdhari babu,

Kameshwar, Sahdev babu, Tarini babu, Darogi babu, Mano babu and many others whose names I cannot now recollect -- became staunch supporters. Their wives discarded the traditional purdah to take part in processions and sit-in protests. Kanhaiyachak became an important village, the charkha was widely adopted and the village later became an important centre for khadi production.

A Khadi Store was opened on the premises of the Jamalpur School and Awadhnarayan Singh was its first Manager.In addition to bales of khadi, the store also sold raw cotton, charkhas and charkha accessories. Villagers from Kanhaiyachak and other places would buy these inputs and return with the khadi yarn, which they would either sell or exchange for khadi cloth. The women of Kanhaiyachak were thus able to not only buy cloth for their use, but could also make some money over and above this.Thus the charkha became the means of livelihood and economic independence for the women, proving one of Gandhi ji's hypotheses about the significance of the charkha. Even after Independence this region remained famous for its khadi production with its resultant sustained economic prosperity.

Once activity levels picked up, space started becoming a constraint at the Jamalpur School. Around that time, Shyamlal Verma started a National High School in Khagaria, and Nandakumar Singh started one in Kharagpur. All three centres had identical activities - education for the children who had left government schools and the production of khadi.

To fund the activities of the Nationalist Movement, the Congress Party started asking its members to contribute an annual subscription fee of twenty five paise. This became the main source of funds for the Party. Leaders like Gandhi, Sardar Patel, Jawaharlal Nehru, Rajendra Prasad and many others toured the country to enlist people for this Movement. Bright and accomplished youth like Jayprakash Narayan sacrificed everything they had to jump into the fray. My brother Suresh, Bhaiya, was one such young man.

There was one other means of funding the revolution -- it was called 'Muthiya' (a fistful). Student volunteers from the National Schools would go from house to house leaving behind an earthenware urn with the request that from the rice or wheat used in every meal, one fistful should be taken out and put in the urn. They would return after a week and take the urn away. The grains thus collected were sold and monies handed over to the Party coffers.

Other methods were also devised to contribute to the Movement. Farmers would give one portion out of every forty portions of the harvested crop, and this was called 'manseri". So manseri and muthiya became the means of creating in the villagers a sense of ownership of the Nationalist Movement, making them an integral part of the Freedom Struggle. Bhaiya and his compatriots would carry the grain thus collected from muthiya and manseri on their heads and deposit them in the Jamalpur School premises. He would quip "This is Gandhi ji's magic-it sits on your head! This is how he is taking the entire country with him against the British."

Bhaiya would explain everything about the Congress, Gandhi and the Nationalist Movement to his friends and followers.

One day I asked him , "Bhaiya, what is this thing called Congress? The girls in school ask me, and I don't know how to answer them."

"Broadly speaking, Congress is the organization that has been created by Indians to fight the British who rule over us."

"Is Gandhi ji its founder?"

"No, it was formed much before him. You will be surprised to know that its founder was an Englishman called Sir Hume, and many famous people are or were in it--Lokmanya Tilak, Lala Lajpat Rai, Annie Besant, Motilal Nehru, Sarojini Naidu etc. Among its functionaries in Bihar are Rajendra Prasad, Brijkishore babu,

Anugraha babu and Shri babu. Rajendra babu has also formed a Youth Wing. These leaders have been travelling all over the country creating awareness among the common people. At this juncture Gandhi ji returned from South Africa, where for many years he had participated in protest activities against the excesses of British rule. He got in touch with the Congress, and infused new life and energy into it.

Gandhi ji had been able to get many rights for the Indian community living in South Africa through his satyagraha (non-violent resistance) movement. With his joining the Congress, many were convinced that he would show India and Indians the path to Independence."

I heard these words many times from Bhaiya, Bhai ji and their compatriots, and they got engraved in my mind.

It was in 1915 that Gandhi ji returned to India and started travelling across the country, to its towns, villages and remote hamlets, meeting people from every strata of society, to feel the pulse of the people. He attended the 1916 Annual Convention of the Congress in Lucknow where Rajkumar Shukla, a farmer from Champaran in Bihar, had come to tell the Congress leaders of the atrocities being faced by the people of that district with the hope that they would help. Gandhi ji said he would personally travel to Champaran to assess the situation first-hand and then decide what was to be done.

Rajkumar Shukla travelled to Calcutta, where Gandhi ji had to attend a meeting of the All India Congress Committee, to escort Gandhi ji to Champaran. They reached Motihari, the biggest town in Champaran, but before Gandhi ji could start his investigations the District Magistrate ordered him to leave the district. He did not obey the orders, but stayed put in Motihari and sent a telegram requesting Rajendra Prasad, Brijkishore babu, Mazrul Haque, Anugraha Narayan Singh, Shambhu Sharan Singh and others to join him in Champaran. This was the beginning of the non-violent resistance movement in the country. It was known that Gandhi would have to go to jail, and the plan was that each of these leaders would court arrest thereafter with their band of followers. These leaders had never gone to jail, but willingly agreed to follow Gandhi.

But they had time to meet the people of Champaran and write down their long list of complaints, more than three thousand people registered their complaints. It was clear that the populace was under severe distress.

The indigo plant was the source of a commonly used dye, and this plant was widely grown in northern Bihar, with Champaran being the largest producer. British agents lived in palatial "indigo-bungalows" from where they supervised extensive indigo cultivation and subsequent production of dyes. These British agents were called 'neelhe' from the Hindi 'neel' for indigo, and the local administration connived with them to force all farmers to dedicate a certain portion of their land for compulsory indigo cultivation, which then had to be deposited with these British agents without any payment in return. Any default in this compulsory quota of indigo resulted in physical assault by hired goons and vandalism of any other standing crop on the farmer's land. This kind of atrocity had become a way of life for the past twenty five years.

A new industrial process for production of synthetic dyes was invented in Germany, ending the British monopoly. This led to a sharp decline in the huge profits being made by the British on the sale of indigo dye, and they devised new means to make up the loss of profits.

Farmers were told that if they paid higher taxes, they would be exempt from the forcible cultivation of indigo. Rapacious taxation followed, often most brutally collected, which further impoverished the cultivators and resulted in untold misery for millions. Then World War 1 broke out and the supply of dyes from Germany came to an abrupt halt. Now the British tried to re-impose the forcible cultivation of indigo. It was in this situation that Gandhi reached Champaran.

The villagers of Champaran had so much faith in Gandhi, that they were willing to risk life and limb to meet him and register their complaints. Thousands gathered just to get a glimpse of him, forgetting their fear of reprisal by the local and district administration.

After extended efforts, a law was finally passed declaring illegal the forcible cultivation of indigo. In addition, several other benefits were announced for the farmers. Several Gandhi Ashrams were opened, and this was how Ramraksha Brahmachari started living there and working for the spread of education, settling disputes through the gram panchayats (village councils) and preaching the benefits of the charkha and khadi.

He gained the trust and confidence of the villagers, whose fear of the indigo agents started diminishing. Now the atrocities of the agents were not suffered in mute silence, voices were raised in protest and cases filed in the courts of law. The profits from indigo started declining and over a period of time the agents packed up their belongings and departed from their palatial "indigo-bungalows".

This was Gandhi ji's first major success against the British, and we were all proud that the first act of non-violent resistance in the freedom struggle of the nation took place in Bihar. Bhaiya had sacrificed everything to follow in Gandhi's footsteps. Gave up studies, took up no job and devoted himself fully to the Fight for Freedom.

It was not only Bhaiya, but also Ma who was now fully involved in this struggle, and the Jamalpur National School started being called Gandhi Ashram.

The nodal centre of Gandhi ji's Freedom Movement was the Sabarmati Ashram in Ahmedabad which had been established in 1918. The Gandhi Ashrams all over the country were patterned on this Ashram. National Schools were being established, and along with Gandhi Ashrams and Khadi Stores, played an important role in the freedom struggle. We gave our time and energy fully to this struggle, and even though I was very young, all these events and beliefs became an integral part of my being. It is no longer possible for me to distinguish accurately between what I experienced personally and what was told to me by my Ma and Bhaiya.

He told me that the Congress leadership had met in Bardoli where Gandhi ji proposed a nation-wide non-violent resistance movement. It was decided to start in Bardoli, and then extend to other parts of the country. Bhaiya had already explained to the Ashram inmates that Gandhi had asked all his followers to take a pledge. All volunteers would sign the pledge and take an oath that they would remain on the path of truth and non-violence, be willing to go to jail, face police bullets and even give up their lives to attain freedom. Gandhi ji even announced the date for the launch of this non-violent resistance movement.

The whole country, our region included, was ready. I accompanied Ma as she went from village to village drumming up support for this great venture. Groups of women protestors were readied by us. Bhaiya had organized many groups of male volunteers who were eager to court arrest. I cannot remember the exact number, but Bhaiya's band of volunteers numbered around seven hundred.

The whole country was agog with excitement and infused with a sense of purpose - freedom! Hundreds of innocent men, women and children had been butchered by General Dyer and his Gurkha troops in Jallianwala Bagh in Amritsar and this incident sent a shock-wave of anger across the country. The campaign to boycott foreign goods , government schools and colleges spread awareness among the masses. Volunteers of the National Schools and Gandhi Ashrams were an important part of this whole movement.

Gandhi ji could feel the pulse of the nation, and picked up causes that struck a chord with the masses. When he was confident he had the support of the Indian people, he would start negotiations with the British authorities and would always try to get these legitimate demands agreed to without any violence. If demands were not met, he resorted to non-violent resistance and protests after giving due notice.

Before the advent of Gandhi on the scene, the Congress would place demands for self-rule, take out processions, hold public meetings and other forms of protest. The British were familiar with Gandhi's non-violent resistance methods from his South Africa days, and knew of its power. So initially they talked of giving some form of representation and rights to Indians in their administrative system, including membership in the National Legislative Council in Delhi. But the infamous Rowlatt Act made it clear that the British were bent on suppressing us. The nation-wide lockdown in protest against this Act, opened their eyes to Gandhi's influence over the Indian people, even in the remotest rural areas where farmers laid down their ploughs in response to the call by Gandhi.

The Muslims were also angry with the British. Turkey sided with Germany in the First World War. The Caliph in Turkey is the Spiritual Head of Indian Muslims, and large numbers of Muslims in the British Indian Army were pressed into action against the Turks. They protested about taking up arms against the country of their Spiritual Head. The British promised them that the might of Turkey would not be destroyed and religious monuments would not be touched, but after Turkey's defeat this promise was not kept. The Sultan of Turkey was treated badly and disgraced, and this inflamed the passions of the Indian Muslims who started the "Khilafat Movement" which was fully supported by Gandhi. This made him popular with the Muslims, large numbers of whom became his ardent followers. The anti-Rowlatt Act protests and the Khilafat movement created a new awakening among Indians from all strata of society, regions and religions.

Now Gandhi was ready to launch his non-violent resistance movement at the national level. He once again toured the country to assess the mood of the people. He visited Bihar also. He was convinced that the people of India were ready for Satyagraha. The Congress High Command had resolved that the objective of this Satyagraha Movement would be the achievement of total Independence, and nothing less. Till now movements were narrow in their scope, directed against specific laws and for specific demands, but now the moment was ripe to launch the drive for complete freedom from British Rule. Gandhi ji gave his blessing to this launch.

Bhaiya returned from Patna full of enthusiasm and patriotic fervour. People were restless to launch the Satyagraha and fill the jails. The women were not behind in this wave of patriotism and large numbers of them signed up expressing their readiness to go to jail if circumstances so demanded.

At this stage a miraculous event occurred in our family. Ma was fully involved in Bhaiya's nationalist activities, while Babuji suddenly started devoting more and more time to the family's farmlands. The Arya Samajis had mostly joined the Congress since there was a lot in common between the principles of the Samaj and Gandhi's social reform agenda. The abolition of purdah, untouchability, social hygiene and cleanliness were an integral part of the Congress agenda and this was precisely the focus of the

Arya Samaj since its inception, so there was a natural convergence and union of the two.Babuji realized that if he did not focus on the family finances, they were headed for severe economic hardship in the days ahead.

From his home base next to the National School and Gandhi Ashram in Jamalpur, Babuji started supervising the family lands on the banks of the Ganga in Shirnia. This came as a big relief and support to Bhaiya, for if Ma and Bhaiji were to end up in jail with him, Babuji would be there to look after me and manage the family properties. I had also started going regularly to school from 1920 onwards.

And then occurred the incident which completely changed the course of the Freedom Movement.

A confrontation took place between the police and the local population in a village called Chaurachori in the Gorakhpur district of the United Provinces (UP). The villagers vastly outnumbered the small police contingent, and in a fit of rage they set fire to the Police Station. Several policemen were burnt alive. Some tried to escape but were beaten to death by the enraged mob and their dead bodies thrown into the fire.

When news of this ghastly incident reached Gandhi, he started having second thoughts about launching the Satyagraha Movement. Doubts arose in his mind about whether the people were really ready to walk on the path of Truth and Non-violence which Satyagraha demanded, and he called off the Movement.

This came as a huge disappointment to Bhaiya and his band of supporters. Gandhi had promised freedom within a year and they were all geared up to court arrest, go to jail and win Independence.

In fact, it was only six years later that under the leadership of Sardar Patel the farmers of Bardoli went on Satyagraha and won many rights from the government. This was a local victory, a far cry from total Independence for the country.

Chapter 3

The Gaya Congress

One day news spread through the Ashram that the annual convention of the National Congress was going to be held in Gaya and everyone should attend it.

This was going to be the first rail journey of my life and I was very excited. Ma made all the preparations for that journey. From our Ashram Bhaiya, Ma, Bhai ji, Avadh bhai and I finally went to Gaya and even though I was very young, I still remember scenes vividly from that historic trip.

Tents had been pitched near an orchard for delegates and visitors to stay in. We stayed in a tent, and while Ma and Bhaiya would go to attend sessions of the Congress, Bhai ji and I would spend our time seeing all that was on display in the Exhibition that had been set up. Everything seemed magical and miraculous to me. The entire process of khadi production, from the harvesting of cotton balls, its ginning, the use of charkha to draw out the yarn, its subsequent weaving into the khadi cloth followed by dyeing and printing of motifs. Dyeing and printing was not done in Jamalpur, and I was repeatedly attracted to that part of the exhibit. For the first time Ma bought some printed khadi for me in Gaya, and I was thrilled. I normally used to wear a *ghaghri* (long skirt) and blouse, my first-ever frock was made from this Gaya printed khadi.

A competition was held to choose the finest yarn producers, and the women of Darbhanga walked away with the top honours.

There was a statue of Lokmanya Tilak, holding a newspaper in his hand. From time to time, as I watched spell-bound, he would put down the paper.

Not far from there were statues of Krishna and Yashoda. I liked this exhibit the most, Yashoda looked so pretty in multiple colours. Krishna also looked very nice. Yashoda was milking a cow, and periodically Krishna would try to steal the milk. Each time he did that, Yashoda would turn her head towards him, and he would quickly withdraw his hand!!

I was mesmerized by these "animate" statues, and kept thinking about them for many days after leaving Gaya.

I also had my first glimpse of leaders of national stature in that Convention, including Chittaranjan Das who was elected President of the Party.

Bhaiya told us it had been decided that the non-violent Satyagraha Movement was going to be launched soon. A corps of fifty thousand volunteers was to be raised, who would be ready to go to jail at a moment's notice. In addition a corpus fund of Rs Fifty lakhs was to be raised from the people of India for this movement.

Bhaiya got down to the task of organizing a band of volunteers, and also decided to relocate the Ashram to an open and spacious area.

Chapter 4

ESTABLISHMENT OF THE GANDHI ASHRAM, GOGRI

In 1924 the Gandhi Ashram was relocated from Jamalpur to Gogri.

The founder of the Khagaria National School, Shyamlal Verma, was an associate and close friend of Babuji's. He was a wealthy man, who had embraced the Arya Samaj principles and social reform programs at the same time as Babuji. His only child was a daughter who died young, and after her death he had devoted himself fully to the service of the country and society. On Bhaiya's urging, Babuji approached him for help in relocating the Ashram to Gogri, and he agreed immediately. With the help of his generous contribution, Bhaiya located a large and open space near the village of Ratan and immediately bought the entire acreage.

Bhaiya had spent some time in the Sabarmati Ashram, and patterned the Gogri Ashram along its lines.

The National High School in Gogri was started with just eight to ten students. There were six large rooms in a row with a veranda in front. The rooms were for the boys to live in, classes were held in the veranda. The students had wooden beds to sleep in, and straw matting to sit on the floor while attending classes. Teachers got a stool to sit on. The kitchen-cum-dining hall was a short distance away from the main building, across the football field, and could accommodate up to fifty people who had to sit on the floor while eating.

Next to the kitchen-cum-dining hall were a row of rooms for the teachers and other Ashram functionaries, which doubled up as both residence and office.

The first Headmaster of the school was Gadadhar Prasad Srivastava, a former lawyer from Chapra.

His residence block was separate from the school and the other block housing the dining room complex, and consisted of two large rooms with verandas on both sides. The front veranda was for meeting visitors, while the back veranda was used as the cooking space. Our house was built on the same design as the Headmaster's house, with an enclosed courtyard at the back.

This entire complex was called the Gandhi Ashram. All construction was of bamboo and straw, but was always kept spick and span and in good repair. There were walking paths connecting the various blocks, and these were lined on both sides with flowers like marigold, *chameli*, *bela* and other shrubs. The Ashram inmates grew enough vegetables to meet their full requirement.

Water was drawn from a well, which was soon lined with brick and cement. A short distance from the well, on the outer perimeter of the Ashram, was a row of lavatories using the soak-pit technology advocated by Gandhi ji. This ensured hygiene and also a regular supply of manure.

Gadadhar babu was joined shortly by his wife. She used to observe purdah (the veil system of orthodox Hindu women) in the beginning but soon gave it up in deference to the Ashram culture.

A big brass gong hung in the veranda and served as the Ashram bell, from the early morning wake-up call to the last bell declaring time to go to sleep. The rules of Ashram life were strictly defined and had to be obeyed by all.

We had to perform all chores ourselves, from washing our clothes and cleaning our utensils, to ensuring our rooms and the Ashram premises were always spotlessly neat and clean. We grew vegetables, fruits and flowers for Ashram use, and even spun enough yarn on the charkha to produce the khadi required for our clothing.

The early morning gong sounded at four am. Students, teachers and all Ashram functionaries would get up and after a quick wash, congregate for prayer. I rarely made it for this early morning prayer. The prayer would be followed by morning ablutions and brushing of teeth using neem or *babool* twigs. After this the Ashram inmates would go in a procession, singing patriotic songs and shouting nationalist slogans, past Jamalpur bazaar to the banks of the Ganga at Rampur Ghat. They would bathe in the Ganga and then return to the Ashram for breakfast, which consisted of soaked gram, *chuda* (flat pounded rice) and jaggery.

After breakfast it was time for studies till noon, when classes would end and lunch be served. Lunch consisted of rice and dal, with one boiled vegetable. Evening was play time where vigorous sports like kabaddi were encouraged. Dinner was served early, at sunset, and consisted of roti and vegetables. Milk was served once daily.

Students, teachers and Ashram functionaries all ate meals together. Food was cooked by Ashram inmates, with Ma helping out if required.

The number of students soon went up to twenty five. I remember some of their names - Satyanarayan Sharma, Ramnarayan, Bhagwat Mandal, Sundarkant, Dhanushdhari, to mention a few. Along with Gadadhar babu, Bhaiya, Mukti babu and Neelkanth babu comprised the teaching faculty. Bhai ji was also one of the students.

The Khadi Store operated from a large room next to the teacher's wing, and Awadh bhai was its industrious in-charge. It was compulsory for all Ashram residents to spin khadi yarn on the charkha and wear only khadi clothes. Ma soon became adept at using the charkha, and I too would join in enthusiastically. In 1924 itself the Khadi Store was handed over to the Bihar Charkha Sangh.

Ma and I would participate in the evening prayers. Bhaiya got us the Ashram Prayer Book, and we would sing from it. Few knew the correct tunes, but the singing was loud, vigorous and enthusiastic!!

Food was totally vegetarian, and all forms of tobacco and other intoxicants were strictly banned.

Bhaiya was a total disciple of Gandhi ji when it came to the dress code and physical upkeep. All Ashram inmates had to have very short crew-cut hair and curls were not allowed. Once when a student allowed his hair to grow long, Bhaiya took his hair in his fist and shook it violently, angrily demanding why he was not following ashram rules about the length of hair allowed.

A labourer was working on a bamboo structure, and paused to smoke his bidi (rolled-up indigenous tobacco leaf) after lunch. Bhaiya was quite some distance away, but smelt the bidi and came running over. Seeing him, the poor man hastily stubbed out his bidi. Bhaiya warned him "If you ever want to work in the Ashram premises, remember never to smoke a bidi here again."

Ashram life was very regimented. The consumption of tobacco or tea was considered a serious offence. The dress code was prescribed: coarse khadi dhoti or pyjama, kurta, Gandhi cap, and later on the Jawahar jacket and a khadi satchel. Women were forbidden any jewellery or ornaments, simple sari and long shirt was the norm. Timings were strictly adhered to and everyone had to assemble by the bell for meals, prayers and exercise.

Bhaiya laid a lot of emphasis on physical fitness and sports. Football was introduced to this region by him, and very soon the Ashram football team had earned a name for itself. Good levels of competence were achieved by the students in various track events, high jump and long jump. The resultant physical prowess and stamina went a long way in enabling the Ashram inmates to keep up with the rigours of Ashram life.

Football matches played in the Ashram field attracted large crowds.

Once someone violated the Ashram rules. I don't remember who violated what rule, but Bhaiya took it upon himself to do penance and went on a five-day fast. Ma was very worried and tried her best to persuade him to give up the fast. "Son, fasting is not for active men like you who exert themselves so much. It is for women who live inside the house"

"Ma, Gandhi ji looks upon fasting as an important means of self-purification and good health, and undertakes fasts himself very frequently."

"Yes, I have heard that too. But it is not necessary for you to do everything Gandhi ji does, you will become weak. Then how will you be able to travel around the countryside spreading his message among the people?"

"Fasting removes all the toxins from our system and purifies body and mind. It will also ensure in this instance that the person who has erred will understand his mistake and never repeat it."

Bhaiya did not succumb to his mother's pressure and broke his fast only after five days by accepting a glass of orange juice.

On one occasion, Bhai ji bought himself a dhoti and kurta made of refined cloth. Bhaiya was very angry at this unnecessary extravagance. A simple lifestyle and bare minimum expenditure was the accepted Ashram maxim. Bhai ji also hated working on the charkha, which led Bhaiya to admonish him and remind him that he could only make clothes for himself in proportion to the yarn he spun on his charkha, another Ashram rule.

In 1926 Gandhi ji introduced the observance of total silence (*moun vrat*) every Monday. Bhaiya observed this discipline for a short while but soon abandoned it as it made Ashram work very difficult on the days of silence.

There would be a Discussion Circle every Sunday evening after prayers, where all Ashram inmates gathered to review the workings of the Ashram to discuss what was going well, what needed improvement and come up with specific improvement plans.

On one such occasion Ma's suggestion was adjudged the best when Bhaiya was chairing the meeting. She had pointed out the lack of warmth and empathy in the Ashram. On another occasion I had suggested the formation of a library. This was how Ashram life was being run, preparing all of us for the trials and tribulations that lay ahead.

Chapter 5

Gandhi Seva Sangh

Bhaiya went to Nagpur in 1923 with his band of volunteers to participate in the Flag Satyagraha, but for reasons I never came to know this Satyagraha was soon aborted and no one went to jail.

It was at this juncture that the Gandhi Seva Sangh was formed and Bhaiya promptly enrolled himself as a member. The main objectives were to spread awareness of the use of khadi (Khadi Prachar) and the upliftment of Harijans (Harijan Uddhar). All volunteers pledged full-time dedication to the National Movement. Bhaiya took this pledge too, but kept himself away from politics. All Gogri Ashram residents, including our entire family, committed ourselves to the Seva Sangh activities. We had no life apart from the Ashram, its inmates and its activities.

I remember one incident clearly, which will show how committed the Ashram inmates were to the protection of the poor and oppressed.

Like every day, after the morning *prabhatpheri* prayers, the Ashram students reached the Rampur ghat for their daily bath in the Ganga. They were aghast to see a burly and bearded sadhu with dreadlocks in his hair, mercilessly thrashing a weak and emaciated boy. Bhai ji, my brother Shiva Kant Mishra, was one of the group of Ashram students. The sight enraged them and they accosted the sadhu ."Maharaj, why are you beating this defenceless boy?"

"He is an untouchable and he can bathe in the ghat only after me. I told him that, but he would not listen to me. Hence I am compelled to beat him", said the sadhu, and continued beating the boy. Bhai ji tried to reason with the sadhu, entreating him to stop what he was doing, but to no avail. Finally, unable to bear the horrific sight, the boys set upon the sadhu and started beating him. The poor boy ran from there while the sadhu was given a taste of his own medicine by the young Ashram students led by Bhai ji.

The sadhu made his way to Jamalpur bazaar and started shouting loudly that he had been set upon and badly assaulted by the Ashram students, led by Suresh babu's younger brother Shiva Kant Mishra.

Bhaiya was out on a trip to the neighbouring district, and happened to return via Jamalpur bazaar, where this incident was the talk of the town. Bhaiya was very upset to hear about it, and berated the boys on reaching the Ashram, especially Bhai ji. "We are committed to the path of non-violence, and incidents of this sort will only damage our credibility in the eyes of the local people".

The success of Mahatma Gandhi's non-violent movement was the sole focus of the Ashram.

In 1924 Gandhi ji had stipulated that to remain a member of the Congress Party, every one must spin a thousand yards of yarn monthly. Very few could actually achieve this target, including Bhaiya and this requirement was soon withdrawn.

Chapter 6

GANDHI JI COMES TO GOGRI

Gandhi ji toured Bihar in 1927.Bhaiya requested him to visit the Gandhi Ashram in Gogri, and Gandhi ji readily agreed. Bhaiya rushed back to Gogri and excitedly announced that Gandhi ji was coming to visit the Ashram. "We must make all preparations to demonstrate how committed we are, what our numbers are and how well prepared we are for the Satyagraha".

Our excitement and enthusiasm knew no bounds. All volunteers who had signed up for the Satyagraha Movement, congregated in the Ashram. The female volunteers came a little later. The largest contingent came from Kanhaiyachak, especially women.

There was a large open ground near Ratan village, and this was chosen as the site for the gathering. Shrubs and bushes were cleared, the ground levelled and cleaned and a huge tented canopy erected on the day of Gandhi ji's arrival. The female volunteers pieced together many bales of khadi to create a large matting which was spread out on the ground for people to sit on. I too participated in this endeavour.

Ma and Yadunandan babu were in charge of the food preparations. Gandhi ji drank only goat's milk, so a healthy milk-bearing goat was brought to the Ashram two weeks before the appointed day and Bhaiya personally ensured that it was fed a nutritive diet. Ma also made ghee from the goat's milk. Farmers of all kinds, from prosperous landowners to marginal farmers, willingly contributed in cash and kind for the Mahatma's visit. Grain, vegetables, milk etc. poured in so that the Mahatma could be given a proper welcome.

The female volunteers also prepared a patriotic song to welcome Gandhi ji, a song composed by Bhuvaneshwar babu, the lyrics of which I still remember:

"Our dear Indian soil, brothers.
Dances immersed in love,
Kisses both the revered feet
For the service of all, O Mother."*

A welcome garland was made from hand-spun khadi yarn. Gandhi ji did not believe in wasting anything, and all yarn presented to him would be used for making cloth.

It was the month of December and cold. Gandhi ji arrived in his trademark dhoti which reached only till his thighs, with a rough shawl thrown over his shoulders. He was touring Bihar with his wife Kasturba bai. He reached Begusarai by car, and addressed a large gathering there. Bhai ji, my younger brother, was in Begusarai to guide the convoy from there to Gogri. Rajendra babu, Shri babu and other Bihar leaders were accompanying Gandhi ji. A large crowd had gathered to welcome Gandhi ji and his entourage when they reached Ratan, and escorted them to the dais with cries of welcome and victory. Then Gandhi ji addressed the gathering. He thanked the people of the region and praised them for their commitment, energy and enthusiasm and urged them to prepare well for the Satyagraha Movement that would be launched soon. He explained that Satyagraha meant walking on the path of Truth and Non-violence in the struggle for Freedom and Independence

---

*Bandau shree Bharat bhoomi
Prem magan jhoomi - jhoomi
Charan yugal choomi - choomi
Sarva sevya mata

from the yoke of British rule.This meant breaking unjust laws, protesting against injustice and inequity. But the jprotest must be strictly non-violent in nature. No violence even in the face of police bullets, lathis and British jails.Not even verbal protest, leave alone violent protest. Jail life would be harsh and difficult, one had to be mentally prepared for the rigours ahead. At the end of the meeting, a large bag of cash was presented to him and Bhuvaneshwar babu sang "Vande Mataram".

After the meeting, all the visiting leaders and volunteers proceeded to the Ashram, where they were served a simple hot meal. Ma could not attend the main meeting because she was bjusy with the preparation of the meal, but she was there for the special meeting of the female volunteers that was held in the Ashram field after the meal. Kasturba made a short speech, and then started a dialogue with the assembled women to find out the problems they were facing. The women were thrilled with this opportunity and spoke at length in Maithili, the local language. Kasturba understood what they were saying, and told them that Maithili was very similar to Gujarati and therefore she had no difficulty in following what they were saying. Not only the language, she said that even the manner of wearing the sari here was very similar to that in Gujarat. This further endeared her to the women present, who now opened up fully. The blight of their lives were the annual floods. While the rich could move to the towns to escape the flood waters, the common folk had no choice but to erect elevated bamboo platforms called machans, or erect simple structures on tree branches, and stay there till the flood waters receded. They had no choice but to use the flood waters for drinking, bathing and other purposes and this posed grave health problems because of faecal contamination.

Kasturba made a careful note of all that was said and assured them that this was precisely what Gandhi ji was fighting against-

-the apathy of the government towards the basic needs of the common man.It was the government's duty to undertake flood protection measures and organize relief activities if flooding did take place. Distribution of food, medicine and clothes was the responsibility of the district administration, and if we were a free nation that would happen. As the conversation warmed up and the women started becoming more and more comfortable talking to this understanding and empathetic lady, they started asking her questions. "How many children do you have? Who takes care of them when you tour the country with your husband?"

Kasturba smiled at these questions. Ma now took the initiative of handing over to her whatever little jewellery she possessed. The others followed suit, taking off whatever jewellery they were wearing and putting them in front of Kasturba. These were poor folk and it was mainly silver jewels that they possessed, but their spirit was something to see and applaud.

Gandhi ji had eaten his dinner at seven o'clock and was sitting in one of the Ashram rooms. There were two simple wooden beds (chowki) covered with spotlessly white khadi bedding. Kasturba joined her husband, and it was there that I first had a glimpse of the legendary Mahatma Gandhi. I had heard so much about this famous man, leader of the Indian people and renowned the world over. I must confess I was disappointed to see him! A frail and unimpressive physique, swarthy complexion, such ordinary clothes, altogether such a lack-lustre personality. Was this really the great Gandhi ji? What was so special about him? And what large ears he had, they were literally sprouting out of his face.

He smiled when he saw us, a simple and innocent smile, eyes gleaming with warmth and empathy. I was captivated by his smile, and felt a strange connection with this person who I had never seen or met before. I felt I knew him, he was one of us. Suryanarayan babu had taken Ma and me to meet Gandhi ji, and he said, "Bapu, this is Suresh Mishra's mother Anoop Devi. She has been actively participating in the freedom struggle since 1921. And this is daughter Kaushalya."

We greeted Bapu with folded hands, and he gently told us to sit down. We sat on the chowki opposite him and Kasturba. I was once again engulfed by the feeling that these two were ours --Ba and Bapu. They had reached out to the common people of India to do something for them. Bapu told Ma, "The people of this Ashram are industrious and full of passion. Seeing such a large group of volunteers, especially the women, gives me the hope that freedom is not far away. The arrangements here are of the highest order, and your family's contribution is truly praiseworthy. If I have a few more workers like Suresh, freedom will be ours very soon."

Hearing Gandhi ji words made Ma feel that all her trials and tribulations had been worth it. I too felt inspired and energized. Kasturba and Bapu made such an impression on my fourteen year old mind, that I took a silent vow to sacrifice everything for my country. If this was the magical enchantment Bapu could cast on all he met, I could well understand why millions chose to follow him and obey his every word.

It was Bapu's bed-time and we got up to take our leave. It had been the most memorable day of my life, and I resolved to follow in Bapu's footsteps forever.

While leaving, Ma handed a small bottle of mustard oil to Kasturba and said, "Your husband must be very tired, he walks so fast and so much. If you rub oil on the soles of his aching feet, it will give him much relief."

Kasturba accepted the bottle with a smile, she knew it was customary for wives in Bihar massage their husband's feet with oil every night before sleep.

After a good night's sleep, Bapu was up before dawn and got ready to leave for Munger with a small band of Gogri men to escort him. The Ganga had to be crossed to reach Munger, and there was a regular steamer service for this crossing. Gogri Ghat, the embarkation point for the steamer, was three miles from the Ashram and this distance had to be covered on foot through fields full of the *arhar* crop. The standing arhar plants were drenched with dew. Bhaiyā had devised an ingenious plan to prevent Gandhi ji from getting his clothes wet from the dew: volunteers stood on both sides to create a passage-way for Gandhi ji and his retinue by pressing down the *arhar* plants, and then releasing them once the procession had moved on. Thus Gandhi ji and his team reached the ghat without getting their clothes wet and simultaneously not a single plant was destroyed! This plan earned a lot of praise for Bhaiya.

Gandhi ji's visit had electrified the entire region. A large number of men and women enrolled for the Congress Party, and great awareness was created for the charkha and khadi. The Gandhi cap became very popular. Those were the days when people really respected -- almost revered -- anyone who wore khadi. Khadi-wearing women rose immensely in society's esteem because khadi was the symbol of sacrifice and hard work, and inspired others.

In response to Gandhi ji's call, in fact far exceeding it, Bhaiya organized more than a thousand volunteers, each one an ardent nationalist and patriot who was ready to sacrifice everything for Gandhi and the nation, to fearlessly brave police lathis, bullets and jail. The Ashram was abuzz with nationalistic fervour, reverberating with the sound of countless charkhas and patriotic songs. These activities were further augmented by daily discourses in which Bhaiya explained and debated the Gandhian philosophy, strategies and tactics, to keep the volunteers ready to launch Satyagraha when the call came.

Gandhi ji's simple life-style, fearlessness and inner equanimity were a constant source of strength and inspiration for the common man. Everyone was waiting for his call to spring into action.

Chapter 7

A Slogan in English

It was February 1928 when one day word spread throughout the Gogri Ashram that protests had to be organized against Simon and soon the air was rent with slogans:

Simon go back!

Simon go back!

Victory to Mother India!

Inquilab zindabad

A crowd gathered around Bhaiya, who waited silently for the sloganeering to die down. One young man asked him, "Suresh babu, who is this Simon and why are we shouting slogans against him?"

Bhaiya explained that an Englishman called Sir John Simon had reached India as the head of a delegation that was to assess whether, and in what form, Indians were ready and competent to become part of the administrative structure. Gandhi ji was told that this Simon Commission would submit a Report on whose basis the British Government would take a final decision on Indian representation in Government.

On perusing the list of members of the Commission, Gandhi knew at once that not one of them was competent to make such an assessment and declared that the Simon Commission must be boycotted. No one must appear before this Commission or submit any statement to it. The people of India must protest against this farce.

When the Simon Commission reached Bombay it was greeted with black flags and cries of "Simon go back".

Bhaiya declared that the Gogri region would do no less. Slogans were raised, protest meetings held and processions taken out.

We later came to know that the anti-Simon protest marchers in Lahore were brutally lathi-charged by the police, resulting in many deaths and a large number of serious injuries. Among the dead was Lala Lajpat Rai, a prominent Congressman, popularly known as "The Lion of Punjab". His death was mourned by many, but the youth particularly were enraged and would not just mourn. A young Sikh revolutionary called Sardar Bhagat Singh shot dead the Lala's "murderer", Assistant Police Commissioner Sanders, who had ordered the fatal lathi charge on the peaceful marchers led by Lala Lajpat Rai. The young revolutionary then disappeared, only to re-surface in the Delhi Legislative Council where he and his fellow-revolutionaries exploded a bomb in the jam-packed Central Hall. They were arrested on the spot.

A few days later, Bhagat Singh, along with his compatriots Rajguru and Sukhdev, were hanged after a speedy mock trial.

The Simon Commission was opposed vigorously across the country,, and had to go back to England without completing its mission. This was an important trial for Gandhi ji, and to his full credit, neither he nor his followers bent before the British might.

The British were also agitated by the success of the Bardoli protest. Bardoli is a rural pocket near Bombay, and under the leadership of Sardar Patel and the overall direction of Gandhi, the farmers carried out a successful Satyagraha to protest against the steep and unfair rise in agricultural cesses. Government officials destroyed many houses, impounded livestock and property, causing untold misery and suffering to thousands of farmers and their families. Large numbers were mercilessly beaten up by the police and hired goons and thousands went to jail, but the protestors remained non-violent and resisted passively. Help poured in from all over the country, there was no shortage of funds, and the protesting farmers remained firm.

Finally, victory was theirs. Cesses went back to the original levels, the arrested farmers were released from jail and even compensated for the loss of crop and property.

This had a huge impact on the mood of the nation. People started urging Gandhi to launch a nation-wide protest. The British knew that it only needed a nod from Gandhi for the entire country to rise in protest against the government. For the common man, seeing the highly principled, frugal and self-denying character of Gandhi, had started looking upon him as a Mahatma (Great Soul). They could see he did nothing for his own selfish interest, accumulated no wealth and did not allow any member of his family to take advantage of his exalted standing in society. This is why people trusted him, and believed in him, and why thousands were willing to give up everything, including their freedom and even their lives, on his call.

Bhaiya believed that the Salt Satyagraha was conceived at this juncture.

Chapter 8

A Freedom Fighter's Wedding

I passed my Upper Primary exam from the Girls School in Jamalpur, and then transferred to the National School Gogri for further studies. I was the sole girl in that school but because I lived in the Ashram, I knew everyone and did not feel odd or out of place. I also spent a lot of time on the charkha. Before I knew it, it was 1929 and I was sixteen years old. All the girls of my age had already been married, and my mother worried that I was getting too old and it would become increasingly difficult to find a good groom. She started remembering all her relatives who could not find suitable husbands, including the pretty, lively and highly accomplished Annapurna who was my grandmother's companion and close friend. The villagers had warned her parents that because she had befriended an Arya Samaji's daughter and even went to school with her, no respectable Brahmin family would accept her as a bride. The parents had panicked and agreed to the first match suggested by the village elders to a young man who had been rejected at the last minute by another family. The boy turned out to be a complete illiterate, and Annapurna was struggling to somehow keep this marriage of unequals going.

The story of my cousin sister Kunti Didi was similar. In her case there was a a potential groom who had been rejected elsewhere at the last moment because of his bad looks, a discolouration on his face and the poor economic status of his family. However, the village elders persuaded my Aunt to agree to this match because the boy belonged to a special subsect of Maithil Brahmins who had high marriage "marketability".

On Ma's urging, Babuji started looking for a suitable match for me. It was clear to him that he would not find someone from an orthodox Maithil Brahmin family since he had been ostracized and ex-communicated by the Shirnia Maithils for his Arya Samaj beliefs and way of life. In fact, he was determined that his children should not marry into the very orthodoxy that he had campaigned against for so many years. Having grown up in the Arya Samaj ways his children, especially his daughter, would never be happy in a traditional Maithil Brahmin household. Babuji accordingly looked for a groom in the Arya Samaj community.

Babuji had cut down drastically on his Arya Samaj duties, but still always attended the Annual Conference in Patna. There he reconnected with Sandhya Devi, who we had first met in the Gaya Congress. The two families had thereafter remained in close touch and had developed excellent relations because of the similarity in background and views.

Sandhya Devi was born to Maithil Brahmin parents, but took to the Samaj and became a preacher. She was well educated by the standards of those times, and had a mind of her own. She scandalized her orthodox community by insisting on marrying a fellow -preacher called Jitendra Sharma. The rumour quickly spread that her husband belonged to the carpenter caste, since no Maithil could have "Sharma" as his surname. But the couple paid no heed to these rumours and continued with their preaching activities as husband and wife.

It was a common Arya Samaj practice for people to drop their caste title-- like Mishra, Jha, Pandey, Singh etc.- and call themselves "Sharma" so that no one would know what caste they belonged to just from their surname. That is why my father called himself Mohit Sharma and not Mohit Mishra. He was disappointed that both his sons Suresh and Shiva Kant used the surname "Mishra" right from the time they enrolled in school. But being very liberal and respectful of other's views, he did not put any pressure on them to use the title "Sharma", which would have been his own preference.

Babuji soke to Sandhya Devi and her husband about me and asked them to let him know if they came across suitable young men from the Arya Samaj. They immediately mentioned one young man.

They had one daughter, Jaydevi, and had been looking for a good school for her. They did not want to send her to a far-away place like Jalandhar or Hathras and in their search discovered a residential Arya Samaj school in the Saran district of Bihar. This was the newly opened Gurukul Harpurjan, which had a girls wing with residential facilities. They went there with Jaydevi, were all very impressed, and immediately enrolled her. It was there that they had met a very impressive and erudite young man, Pandit Ramavtar Sharma, who was also currently attending the Patna Conference. They suggested that Babuji meet this young man, they would be very happy to make the introduction.The introduction took place at the Steamer Ghat on the banks of the Ganga River where the crossing from Patna to Chapra took place. After a brief introductory conversation about the two families, the young man invited Babuji to come for the Annual Meet in Gurukul Harpurjan next month.

Babuji talked to Ma and Bhaiya about this meeting on his return to the Gogri Ashram. "The young man is good looking, fair complexioned and of medium height, not tall like Suresh and Shiva Kant. Looks more like a Brahmin from the Himalayan regions of the North".

Bhaiya was attracted to this proposal. "The atmosphere in a Gurukul is akin to that in an Ashram. Kaushalya has never really lived in a village or city and is not familiar with the ways of either. She will adjust easily to life in a Gurukul. What particularly appeals to me is that she will be able to study further. I will accompany you to Harpurjan."

Eventually Bhaiya went on his own to Harpurjan. The Administrator of the Gurukul was Shri Krishnabahadur Singh, the local Zamindar (landlord). He was a highly respected person and a renowned Vaid. After entering the Arya Samaj, he had dedicated his life to social reform. He was convinced that social reform and economic development were not possible without education, especially of the girl child. He donated his own land to establish a Gurukul and a Girls Gurukul, and his entire family plunged whole-heartedly into the pursuit of this noble mission of spreading education.

Bhaiya was very impressed by the Gurukul and by Pandit Ramavtar Sharma, who taught the Vedas in the Gurukul and was referred to as "Vedic ji". He expressed the desire to go to the young man's native village and meet his guardians. "You are Maithil Brahmins, I am a Saryupari Brahmin. The other members of my family use the surname Tripathi and follow the Sanatan Dharma. My father is no more, my elder brother is very angry with me for having joined the Arya Samaj and has severed all relations. Now the Gurukul is my family and my world, and the Administrator Shri Krishnabahadur Singh is both friend and guardian."

Bhaiya spoke to Krishnabahadur ji and the marriage was agreed upon. The marriage would take place from the Gurukul, and that would be my home too.

Sharma ji was twenty-eight years old and had been married before but his wife had died before any children were born. He shared all this information frankly and openly. On returning to the Gogri Ashram, Bhaiya shared all this information with Ma and Babuji. His being a widower was overshadowed by all the positives, and Babuji finalized all arrangements for the marriage. The young man was highly respected in the region as a fine human being and a great scholar. He was also a regular visitor at Rajendra Prasad's nearby home in the village of Jiradei, and had very good relations with that family, a relationship that he kept up even after Rajendra Prasad became the first President of free India.

The Maithil Brahmins of Shirnia believed in austere marriage ceremonies sans any ostentation and fanfare. In any case, my family did not observe any traditional Sanatan ceremonies and hence my marriage was a very simple affair.

Babuji wanted to give some jewellery to me as a gift for my marriage, because he believed this would be an insurance against bad times. Bhaiya suggested that he check with me, and if I agreed he could give the gift to me.

I flatly refused. Normally it is the Indian mother who organises the things her daughter would take to her new home, but here it was Ma who stood up for my decision "If she does not want any jewellery, that is fine. After all, since childhood we have brought her up to believe that materialism was a bad thing."

Babuji reiterated his conviction that a bride should be given jewellery as an insurance against bad times, since jewels could always be sold for required cash. After much persuasion, I finally agreed reluctantly to accept gold bangles. In Bihar the tradition is to give gold bracelets, not bangles. As a compromise, I was given thick gold bangles, very similar to bracelets. My trousseau comprised khadi saris, blouses and slips. Petticoats were not worn those days, a yard of thick cloth was worn below the sari and this was called a "*satua*" in Bihar. Bengali women wore a *shamij* below their sari and blouse, and influenced by my Bengali teacher I had started wearing *shamij*, so Ma had several of them made for me along with the other clothes. One box contained clothes, the other utensils for household use. Ma also gave me ample bedding material. For the groom, khadi dhotis, silk kurtas and one gold ring.

Elaborate arrangements were made to feed the wedding party. Bhai ji had always been interested in food, so he was made in-charge of all arrangements for feeding the guests. He supervised the actual cooking, which had been organized by Yadunandan Choudhry ji. The marriage ceremony itself was not done in the traditional "mandap" but under a shamiana around a *havankund*. The wedding guests numbering twenty-five all came from the Harpurjan Gurukul, led by the Chief Administrator of the Gurukul. The actual marriage rites were performed in pure Vedic style by a learned scholar.

Word had spread in the neighbouring areas that a "nationalist" wedding was taking place where the bride would not cover her head, there would be no music or fancy lights, and no Maithil Brahmin ceremonies. A large crowd of onlookers gathered around the shamiana and watched the entire marriage proceedings.

Bhaiya's political companions and local leaders were also present. Shrikrishna Singh (who would go on to become Chief Minister of Bihar), Singheshwar babu, Chandi Prasad, and Dr Kartik Prasad are some names that I can recollect. Of course, the Ashram residents in any case were like family and were all there. Sandhya Devi also came. The food and other arrangements were excellent and everyone commented on it.

Babuji's Arya Samaji friends were very happy that Mohit Sharma's daughter Kaushalya had married a good Arya Samaj boy. They had come in large numbers from Jamalpur, and prominent among them were Shri Sundar Choudhary and his son Valmiki, and Shri Gokul Prasad. The latter's wife sent a gold ornament as their wedding present.

Rajendra Prasad had promised to come but could not make it because he fell ill. He sent me a fine printed sari woven from yarn spun by him personally, and it was in this sari that I got married. I treasured this sari for a long time. Singheshwar babu presented me a Murshidabadi silk sari along with a book. Shri babu also presented me a book. Altogether I got ten books as wedding gifts, and I kept them very carefully with me.

I was not at all familiar with household chores, nor did I know how to manage household finances. In the Ashram it was a collective life where everything was shared, food came from the surrounding farmers and we spun our own cloth. I had no idea about the market price for anything since I never went to buy things from the market.

Before I left home, Sandhya Devi explained to me how I should manage the household in Harpurjan. Her daughter Jaydevi was there, and she suggested I should look upon her as my younger sister. She would be my friend and companion, and together we would be able to manage things easily.

Ma advised me that while I should get into the rhythm of cooking food and managing the kitchen, I should continue to focus on further studies. My husband could easily continue with the Gurukul food that he was used to having.

I broke down when it came time to leave for my new home. I had never lived away from Ma and was used to the love and affection of not only Babuji, Bhaiya and Bhai ji, but of all the Ashram residents. Mukti babu, who had taken over from Gadadhar babu as the Headmaster of the Ashram School and who also taught me separately, tried to stop me from crying. "Do you want people to laugh at us? Everyone is talking about this 'nationalist' marriage and how gracefully it has been conducted. What will they say if they see you crying like any other illiterate village girl?"

I felt like telling him, as I struggled to hold back my tears, "Educated or not, a girl's emotions don't change. It's not only uneducated village girls who experience the pangs of leaving the safety and love of home." But somehow I managed to control the flood of tears that threatened to start flowing again.

A bus was waiting on the main road to take the young couple and the groom's party to the railway station. We had to walk from the Ashram to the main road, and I bade farewell to my parents before boarding the bus with my husband.

The bus dropped us to the Maheshkhunt railway station, Bhaiya and Bhai ji came with me till there. Sandhya Devi boarded the women's compartment with me, while the rest of the party boarded another carriage. Her presence was a big comfort to me, but she got off at Sonepur to catch the connecting train to Patna. I could not control my tears as I saw her leave, it felt as if I was finally severing connections with home and family now that she was no longer with me. I kept crying for a long time, there was no one to stop my tears.

We disembarked at Chapra to take the narrow gauge train to Harpurjan. Now I got to sit with my husband, Sharma ji, while the others went to a different compartment. Ma had packed some food and given it to the departing guests, someone should have thought of the two of us and given us some of that food since it was morning now and time for breakfast. But they forgot. I had freshened up in the station waiting room and was feeling very hungry. Sharma ji assumed that I would not eat in front of him, and therefore had not thought of asking me before he started eating the cucumbers that he had bought for breakfast. After some time, perhaps unconsciously, he offered me a cucumber and without any hesitation I took it. I think he was quite surprised for he said "I have never seen any woman of my family eat in front of the men, and hence had assumed that you too would follow that tradition." I, of course, was not even aware of such a tradition, never having experienced the "purdah" system because my Arya Samaj parents had campaigned against it for as long as I could remember. I had automatically assumed that it did not apply to me.

We got off at Mashrak, where a motor vehicle was waiting for us. Adhistata ji (the Chief Administrator of the Gurukul and also the local landlord) sat with us in the car. A short while later I saw a large crowd of people. Sharma ji explained that this was the famous Dumarsan Fair which took place on the festive occasion of Ram Navami. It was renowned for the large number of cattle that were bought and sold, in addition to a smaller number of elephants, horses, goats, donkeys and even camels occasionally. Of course, there were household utensils for sale and performing acrobats and dancers to entertain the visitors to the fair.

Looking around, I saw large numbers of men, women and children on foot and on bullock carts, all headed for the Fair. Adhishtata ji asked the car to stop and got off for some work, while I kept sitting comfortably in the car with Sharma ji. Everyone seemed to know Adhishtata ji and Vedic ji (my husband's local name), and soon word spread that Vedic ji was with his newly-married wife. A bride whose face could be seen because she was not observing purdah, was an unusual spectacle for the milling crowds. Women with faces covered with the fold of their saris, with little children clutching their hands, gazed at me in amazement. "All these people recognize me" Sharma ji said, "and we are also very close to the Gurukul".

"Should I cover my face?" I asked.

"No" he replied. "Just cover your head."

Chapter 9

Gurukul Harpurjan

My heart leapt with joy to see that the Gurukul building was surrounded by trees and thick foliage.

The Gurukul and its surroundings were very pleasant on the eye, far more than the Gogri Ashram. Adhishtata ji got off after we had crossed the main building of the Gurukul. We continued on to the Girls School, where we found no one to open the locked gate. On the wall was written "Speak the Truth, live your Dharma".

As we were wondering what to do, we saw a group of eight to ten girls come running towards us. One of them folded her hands in respectful greeting and said, "I am Jaidevi". I embraced her and, surrounded by the group of girls, entered my new home.

The main building of the Girls School was a replica of the Gurukul building, but was a newer construction--in fact, a small portion was still not fully ready. It had concrete walls, a sloping roof with earthen tiles and huge windows and doors, two large rooms and a hall, all opening on to a wide corridor. The campus was very large, with a high brick wall along the perimeter. Kitchen on one end, a toilet block on the other end. A big well near the main building, with two large trees for shade. A huge playing field, and neem, mango and *seesham* trees along the perimeter walls, along with many banana trees. And plenty of flower beds.

In preparation for my arrival, the earthen floors had been freshly plastered with cow-dung, which has disinfectant properties. There was a bed kept in the corner-most room. However, none of the rooms had doors, just open entrances. This did not come as a surprise to me, because even in the Ashram there were many rooms with no doors that could be closed.

Jaidevi and the girls took charge of me. After arranging my belongings in the room, they took me to the well for a bath. Sharma ji had gone off to Adhishtata ji's house. The girls drew water from the well and kept it on the bathing platform along with soap and towels, and then went and sat down in the veranda. Adhishtata ji's wife reached just as I had finished getting ready after a refreshing bath, with a maid in tow. She sat me down lovingly, and served me a delicious meal of kheer with puris, which was the traditional meal with which a new bride was greeted into the household. She was performing the role of my sister-in-law. Not only that day, she continued to shower on me the love, affection, friendship and companionship of an elder sister, friend and sister-in-law all rolled into one. She brought a lot of joy and succour to me in the days ahead.

Adhishtata ji's younger daughter was called Munni, though her actual name was Vidyadhari, and her mother was referred to as "Munni ki eeya" which sounded like "Munnikeeya". Everyone addressed her thus.

Munnikeeya was indeed a true life-partner and kindred soul for her husband. She had not studied much, but was a very mature and wise person, and was in-charge of the Girls School. Residential accommodation for the girl students were made in her own home, which was a palatial mansion. The mansion was divided into two parts, of which the front portion was the male wing. It had four large rooms which opened onto a large living room. The living room was connected by a passage-way to a raised platform in front of the house, which was open on three sides. A wooden divan was kept there permanently with eight to ten chairs in front of it. The Adhishtata ji would sit on this chowki while his visitors sat on the chairs. On one side was a large lawn which was a frequent venue for a host of cultural and artistic events ranging from the recital of classical music to local bards singing ballads of Allahudal, hudka dances etc.--this way, even in this remote village, there was always some secular activity or the other for body, mind and soul.

The rear portion of the mansion was known as the haveli and consisted of a large courtyard surrounded by rooms on all sides, ten rooms in all. A wide veranda ran in front of all the rooms. The girls hostel was located here. Adhishtata ji had three daughters: Vidyavati, Vidyottama and Vidyadhari, and two sons Rajendrapal and Narendrapal. Rajendrapal was studying in the Gurukul and two daughters in the Girls School, while Vidyavati taught there. There was a pundit to teach Sanskrit to the girls and his name was Ganeshdutt.

The atmosphere in the Gurukul was similar to that which must have prevailed in the ancient gurukuls situated in the midst of forests. I remember the names of some of the ten girl students - Satyavati, Radha, Jaidevi, Janaki and Damyanti. Within a month of my arrival, Adhishtata ji asked me to teach Hindi, History, Geography and Mathematics and so, instead of becoming a student, I became a teacher!!

The girls would get up every morning at five and taking a change of clothes, would troop from the haveli to the Girls School. After dance and morning exercises, they would wash their clothes, bathe and then do morning havan, after which they would return to their hostel in the haveli for breakfast. The distance from the school to the haveli was barely a hundred yards, you could be clearly heard from one to the other if you shouted loudly. Breakfast consisted of puris or rotis with vegetables, after which they went back to school for classes. Dress was sari and a long shirt, both dyed in *ramruj*, which was a kind of yellow mud that imparted a turmeric-yellow hue to the clothes. This dye was strong and long lasting. Hair was to be cut short in the manner of boys, no ornaments were allowed--no chappals, bangles or *bindis*. Adhishtata ji's daughters finished their studies in the Girls School shortly after my arrival and went on to the boys gurukul for higher studies where they wore a dhoti and kurta like the other boys, but draped a sheet over it. All girls had to have the sacred thread ceremony, for Swami Dayanand wanted no difference in the treatment of girls and boys.

In accordance with the ancient traditions, once students entered the Gurukul they could return home only after completing their studies. All religious rites and initiation ceremonies were performed in the Gurukul itself, like the sacred thread ceremony. Parents and relatives could visit once a year during the Annual Meet. All necessities like food, clothes, books, etc. were taken care of by the Gurukul from the monthly fee of five rupees. There were also a number of orphans and poor children in the Gurukul, who were all exempt from paying any fees.

As a teacher in the Girls School my life was simple, disciplined and regimented. Early morning prayers and havan, followed by teaching and then joining the girls in the evening on the playing field. The games popular with the girls were kabaddi, *ekath-tookath* and hide-and-seek, simple games which did not require any kit or gear. The boys followed a similar regimen, with the big difference being that wrestling was encouraged in the mornings. Vedic ji would leave early for the boys gurukul because it was his responsibility to supervise the morning wrestling activity.

The Gurukul had a large fruit orchard which ensured a steady and plentiful supply of seasonal fruits. Mango, jamun, lychee, banana, sweet lemon, amla, *shatalu* were consumed in large quantities. There was also sufficient availability of milk, curd and ghee for students and teachers alike.

In the Girls School, havan was done only in the mornings while mantras were chanted in the evenings. A large space (*yagyashala*), ringed by trees and flowering shrubs, was set aside for performing *havan* and other Vedic rites. The gymnasium was also very impressive, with the wrestling enclosure next to it. There were also open spaces for the boys to perform traditional Indian fitness exercises, including the heavy wooden clubs called *mugdars*. Physical fitness was stressed and indeed the Gurukul residents were all in very good physical shape.

Adhishtata ji was also a renowned Vaid, and used to attract patients from afar. He had opened a hospital for Ayurvedic treatment, which was called an *Arogyashala*. This *Arogyashala* had excellent facilities including rooms for the in-patients, a kitchen, and its own cowsheds, orchard, kitchen garden and fields for growing crops. All facilities were kept spotlessly clean and hygienic. This complex was about a mile-and-a-half from the Gurukul, and away from all human habitation. There was thick greenery all around the main building, with a large well for water supply. The pure air and sylvan surroundings were considered important for the curing process, especially since a large bulk of the patients came for the treatment of tuberculosis (TB).

Adhishtata ji personally supervised the preparation of the medicines, which was done in a separate outer part of his mansion. Vedic ji was very interested and heavily involved in this process of preparing and dispensing the ayurvedic medicines, constantly referring to the Vedic scriptures for process details. In due course, he became quite an expert in Ayurved.

Those close to Vedic ji called him "Pandit ji" and soon everyone started calling him Pandit ji, while addressing me as "Panditayin ji". Pandit ji had first come to the Gurukul Harpurjan to seek a cure for his stomach ailment. He had then gone to Motihari for higher studies, moving from there to Calcutta where he mastered the four Vedas and earned the "Tirtha Chatushtaya" degree. It was in Calcutta that he came in touch with a Brahmin family from UP who had a trading business. Their daughter Jwaladevi got married to Pandit ji, who came to Harpurjan as the Head Master after completing his higher studies in Calcutta. In Harpurjan he further acquired the difficult "Shat-tirtha" degree.

His wife Jwaladevi came with him from Calcutta. Pandit ji insisted he would accept no dowry, but could not prevent his in-laws from giving a lot of household items to their daughter. The young couple lived in one of the rooms in Adhishtata ji's haveli.

For a city-bred girl who had grown up in Calcutta, Jwaladevi found it very difficult to adjust to life in this remote rural Gurukul. She would cry all the time, pining for home and family. Her brother came and took her back to Calcutta. Unfortunately she never returned because she contracted typhoid and died. This happened three years prior to my marriage and Pandit ji had shared all these details with Bhaiya in the first meeting itself in Harpurjan.

For the first two months we ate food prepared in the girls hostel. This was not a very convenient arrangement, and Pandit ji suggested that we start our own kitchen facilities. I got a lady called Mahungu bahu to help me with the household chores. She took charge most efficiently and was overjoyed when I gave a monthly salary of two rupees plus food for her child. I would pay her extra for any additional chores that came up from time to time. I did not have some important utensils, and when my mother pointed this out on her first visit to Harpurjan, Pandit ji went personally to the market and got all that was missing.

I struggled a bit with the cooking in the beginning, but soon became an adept, including adapting to the much bigger cooking-oven in this part of Bihar as compared to the Gogri ovens.

The Gurukul teachers were not paid any cash salary, but their entire needs of board and lodging were taken care of. Plus all other essentials. A weekly *haat* (market) was held in Bashan from where all essentials were procured. We would send our full list of requirements weekly to Adhishtata ji's house and someone would get them from the *haat*. Rice, dal, wheat, edible oils, sugar, soap, salt, turmeric and spices of all kinds were available in the *haat*. Khadi was available in Chapra, from where Pandit ji would get summer and winter clothing. Maybe other women would have felt deprived at not getting cash in hand, but I was used to life in the Gogri Ashram where we never handled cash for our daily needs. It was only after coming to Harpurjan that I came to know the prices of things in the market!

Milk and ghee would be delivered to our home by the wife of a cowherd who would be paid monthly by Adhistata ji.

Pandit ji's entire family were staunch Sanatani Saryupari Brahmins and were from Teliya-Basuali village, three miles from Harpurjan. His widowed mother lived there with her elder son Ramprasad Tiwari, her husband having died many years ago. She had heard the rumour that her younger son Ramavtar had gone to a distant village and married out of caste, in fact had married a widow. Pandit ji went to his mother and told her what the facts actually were, and brought her to Harpurjan to meet me.

Her name was Budhadevi, a good-looking woman of very fair complexion, but bent almost double at the waist. She had come wearing a sari and was bedecked with jewels for the occasion. I could see she was happy to see me, and in a short while of talking with me all her apprehensions created by the rumours, vanished. But she was disappointed by the fact that I wore a simple white khadi sari and no ornaments. Her image of a new bride was of someone dainty and wearing a lot of finery as she tip- toed in the courtyard. And here I was, bustling around in my simple clothes sans any jewellery, attending to the heavy household chores!!

She immediately took out the heavy "*hasuli*" from around her neck and with some difficulty managed to put it around mine. It was heavy and uncomfortable, and my neck started to hurt, but there was no way I could remove it in her presence.

She later told me in her Bhojpuri dialect, "Parents are supposed to load their daughter with jewels and ornaments when she leaves for her husband's home. If not gold and silver, copper and brass will do, but it is inauspicious to send her with nothing. My parents had loaded me with so much jewellery, that we needed a buffalo to pull my palanquin!"

Thinking that poverty was the reason for my not wearing any jewellery given by my parents, in her own way she was trying to make up for it by giving me her jewels. The simple life of the Gurukul did not suit her, and she returned home to Teliya after a week.

Pandit ji started visiting his mother weekly. I would make delicacies like halwa and *khajur-nimki* and send it for her in a tiffin-carrier, which he would sling on the front handle of the bicycle which he had newly bought to save travel time. This would please my mother-in-law and she would send back eatables like *sattu*, *chewda*, roasted sweet potatoes etc. for me.

I was not ostracized by my husband's orthodox Brahmin family for being an Arya Samaji. My mother-in-law had eaten rice cooked by me when she had first visited us, and my brother-in-law too came to see me. But Pandit ji's three sisters were not being allowed by their in-laws to visit me because of the rumour that I was not a Brahmin but from the lowly '*ahir*' caste.

My middle and younger sisters-in-law, Sampato and Sanmato, were married into a family from Katalpur, a village three miles from the Gurukul. Sampato's husband, Pandit Sheetal Pandey, was an educated and erudite person, a prosperous farmer with large land-holdings, and highly respected. Hewas the first to send someone to meet me, his elder son Vidyanidhi.

He sent word through a traditional 'kahar' messenger that his son Vidyanidhi would come to meet me, his aunt, on the following Tuesday bearing gifts for me. We gave the messenger a hearty meal and a generous tip before he set out for his return journey to Katalpur.

Vidyanidhi arrived on horseback on Tuesday morning, wearing a yellow dhoti with matching top, a turban and religious sandalwood paste symbol on his forehead--every inch a Brahmin. He was all of four years old! Fair complexioned and a very sweet-looking child, he was accompanied by a person carrying the traditional 'bahangi', wicker baskets laden with gifts on the two ends of a flexible bamboo pole slung over the shoulders of the kahar porter. There was instant rapport between Vidyanidhi and me, a rapport which continues to this day.

The gifts included clothes of all sorts, cosmetics, bangles and also foodstuffs. By sending his son instead of coming himself, Pandey ji showed great wisdom. He signalled the start of a relationship and yet avoided adverse comments from his orthodox family members. My sisters -in-law came to visit me only after the birth of my first child, but relationships with my husband's family kept improving steadily by the day.

Unfortunately Vidyanidhi's father suffered a stroke and died, causing a lot of sorrow and grief in the extended family, because he was loved by all. I asked his elder daughter Savitra to join me in the Gurukul because it would do her good to get away from the grief-laden atmosphere in Katalpur. She would also provide companionship to me during my pregnancy. Ma had got news of the impending birth and was scheduled to arrive soon. Savitri was twelve- years old and a lovely looking child, but painfully shy. She would run away to her room the moment she saw any male in the house, and would also not eat in front of anyone. She would take her food, sit on her haunches facing the wall and eat small morsels, in total silence. I now understood why my husband had never seen any woman eating food till he met me!!

The drive against the scourge of Untouchability was a central pillar of Gandhi ji's social reform movement. The Arya Samaj had embraced this drive and in the Harpurjan Gurukul's annual function when parents and guardians visited their wards, along with many other events a special event was organized. Local Congress and Arya Samaj leaders joined the Gurukul inmates for this occasion, where a Harijan drew water from the well and all assembled drank it.

This news reached Katalpur, and a person was immediately despatched to the Gurukul to bring Savitra back home. I was left alone without a female companion.

Vidyanidhi had moved to the Gurukul after his father's untimely death, and started studying there, under the watchful eye and guidance of his Uncle, my husband Pandit ji. With the passage of time, Vidyanidhi got drawn into the freedom struggle, went underground and participated in several important events in the fight for Independence.

Ma reached Harpurjan a week before the baby arrived on 23rd March 1930. Ma was not sure how long she would be able to stay in Harpurjan and wanted the child's naming ceremony to be conducted in her presence before she returned to the Gogri Ashram.

Swami Dayanand Saraswati's books *Satyarthprakash* and *Sanskar Vidhi* had a special place in the Arya Samaj way of life. The sixteen rituals prescribed in the *Sanskar Vidhi* were observed religiously and with great reverence by all Arya Samajis. Arya Samaj did not discriminate between the genders and Pandit ji followed all the prescribed Vedic rituals, including the 'Jatkarma', followed by the naming ceremony. This havan was done with the full support of Adhishtata' ji's family and the little baby girl was named Savitry. This name was chosen by Ma, and Pandit ji did not object despite the fact that Vidyanidhi's sister's name was also Savitry, though everyone called her Savitra. Ma said that for a long time she had harboured the wish that if a girl was born in the family she would be called Savitry. My husband deeply respected Ma and obeyed her every wish. It was reasoned that despite having the same name, the two girls would grow up in two separate places and hence there was no possibility of any confusion with the same name for both!

Chapter 10

MA'S FIRST TRYST WITH PRISON

When my father became an Arya Samaji and plunged into its social reform activities, neglecting all responsibilities of family and home, his father Yagyadutt Mishra was very disappointed. Whenever he tried to persuade his son to attend to family and property, Mohit would remind his father of the ditty:

"The vehicle runs on the road well-travelled
So does the wayward one
The three who don't take the well-trodden path
Are the poet, the lion and the obedient son" *

He would thus justify that he was being a dutiful and good son. History was now repeating itself, the wheel had turned full circle. Bhaiya Suresh Mishra was a brilliant student, always topped every exam and was a recipient of scholarships from a very early age. He came first in the Matric exams of the combined Bihar, Bengal and Orissa board and got direct admission with scholarship to the Science College. Not only was he a brilliant student, he also excelled in sports with football being his favourite-and to top it all, was also very good-looking. In response to Gandhi ji's appeal,

---

*Leek leek gaadi chale
Lokhain chale kapoot
leek chhode theeno
Shayar, Singh, Sapot

he gave up College studies. His British Professor counselled him not to give up his studies. He was so brilliant that even if he did not want to work for the British, he could always dedicate himself to research where he was destined to make a mark for himself. But Bhaiya had made up his mind and walked away from everything to follow in Gandhi's footsteps.

Then Ma had joined him in the freedom struggle. Babuji's ardour for social reform had waned, and he now stayed at home supervising the farming. This helped to stabilize the family's economic situation to some extent. Ma had been walking the path less trodden by women and I too had imbibed those values and that indomitable spirit. My daughter was barely two weeks old, but while Ma was physically in Harpurjan her thoughts were in Gogri. She told me that Bhaiya had returned from the Lahore Congress infused with the fire of 'Total Freedom" and had plunged body, mind and soul into preparing for it. He had brought with him the proclamation of 26th January as Independence Day. The national flag would be hoisted in locations across the country that day and volunteers would take the vow to do Satyagraha to achieve the goal of Total Freedom. People were fired with patriotic zeal and fervour once more.

Independence Day was observed in the Gogri Ashram with great enthusiasm. Surya Narayan babu, Bhubhaneshwar babu and Awadh bhai came from Kanhaiyachak along with a large contingent of women and youth volunteers. A flag pole was erected on a circular raised platform, and in the early morning the Tricolour was hoisted -- the flag had three horizontal bands of saffron, white and green with a charkha in black in the centre. All present took the solemn vow that they would participate fully in the Satyagraha movement till India became free. It was from this heady milieu that Ma had left Gogri to join me in Harpurjan. It was my first child, there was no one who could be with me full-time and so Ma had come. But I could see she was feeling restless and her mind was pre-occupied with the pre-Satyagraha activities that were in full swing in Gogri. She would often tell me that she would have to leave when the Satyagraha call finally came from the Congress High Command, to which I would reply. "Then I too will accompany you. I had made a pledge (to myself) when Gandhi ji came to the Gogri Ashram that I would join the freedom movement whenever he gave the call for the masses to join."

Ma tried many times to dissuade me, reminding me that I had a baby who was just a few weeks old and the summer heat had started. If anything untoward happened to the baby, she would never be able to forgive herself. There would be many opportunities in the days ahead, once the baby was a little older.

Bhaiya had sent Ma a letter in end-March. "This time around, Gandhi ji is going to start the Total Freedom movement with the Salt Satyagraha and I am going to join him. What awaits me are lathi charges, imprisonment or even death by police bullets. I seek your blessings that I may have the courage to make the supreme sacrifice for Mother India. This Satyagraha is likely to be in Garhpura."

On receiving this letter, Ma was desperate to leave, and Pandit ji started making arrangements for her return journey. I was perplexed about the novel form of this Satyagraha. What could possibly be the relationship between salt and independence?

"I too am not clear," she replied. "What I do know is that whatever Gandhi ji does, it will be the right thing. We have taken a pledge to support him fully whenever he gives the call, no matter what he asks us to do. This time going to jail is almost certain."

"Ma, where is Garhpura?"

"This is a village near Beguserai, and I will disembark at Beguserai on my way back to Gogri from here. There will be many volunteers going to Garhpura from there, and I will join them."

Ma went straight to Garhpura from the Beguserai railway station in the company of a large group of volunteers. Salt was found in the local soil and the "noniya" caste extracted this salt. Gandhi ji said that this salt was nature's bounty like air and water, and it was criminal for the British to tax, and restrict production of something that God had intended to be consumed for free. Gandhi ji had declared that he would first make salt with his own hands on the sea-shore in Dandi, a small village in Surat district of Gujarat. This would be the signal for salt to be made by volunteers all over the country. April 6th was the appointed date for the Dandi salt march.

Bhaiya had readied a large number of volunteers, who were ready and itching to leave for Garhpura for the salt satyagraha. He would read aloud to them the news reports of Gandhi ji's march to Dandi from the Sabarmati Ashram in Ahmedabad, of how the size of the marchers kept growing along the way as people kept on joining him, not only the locals but volunteers who had travelled from all over the country. The 'Dandi March' caught the imagination of not only all Indians but indeed of the international community. Gandhi ji collected a fistful of salt on the Dandi beach, and this was the pre-appointed signal for thousands of his countrymen to start doing the same thing in hundreds of locations along the length and breadth of the country.

A *shamiana* was erected in Garhpura, a brick oven installed and a big metallic pan placed on the oven to start the process of extracting salt from the local soil. Water was poured into the pan, and the soil added into the boiling water, which on evaporation would leave behind the salt. This salt was made into packets that were then auctioned to the highest bidder from the assembled volunteers. All the auction proceeds went into a Satyagraha Fund.

Bhaiya had left College in 1921, and shortly thereafter had come in contact with Shri Krishna Singh, who was popularly known as Shri babu. He was also often referred to as "Bihar Kesari" because he used to "roar like a lion" while giving speeches. During the non-violent movement Bhaiya had accompanied Shri babu throughout his tour of Munger district, visiting villages and remote hamlets in every nook and cranny of the district. Whenever Shri babu asked for volunteers for satyagraha, Bhaiya would be there at the appointed hour with the required number of enthusiastic young men and women. Shri babu had come to admire and respect Bhaiya's organizational ability and leadership qualities.

He had visited the Jamalpur National School many times and loved to eat the food made by Ma.

The organizational work done during the non-violent movement days came in very handy during the Salt Satyagraha. Shri babu travelled on foot from Munger to Garhpura, and when the police tried to disrupt the salt making on the 17th of April he had shielded the pan of boiling salt solution with his chest. The police had to drag him away forcibly. Bhaiya had marched on foot from Gogri to Garhpura with a large band of volunteers. Batches of twenty volunteers worked for five days to produce salt. They would come shouting slogans like 'Victory to Mahatma Gandhi', 'We will make salt', 'Make salt', 'Vande Mataram', 'Victory to Mother India'. Then they would start boiling the salt solution in the pan. The police would spring into action, beat up the volunteers with staffs and canes, drag them away and destroy the oven and other structures. But fresh volunteers would turn up and rebuild the ovens and the process would start all over again. There was police firing in Garhpura but no one died.

My first cousin Murlidhar was one of those who shielded the pan with his chest and, as the police beat him mercilessly, he kept on repeating "Gandhi ji has said that the fist may get broken but must never open". He was dragged away almost unconscious and left in a ditch some distance away from the salt- making site. Shri babu was arrested in Beguserai and Bhaiya met the same fate a short distance away from Garhpura. Volunteers had come not only from all over Munger district, but from other districts as well, and they took the salt back home where large processions carrying the packets of salt would congregate at some central point, and the salt would then be auctioned. Garhpura became an important symbol of the Salt Satyagraha.

On Gandhi ji's appeal, the masses responded enthusiastically and salt started being manufactured all around the country. There were lathi charges and police firings, the jails started filling up. But this did not deter thousands of Indians, men and women, from taking part in the Satyagraha, which remained non-violent despite all the excesses of the British administration. The people suffered the atrocities with grim determination and without retaliating, even under extreme provocation. The top leaders, starting with Gandhi and Nehru, were all put in jail.

The Satyagraha continued with full gusto till mid-May. Ma was not arrested in Garhpura, but was sentenced to a month in jail for participating in a demonstration in Jamalpur in the company of women volunteers from Kanhaiyachak, Samastipur, Gohchari and Chak. All were sentenced to a month in jail. Gandhi ji wanted the movement for boycott of foreign goods and abolition of liquor to be conducted simultaneously with the Salt Satyagraha, and wanted women to take the lead in these two. When I heard about all this, I became very restless and repeatedly told Pandit ji that I wanted to go to Gogri to join the Movement. He replied that our daughter Savitri was just two months old and it would not be safe to expose her to the heat and dust and crowds. I decided to do satyagraha at home to press for my demands!!

Pandit ji responded that the nishkraman-ceremony had not been done and there was no question of the baby stepping out of the house before that ceremony.

I countered by saying the ceremony could be done that day itself, after all he was a Pandit himself and eminently qualified to do so. But eventually the ceremony was only done after the child was three months old. On my insistence, Pandit ji then dropped me and Savitry to the Gogri Ashram and returned soon to the Gurukul. Ma had been released from prison and was home by then.

I now plunged into the freedom struggle. The fact that I had a young baby to care for, was no hindrance.

Jamalpur was our theatre of operation. Groups of five or ten women would land up at shops in the bazaar that were selling foreign garments and sit in demonstration outside, shouting slogans against the sale of imported material. Many of the shopkeepers responded by making bundles of such garments, putting a 'Congress Seal' and consigning them to the godown. Those who did not, were the object of our demonstrations. This was called 'picketing' and Bhaiya too was involved in the organization of these picketings.

Ma and I would spend our days visiting villages and rallying women volunteers for the picketing. Travel was mostly on foot, I would lead the way carrying a large Tri-colour and Ma would follow with Savitry (who we had started calling Sabo) in her arms, protecting her from the strong sun in the shade of the flag.

We would try to get the women-folk together for a meeting as soon as we reached a village. This was a very difficult task. Women would hesitate to step out of their homes and congregate in an open space, and meetings would have to be conducted in inner courtyards, with many coming out of pure curiosity to see the "women freedom fighters". Inevitably the village children would fall in behind us, shouting slogans---this was like a game for them!

The men-folk would often get alarmed the moment they saw us enter the village, fearing that the police would follow us to the village and harass them. Lathi charges and mass arrests had become common-place. The government was visibly shaken by this wide-spread movement, and we were confident that the downward spiral of British rule in India had started.

I remember one incident vividly. Ma, I and Naval (an enthusiastic and committed young man from Jamalpur) were, tired, hungry and thirsty by the time we reached Baisa village in the late afternoon. But it was our practice not to ask for anything, the village women would themselves offer us food and water. We sent the village children ahead to inform the women of our arrival, and they did so most willingly, going from house to house with the message that the "Freedom Fighter Mother" (which was the name by which Ma was known in that region) had come. The women of the house in which we were going to meet were excited and were preparing to receive us with refreshments, when the man of the house happened to return from Jamalpur bazaar. He exploded with anger and shouted at us at the top of his voice. "The police knows that you are here to organize a meeting, and they are on their way to arrest you. They will harass all the villagers. What does it matter to you--you will be arrested and go to jail. But the police will seize and destroy our homes, we will be finished. Leave the village at once".

My mother replied immediately with equal force. "You are a coward, fit only to wear bangles like your women folk and hide in your house. Go and hide in fear, we will carry on the work we have set out to do."

Having spoken thus, Ma got up and we prepared to leave. But the women felt ashamed and requested us to stay on and have food. However, we felt so insulted that we left at once. This same man joined the Congress after Independence and took a lot of advantage of his political status!

It was dark by the time we left the outer limits of the village, and we were worried where to spend the night. As luck would have it, we saw a thatched temple in the darkening gloom and reaching it, prepared to spend the night there. As we prepared to bed down, the temple priest arrived to light the evening lamps for the goddess, Bishari Devi. He was surprised to see us sitting on the floor with a small child. "It is getting dark, what are you doing here? This is a lonely place and even the locals don't come here at night because this is the temple of the Goddess of Snakes."

We explained who we were and how we came to be here at night. He went back to the village and returned shortly with a few other people, carrying food and mattresses to sleep on. The coarse rotis and meagre portion of simple vegetables tasted heavenly, and we had a good night's sleep.

We decided that organizing large meetings was increasing the risk of arrest and would result in the discontinuation of our work, and hence our purpose would be better served if we went from house to house and had individual meetings.

Gandhi ji's teachings were imprinted in my mind through my interactions with Bhaiya over the years, and I would share them with the village women. They would treat us with a lot of respect and affection, seating us on straw mattresses and surrounding us in a circle to listen with rapt attention to what we had to say about Gandhi ji and the Freedom Struggle. I would tell them ,"Imagine someone enters your home, takes hold of all your possessions and sends them back to his home. Then he sells you back your own things at extortionate prices. What will happen to you? You will become impoverished. This is exactly what the British are doing. They are lording it over us, and live lives of luxury, while we become poorer and poorer. They have even imposed taxes on an essential item like salt, which even the poorest must consume. Gandhi ji is fighting to end this reign of atrocity and injustice. He wants all our countrymen and women to boycott the use of foreign goods, especially garments. Wear khadi and spin yarn for it on the charkha. He has appealed to his sisters and mothers, the women of India, to demonstrate outside shops that sell foreign garments and alcohol, to stop their sale. This is the reason we are going from village to village, spreading Gandhi ji's message. Will you join us?"

The women would be inspired by what we said, but most found it difficult to come out of their homes and join the Satyagraha. But still many families plunged into the freedom struggle, including their women.

The children made this into one big game. Singing songs as they walked around with make -- shift flags on their small shoulders became a favourite past-time for them. In this way, young and old, men and women, joined the flood unleashed by Gandhi.

Some of the songs were:

Song 1

"Don't think we are small
We will become leaders,
In the service of the nation
We will become accomplished"

Song 2

One child "One"
The whole group -- "Throw the red turban"
One child: "One, two"
Group – "Throw the red turban"
One child: "One, two, three"

Song 1
Hamko Chhote na Jaano
Hum Sardar baneinge
Bharat ki seva kar
Ham honhar baneinge

Song 2
Ek bachha - ek
Poora dal - lal pagree phek
Ek - ek do
Dal - lal pagree phek do
Ek - ek do theen
Dal - lal pagree chheen
Ek - ek do teen char
Dal - police ko maar

Group – "Seize the red turban"
One child; "One, two, three, four"
Group – "Kill the police"

Song 3

The favourite of the older children and youth was:
"The procession of martyrs ventured forth
With coffins on their heads.
Grandfather's daughter Maina
Was burnt alive till she was dead,
It is to keep her company that we have tied the coffins to our heads"

Song 4

"Step out as soldiers
Be not afraid for your lives
The police will blindly rain their lathis on us
But not a sound will escape our lips
Our homes will be confiscated and destroyed
We care not for that."

Some of the songs the women sang as they marched:

Song 5

"Who can call us weak
We are the brave tigress women

Song 3
Shahido ki toli niklee
Sar baandhe kafiniya ho
Nana ji ki beti maina
Zinda dayi jalaaye
Unhee ki
Humjoli niklee
Sar baandhe kafiniya ho

Song 4
Nikal pada ab bankar sainik
Bhay na karo kuchh ptaano ka
Andhi ho kar police chalaave dande
Nikle muh se aah nahin
Ghar ka maal kurk kar jaaye
Humko kuchh parvah nahin

Song 5
Ab kaun kehe abla hamko
Hum veer singhni naari hain
Darti nahein hum goli se
Hum matribhumi adhikari hain

Bullets do not frighten us
The mother-land belongs to us"

Song 6

"Oh villagers, who are you trying to scare?
The tiger who walks ahead is mine
His roars will
Frighten even the king of the jungle.
To think you will frighten his mother
Is the height of ignorance"

Song 7

"Come friend let us see
What the jail has in store
Imprisonment is a mere game
We are ready to be hanged"

These were the popular songs which were sung with feeling and passion. I have no idea who wrote them and when.

There was one particular ditty sung by the children which really caught my fancy:

Song 8

One: "Brothers o brothers"
Many: "What brother what?"
One; "Will you come to jail?"

Song 6

Are gramwalo tum daraate kise
Aage--aage jo jaata mera sher hai
jiski hunkaaro se
sher bhi dar jaate hain
Uski ma ko daraana
Ek andher hai

Song 7

Chaloo sakhi dekhan
Jail ke jabaiya hay
Jail ke to khel samjhe
phaansi pur chadhvaiya hay

Song 8

Ek bachha - bhaiyon te bhaiyon
Poora dal - Kya bhai kya?
Bachha - jail Chaloge?
Dal - kyo bhai kyo?
Bachha - mil jaayegi
Dal - Kya bhai kya?
Baacha - aazadi
Dal - wah bhai wah!

Many: "Why brother why?"

One: "You will get"

Many: "What brother what?"

One "Freedom!;

Many "Yeah brother yeah!"

These songs typified the mood of the masses in India. In the Gogri Ashram this created an atmosphere of alertness and readiness for action.

From Kanhaiyachak the wives of Suryanarayan Sharma and his brother, Bhubhaneshwar babu, Lakhanlal and many other women set out from home to join the Movement. Between 1930 and 1932 these brave women took part in protest marches and the picketing of shops selling liquor and foreign garments. Many went to jail. These are just a few names I am putting down, there were large numbers of women who did the same things.

Awadh bhai was a long-time functionary of the Gogri Ashram and Manager of the Khadi Store. Seeing me go out on Satyagraha work with Ma and young Sabo, inspired him to think of bringing his new bride Sushila Devi to the Ashram so that she could join Ma and me in our work in the villages organizing women volunteers. He came from a well-to-do Rajput family.

When he mentioned this desire to his family members, he met with strong resistance. "Is it not enough that you have become a member of the Ashram and a revolutionary? Why do you want to drag the women of our house into that activity?" But Awadh bhai was a determined young man. He persuaded his wife to join him, and she readily agreed to give up the confines of a traditional Rajput home for the company of her husband and the vigorous open-air life of the Ashram and surrounding villages. They schemed to run away from home. Awadh bhai was a lean and wiry six foot tall person. His wife was small and petite, beautiful and wise. He manged to a get a dhoti, kurta and turban for her so that she would look like a young boy. Late one night, when the entire household was fast asleep, the two lovers of freedom slipped away in the darkness and made their way on foot to the Ashram, where they were received with joy and open arms. Sushila Devi became our close friend and companion, and a fellow revolutionary.

It was around this time that a young and inspired resident of Kanhaiyachak arrived at the Ashram-Kashi Jha. He threw himself with gusto into any task assigned to him, from cooking food to leading protest marches with the national flag in hand. He was an eager volunteer for travelling large distances to convey Satyagraha instructions, often running for miles to ensure messages reached on time. All this with an ever-ready smile on his face. He had composed a song after his imprisonment in 1930, which he would sing as he went about his work:

"In the Jamalpur picketing
Was arrested the mastana Kashi Jha
Six months in jail later
Returned mastana Kashi Jha
In the bomb conspiracy was arrested
Mastana Bhagat Singh
In the Jamalpur picketing
Was arrested mastana Kashi Jha"*

Ramdev from Malpa village arrived in the Ashram. A staunch Arya Samaji, he was totally committed to the freedom struggle. From Temta came the courageous Bhubhaneshwar Singh,

---

* Jamalpur ke picketing mein
Pakda gaya mastana Kashi Jha,
Chhe maheenay jail bhog kar
Aa gaya mastana Kashi Jha,
Bum case mein pakda gaya
Mastana Bhagat Singh.
Jamalpur ke picketing mein
Pakda gaya mastana Kashi Jha.

who went on one dangerous mission after another without ever flinching. The Ashram residents later started calling him "Bose Bhai". Nandkishore Singh of Basudevpur was living in his sister's house to study. He gave up his studies, moved into the Ashram and offered himself up to take part in protest marches and go to jail. That was the era when countless youth sacrificed all that they had to join Bhaiya's band of volunteers, risking life and limb for the Motherland.

Mother and I were out enrolling women volunteers in Temta. We managed to hitch a ride on a bullock cart on the return journey to the Ashram. We had hardly left the village when we saw a young boy of twelve or thirteen, a bundle of clothes clutched under his armpit, come running after us. As he drew level with the bullock cart, he said, "I want to join you in the Ashram and devote my life fighting the British. Please take me with you."

Ma tried to reason with him, "You are very young, your family must be looking for you. Please go back home to them."

"I will not go back", the boy replied. "I do not have any parents. You are Mai ji, everyone's mother. Please take me with you to the Ashram."

Ma persisted. "Son, the police follows us everywhere, we can be arrested anytime and thrown into jail. The police is brutal and beat people mercilessly. Recently, after beating a young man black and blue, they pumped air into his ears from a bicycle pump and burst his eardrums (this young man was from Bihpur, I cannot remember his name). You are young and frail, and if you start being beaten you will beg the police for mercy. This will bring dishonour to the Ashram's reputation."

"I will not utter a word even if the police beat me to death. I have come because I am ready to sacrifice my life."

That young boy joined us and never went back to his village, the Ashram became his home. His name was Ugramohan Mishra.

All the people I have named were hard-boiled freedom fighters. They bore police beatings and went to jail countless times. They sacrificed the prime of their youth to the War for Independence and would never be able to find a remunerative livelihood because they had given up their studies.

Ma was arrested in early 1930 while picketing in Jamalpur bazaar, along with the group of women from Kanhaiyachak. The women, many of whose names I have mentioned in the last few pages, would offer themselves in group after group for picketing and subsequent arrest, creating a chain which never seemed to end. Ma had entrusted me with the responsibility of ensuring that the picketing continued despite the repeated arrests, and I would return to the Ashram every day to ready the next few batches of volunteers for picketing and subsequent arrest the following day.

Bhaiya was released from jail six months after his arrest in the Salt Satyagraha. In November 1930 Bhaiya was leading a large protest march through Jamalpur bazaar, shouting slogans against the government, when he was again arrested together with many of his fellow demonstrators.

Ma was interned in Bhagalpur Jail, and released after a month and-a-half. She resumed the picketing immediately after her release. I now insisted that my job of organising volunteers be given to someone else and I be allowed to join the picketers, so that I too could court arrest and go to jail. Ma said, "First write to your husband, take his permission and then go to jail."

"I had taken his permission before coming, but I will write to him immediately and take his specific permission for going to jail", I replied.

Having seen the conditions inside a jail, Ma knew how difficult it would be for me to stay there with a small child. You had to sleep on a raised concrete platform for a bed, with a thin mattress as the only bedding, wear the striped jail uniform made of coarse and heavy cloth, and eat the coarse jail food which inevitably contained small stones mixed with the rice and dal, the rotis half cooked and the vegetable portions small and quite inedible. Khichdi for breakfast. Jails now kept political prisoners separately under different rules and conditions from the ordinary criminals, a practice recently introduced after Yatindra Nath Das had gone on a protest fast in 1929 and died after sixty days. The jail authorities had created categories A, B and C for political prisoners, but most were kept in Category C, including Ma.

However, when I asked her what it was like inside the jail, she said, "Very nice."

This was the energy and enthusiasm of those freedom fighters.

One day, when Bhai ji and Kashi Jha were in the Ashram, Ma and I were visiting Khajraitha village. The police suddenly appeared and arrested the two of them, along with Bhagwat bhai who was visiting. The Ashram was seized and confiscated, a lock and seal put and a police picket posted.

One of the Ashram inmates managed to slip away and came running to Khajraitha to tell us what had happened in the Ashram. He also carried a message from Bhai ji that Ma and I should somehow come to the Maheshkhunt railway station and see him there. He was being taken to Bhagalpur, it was still a few hours for the train departure. He told us we could reach Maheshkhunt in time if we took the train from Pasraha to Maheshkhunt. We somehow managed to reach Maheshkhunt just in time to see Bhai ji sitting in police custody, and were allowed a few minutes to meet him. He told us "Now both of us brothers are in jail, we have no idea when we will be released. The main functionaries of the Ashram are all in jail and the Ashram has been seized and confiscated. I have called you here to tell you that now all the responsibility will be on your shoulders. I know it will be very difficult, but you must continue the work with faith and courage. You must ensure a steady stream of volunteers for picketing and arrest, the Satyagraha movement must not suffer."

We saw Bhai ji being led to the train by his police escort, and we began our trek back. But our home, the Ashram, had been seized and we had nowhere to go. Within two days, a tented camp was set up in Jamalpur and we moved in there. However it was not possible to spend the nights there, and we would find it difficult to find someone brave enough to put us up for the night, since the government was going all out to destroy the Satyagraha Movement and would come down heavily on people giving refuge to known revolutionaries like us. But there were brave souls who stepped forward to help, chief among them being Bhumni Mishra, Jagdish Prasad, Gokul Prasad and Sundar Choudhry (Balmiki Choudhry's father). They were ardent nationalists, and they opened their homes for us to spend nights in. We would come in late at night, and leave before day-break for the Jamalpur Camp to resume the daily picketing activity. Ma was arrested again and this time sentenced to six months imprisonment. I was expecting a reply from my husband, Pandit ji, who was in Calcutta to take an exam for a higher Sanskrit degree. However, in the absence of the awaited permission from him to go to jail, I could not stop Ma's work now that she was in jail. So I kept on with the work Ma had been doing.

Pandit ji meanwhile had left Calcutta for Gogri on getting my letter and landed up at the Ashram, only to find a big lock at the entrance gate and a police picket. Several of the policemen were our sympathizers, they treated Pandit ji with courtesy and offered him a seat and water to drink. They told him a Camp had been set up in Jamalpur and he could expect to find ''Behen ji" (i.e me) there. By now Ma was famous as "Mai ji' and I as "Behen ji" in the whole region.

The incident that catapulted Mai ji to fame is worth recounting. Ma, Bose bhai, Sabo and I were touring the Choutham area in the immediate postmath of the Salt Satyagraha. Our main activities were centred around creating awareness about Self-rule, village development and reform, abolition of liquor etc.

We came to know that there was a pond in the village of Kaithi about which it was believed that if a person bathed in its waters on Tuesday or Saturday and then made offerings to the Lord Hanuman in the temple located there, all diseases would be cured and all wishes granted. Crowds gathered every week on those two days and the atmosphere was like that of a large fair, with sweet-sellers and other vendors setting up shop to cater to the needs of the worshippers. The person on whose land the pond was located had set up facilities for visitors to rest in and have meals. All in all, it was a steady revenue generation opportunity for him.

Ma thought this would give us a ready audience, and with this objective in mind we reached Kaithi. Sabo was unwell, and so I decided to stay on in Choutham and did not accompany Ma and Bose bhai to Kaithi. It was nine o'clock at night by the time the two returned to Choutham and Ma was too tired to do anything but collapse in bed and go off to sleep. It was Bose bhai who narrated what happened in Kaithi. "Sister, Mai ji performed a miracle today. On reaching Kaithi we discovered that what was once a pond was now merely a mud-hole. Huddled around it were the maimed, deformed and diseased, with a large number of lepers among them. They would enter and wallow in the oozing mud, and that sight saddened and enraged Mai ji."

"Sister! You should have heard Mai ji's passion-filled oration, which drew and mesmerized all the people who had congregated around that so-called pond. 'Do you see the pond? it is nothing but an oozing mud-hole. Those who enter the mud will worsen their sores and wounds, those who are not infected will expose themselves to all manner of infection. Instead of curing ailments and disease, you are spreading them. Go to the hospitals for your cure. Those who consume the water of this pond are inviting cholera, typhoid, leprosy and other infections. I beg you, stop coming here for cures, save yourself from this false belief. I know this place has a reputation for cures, but does any of you personally know a single person who has been cured by bathing in this mud-filled pond?'

"No one stirred. Mai ji continued 'There is a hospital in Jamalpur, please go there and get proper treatment and medication. Please trust what I am saying. Today is Saturday. I will be waiting for you at the hospital on Tuesday and will ensure that each one who comes there gets proper medical advice and treatment'."

The next Tuesday indeed the crowds at Kaithi thinned, and increased at the hospital in Jamalpur. The local priest at Kaithi told those who went there that it was a big mistake to forsake the gods for doctors, and it would not be long before people started thronging the Kaithi pond again. But in fact the opposite happened. The hospital doctors cured several people, who spoke about their experience to others and over time Kaithi's fame as a place for wonder cures faded away and became history.

When I look back, I am surprised how even after Bhaiya's imprisonment there was no shortage of volunteers for picketing and courting arrest. It is difficult to describe the solidarity and zeal of the people in those heady days. Such a large number went to jail, that I cannot remember their names or even their faces. Many used codenames so that the police would not be able to trace their family connections and harass them. So many adopted names like Bose, Ghosh, Leader, Soldier, Follower, Monkey etc.

By the time Pandit ji arrived at the Jamalpur Camp from Gogri Ashram, we had set out for Baisa. A volunteer accompanied Pandit ji from the Camp and finally they caught up with us. He said his mother was seriously ill, and he wanted me to go back with him to look after her. Much against my inner desire I agreed to go, but frankly I thought this illness was just a ruse to take me back. I had never thought of backing off despite all I had heard about the living conditions in jail, and every morning I would leave the camp fully prepared to be arrested and packed off to jail. The image of Gandhi ji and Kasturba in the Gogri Ashram was imprinted in my mind and was a constant source of inspiration and courage to help keep me walking on the path prescribed by him.

We reached Harpurjan with Sabo, and immediately Pandit ji went to his village home to get his mother. She was indeed very unwell, and all my doubts about Pandit ji vanished. It took two months for my mother-in-law to recover. It was the combination of Adhishtata ji's medication and my constant care that restored her back to health.

The number of students in the Girls School had halved from sixteen to eight. There was no one to teach some of the subjects I had been teaching-Hindi, Sanskrit and Mathematics. Parents were worried about their wards. The Satyagraha and protest movements were gathering momentum, police beatings and arrests were becoming common-place. All Arya Samaj establishments were under government surveillance because a large number of Samajis had joined the Congress. When the news of my having gone back to Gogri to participate in the freedom movement reached them, parents had become even more worried. Many came and took their daughters back home.

I tried my best to improve things at the school. The girls started to take interest in their studies once more and things were returning to normal when a telegram came from Bhai ji "Bhaiya very unwell. Please send Adhishtata ji to the Camp Jail in Patna."

The next day we got a postcard stating Bhaiya was down with pneumonia.

It took us a day to organize funds for the trip to Patna. Cash was never kept in the Gurukul but across the river was a village named Gopalpur where there was a merchant named Shivathal

Sah. He was a social reformer and had good relations with the Gurukul residents. Pandit ji went to him and borrowed thirty rupees, and the next day Adishtata ji left for Patna accompanied by a student named Vidyasagar.

Chapter 11

PATNA CAMP JAIL

The number of political prisoners had become so large, especially after the Salt Satyagraha, that the normal jails could no longer accommodate them and the Patna Camp Jail was created to house political prisoners. This was a facility situated near the Patna Railway Station and its walls and roof were made of steel/tin sheets, which meant that it became unbearably hot during the summer and very cold during the winter. Subterranean water seeped through the floors which were wet all the time, and this resulted in the jail being infested with flies and mosquitoes. Disease was rampant, particularly dysentery and malaria.

Bhaiya and his companions were lodged in this jail. The first stint was for six months, but they were back in again and had to spend the winter months there. The health problems started with the advent of summer.

Bhaiya had started a cleanliness campaign. Working in the blistering sun, they would cut brushwood and bring in dry soil to spread on the wet floors, clean the drains and the jail premises with brooms. Bhaiya developed a cough and low fever but kept on working till one day he could not stand up and his friends carried him to his cell bed. He had very high fever and the jail doctor had to be called.

Bhai ji was with him for the two weeks that the high fever raged. The jail doctor was not sure whether it was typhoid or pneumonia and kept changing his treatment. Seeing no improvement, Bhai ji decided it was time to call Adhishtata ji and approached the jail authorities for permission to do so. The jail authorities too were worried, and agreed. That was when the telegram and postcard were sent to me.

Adhishtata ji saw Bhaiya in the jail, and stayed on in Patna for two days. He gave Bhai ji the Ayurvedic medication and explained how to administer it. He then returned to Harpurjan.

I was very worried, but Adishtata ji assured me that Bhaiya was out of danger, but very weak. He had advised Bhaiya to come to Harpurjan for a few days after his release from jail, so that he could rejuvenate his body and mind under Adhishtata ji's supervision and care.

Ma was in Bhagalpur Jail, and news came that she too was suffering from fever. Bhai ji was fortunately with Bhaiya and managed to safe his life, but with no one there with Ma, I was really worried for her.

Bhaiya was released in early 1933 and came straight to Harpurjan along with Bhai ji. It took two months for Bhaiya to regain his strength and vigour. The brothers used to have their meals and spend time with me, but nights were spent in Adhishtata ji's house.

By then news came that Ma's fever was persisting and she had become very weak.

The Freedom Movement had started losing momentum. The Gogri Ashram had been seized by the government and the premises locked up, large numbers of Congress men were in jail. All the important women volunteers, who along with Ma were the heart and soul of the women's protest movement, were in jail. Bhaiya told me I should return to Gogri with him, we would try and put life back into the freedom struggle in that region. The participation of women had almost come to a complete halt, and I was the only one who could revive it. He was also confident that if I was with her, Ma's health would improve. I was restless to go back, and when Bhaiya finally left for Gogri, I accompanied him.

The first problem was to find some place to stay. The days were spent travelling from village to village, organizing women volunteers, and I would eat whatever food was offered by the villagers. The problem was the night stays, since people were now even more afraid to give shelter to us for fear of police harassment. Homes that gave shelter to Congress workers were seized and often vandalized, but we still always found someone who was willing to put us up for the night. One night we could not find anyone who could accommodate us, and decided to spend the night in a haystack. I spread a sheet on the hay and I tried to go to sleep with little Sabo next to me, but sleep was hard to find. I was finding it difficult to breathe with all the dust and hay-particles assailing my nostrils, when suddenly Sabo shrieked. A centipede was crawling on her face.

I sat up all night with Sabo in my arms.

I managed to enrol eight volunteers and was making plans to go to Jamalpur and re-start the picketing when Bhaiya arrived. He told me that Gandhi ji had gone on an indefinite fast, and Satyagraha activities all over the country had been halted. I should return with him.

There was no place to stay in Gogri, all ties with Shirnia had been broken. I went to meet my old teacher Ambika Devi, and she invited me to stay with her. I spent about two weeks in her house.

Chapter 12

Camp Diyara

Babuji was now fully immersed in managing the family's economic affairs. With Ma and Bhaiya fully devoted to the freedom struggle, he had taken it upon himself to manage the finances, and used to supervise the farming on the family landholdings in the Shirnia Diyara (land on the banks of the Ganga river).When the Ashram was seized he had relocated to the Shirnia Diyara, had a thatch hut constructed and started living in it. Farming was good, and as part of a family agreement the Patharghat lands were given to his elder brother's widow while all the Shirnia diyara land came to him. My widowed aunt lived in the family home in Shirnia with her son Jageshwar, while Babuji was on the Shirnia diyara with Nandkishore and Bandar Namdhari. I decided I would join him there till such time that Gandhi ji ended his fast and Satyagraha activities resumed.

A Satyagrahi had come to meet me in Jamalpur after his release from jail and he advised me to move to Camp Diyara. "Whoever is released from jail finds his way there, it is the nerve-centre of all future plans. Sometimes we can find Suresh babu (Bhaiya) there, sometimes we can't. But we always get to know where he can be found."

I set out for the Diyara on foot, Sabo in my arms. After walking twelve miles we reached the banks of the Ganga, where we got on to a boat for the river crossing to the Shirnia Diyara.

By the time we reached, we were extremely tired, hungry and thirsty. But to our dismay we found that the hut was empty. Babuji was out in the fields supervising the farm labourers, Nandkishore and Bandar had gone shopping for food. No one was aware that I was coming. The hut had no door, so I went in. Babuji had made a large wooden chest in which he stored food items since any food left outside would be eaten up by the jackals who frequented that area. I opened the chest and saw something that looked like a roti, but it had a terrible taste and could not be eaten. Fortunately there was also some milk, which I heated and gave to Sabo. She had it and went off to sleep.

By then Nandkishore and Bandar returned with rice, dal and vegetables. The boy who had accompanied me from Jamalpur drew water from the well and I cooked a large portion of khichdi, which we ate to our heart's content. You only realize the joy and significance of having a roof over your head and food to eat, after experiences like this.

We were all waiting for Bhaiya. He came after three or four days, with Bhai ji and two other volunteers, and soon Camp Diyara started humming with the presence of revolutionaries even though the resumption of Satyagraha was going to take some more time. It was the summer of 1933 and Sabo had started talking a lot. I had told her we were going to visit the Jail, her grandmother (Nani) was there. She now started asking, "What kind of jail is this that we have come to? Nani is not here."

I explained that this was her Nana's diyara, not a jail and that I would take her soon to meet Nani in jail. She kept crying to be taken to meet her Nani and it became increasingly difficult to make her feel happy in the diyara without her Nani. Finally Bhai ji told her we would go the next day itself to meet Nani. In preparation for the jail visit, I washed all our clothes and made some dry snacks for Ma.

The shortest route from the Shirnia diyara to Bhagalpur was via Bariyarpur. We travelled by bullock cart to the river crossing point at Jhouya Bahiyar and crossed the broad Ganga by boat. But by the time we reached Bariyarpur we found that the last bus had already left for Bhagalpur. However, there was a bus about to leave for Munger and Bhai ji suggested we board this bus and go to Bhagalpur from Munger.

The bus reached Munger at ten o'clock at night. Awadh bhai was the Khadi Store Manager in Munger and we spent the night at his place. Next morning we took the train from Munger to Bhagalpur. At the Bhagalpur railway station we hired a horse-pulled tonga to take us to the Bhagalpur Jail. Visiting hours at the jail were limited and Bhai ji urged the tonga driver to make haste. But suddenly the horse came to an abrupt halt and despite all effort, refused to budge -- almost as if he was doing Satyagraha! The driver explained that they were passing his house and this was the horse's feeding time, that is why he had stopped!!He got us another tonga and we somehow managed to reach the jail in time.

We informed the prison security that we had come to meet Anoop Devi and were led to a waiting room near the jail entrance. After a short while, the Jailor appeared along with Ma. It was so sad to see Ma in the striped clothes of the jail. Sabo started crying that she wanted to go to her Nani's lap but iron bars separated Ma and us. MA told us that till a short while ago women visitors were allowed to come inside the jail premises, but recently all security measure had been tightened. The good news was that her fever had subsided and she was feeling much better. Bhai ji had not even started talking when the Jailor re-appeared and told us that visiting time was over, and led Ma back into the Jail. Sabo started crying that she wanted to stay back with her Nani, and it was with great difficulty that we managed to placate her and make our way to Bhagalpur town. After a short halt, we started on our return journey to the diyara.

I think Sabo felt that jail was some very nice place where her Nani lived!

Chapter 13

Back to the Girls School in Harpurjan

The freedom struggle had lost all momentum. It was June of 1933 and terribly hot in the riverine diyara tract on the banks of the Ganga. I decided it would be better if we returned to Harpurjan instead of hanging around in this desolate place on the diyara.

Vidyavati had completed her Kavyatirtha exam in the Gurukul and had got married a year ago to Mangal Singh of Pokharpur, a village near Chapra. Mangal Singh was a prosperous landlord, a Congressman and a believer in the Arya Samaj view of the world. He was studying for his M.A degree at the Banaras Hindu University, and had taken Vidyavati with him to Banaras so that she too could continue further studies.

The state of affairs at the Girls School had deteriorated sharply since my departure. Vidyavati and I had been the main teachers and a major crisis had developed after both of us left, since it was not possible to find replacements.

Satto Bhai's (Satyanarayan Singh) wife Bindeswari Devi fell ill in jail, and was released before Ma. On his release Satto Bhai hired a house in Jamalpur for his wife's treatment in the Jamalpur Hospital. Bhaiya suggested that she go to Harpurjan for treatment and so Bindeswari Devi accompanied Sabo and me.

Before my arrival, Bhagwat Bhai's wife Kamala Devi had come to Harpurjan and experienced a successful cure. Likewise, Bhaiya sent many of his Satyagrahi friends and compatriots to Harpurjan for treatment because of his faith in Adhishtata ji, and indeed all returned home happy and cured.

Pandit ji had started feeling uncomfortable with not having his own house to live in and had decided to construct one even before I returned. Adhishtata ji gave him some land between his house and the Gurukul, and construction work was going on when I arrived. There was no formal paper-work for the land transfer, everything was on faith and word-of-mouth.

I plunged headlong into the work of reviving the Girls School. Goraiya Kothi was a progressive village and its landlord Narayan Singh was a Congressman. Two girls from his family came to study in Harpurjan, two more girls came from Chapra and Bhagyavati also came around this time. In later times she would get married to my sister-in-law's younger brother, Ramdhari Upadhyaya. Vasudev, a Brahmachari in the Gurukul, who was studying to become a Snatak, taught PT to the girls.

Babu Gunraj Singh, who was a lawyer in Chapra, sent his daughter-in-law Kaushalya to study in the Girls School at Hapurjan.

The Annual Convocation in the Gurukul was an event everyone looked forward to and was an important day in the life of the Gurukul. It was on this day that students who had completed all the study requirements of the Gurukul curriculum were awarded the Snatak degree and could finally go home. This was also the only day in the whole year that parents could meet their sons and daughters studying in the Gurukul. As I have already mentioned earlier, Gurukul rules required students who came to study not to leave the Gurukul and go home till they had completed their full course of studies, which took many years.

The Gurukul students would exhibit their prowess in drills, wrestling and other traditional physical fitness practices. The actual Convocation ceremony was very impressive and worth seeing. Wearing yellow clothes, graduating boys and girls would assemble in the massive Yagyashala where a traditional Vedic havan was performed to the accompaniment of mantras chanted by both students and teachers. In the afternoon a general assembly was held where many residents from the surrounding villages also gathered to hear the Arya Samaj preachers and scholars hold forth against prevailing social evils, followed by a session of melodious bhajans. A separate assembly would be held for women so that even those who observed purdah could participate.

That year Vasudev and Satyadev were awarded the Snatak degree. Kaushalya was very good at drills, and we had decide she would lead the girls drill. At the appointed time the girls lined up smartly in front of the vast gathering, with Kaushalya in front. She had never gone out of her house, and even in the Girls School always did her drills inside the school compound. The sudden sight of so many people, mostly men, unnerved her and she fell down in a swoon. The girls drill had to be cancelled.

Vidyasagar and Dayasagar were two brothers studying in the Gurukul. Both were in peak physical fitness and had magnificent physiques. They demonstrated a range of feats of amazing physical prowess including acts of supreme skill with the staff and bow-and-arrow by Dayasagar while Vidyasagar stopped a car from moving and even allowed it to drive over his body! Watching these extraordinary feats, people forgot their disappointment at not being able to see the girls drill.

The women's assembly was also a big success. Many female preachers, among whom the most prominent was Sandhya Devi, held the women spell-bound.

That year Jaidevi went home with her mother and got married.

Chapter 14

Our New Home

Pandit ji took great pains to supervise the construction of his new house. It was going to be a big house with large hall-like rooms, each with four windows and two doors. In this part of the country, the rooms in the women's section of the house had very small windows and that too at near ceiling-level. This was to prevent outsiders from looking in, and that too explained the small doors where one had to bend to enter. This resulted in the women of the house being denied sunshine and fresh air. It was only when they grew old that they ventured to sit out in the courtyard. New brides did not venture out of their rooms, not even onto the veranda in front of their room. These were manifestations of the purdah system, against which the Arya Samaj campaigned relentlessly.

Consequently, all new Arya Samaj houses were open and airy, and so was our house too. Four large bedrooms with a wide veranda in front opened on to a big courtyard which had provision for shrubs, fruit trees and flower-beds. The kitchen, store-room and other utilities were on one side of the courtyard, each one as large and spacious as the bedrooms.

All this took time to make. Meanwhile, in October 1933, my second daughter was born. Ma had been released from jail and came to Harpurjan to help me. We were still living in the Girls School and had not yet moved to the new house, whose roof was by then just half complete. We named the baby Indira, a name chosen by Ma.

Ma returned to the Diyara shortly after the delivery, taking Sabo with her because it would have been impossible for me to manage both the girls by myself.

The traditional latrines in Harpurjan required manual removal of the excreta by members of an untouchable caste called 'Halkhor'. There was no container for the human waste, which fell onto the ground and was removed by these folk. I insisted that we construct a latrine like the ones used in the Gogri Ashram. It was Gandhi ji's constant endeavour to improve the living conditions of the Harijans (his term for the Untouchables). In fact he was on a hunger strike for the cause of the Harijans when I came to Harpurjan from Gogri in 1932. The government had mooted a plan to reserve election seats for Untouchables, but Gandhi ji opposed this move saying this would further strengthen the divide between the Harijans and others, what was required was their integration with the rest of society. The later developments in Independent India showed how correct his thinking was.

Anyway, I could not bear the thought of a Halkhor clearing our excreta, and Pandit ji concurred with me. So we adopted the Gogri Ashram latrine design, where the latrines were situated outside the house, no manual evacuation was required, hygiene was much better and the waste was converted into manure for subsequent use.

Chapter 15

Earthquake

It was January of 1934.Pandit ji had gone to Teliya to give winter clothing to his mother. Ugramohan was living in our house, Ma had sent him to help me when she returned to Gogri. Ugramohan was still very young and he had not been allowed to court arrest. He had gone to Adhishtata ji's house to see the panchayat in session there. I was lying with Indira (Indu) on a cot, soaking in the mild winter sun and had almost dozed off when suddenly the cot started vibrating. I got up startled, and looked in all directions to see who it was that was trying to move the cot, thinking it was some of the girls up to their usual pranks again. But the vibrations continued, and the trees started swaying wildly from side to side. Then the compound walls started collapsing in front of my unbelieving eyes. I picked up Indu and ran for the main gate, but as I neared it the surrounding walls collapsed. Only then did I realize that this was an earthquake.

I was lucky that the collapsing walls did not fall on me. The nearest portion of the collapsed wall had fallen no more than one foot away from me, but our cow's young calf was not so lucky. Its head and torso were buried under the debris, I could see only the thrashing legs. I could not bear that sight, and putting Indu on the ground I started removing the debris which covered its body.

By this time a few villagers arrived running, and soon Ugramohan reached with some of the girl students. Together they extricated the calf from under the debris, but unfortunately it was dead by the time they did so.The mother cow was tethered nearby, and seeing its dead calf it burst into mournful cries. The dead calf's body was quickly removed, but the mother cow kept crying for days and refused to eat or drink anything.

While the calf's body was being removed, some of the girls were attracted by a strange sound from the well and they rushed to it. To their surprise, they saw that the water table had reached the upper brim of the well. As they watched in astonishment and horror, the water suddenly disappeared and the well filled up with sand. This happened to wells all over and many of the rivers too dried up, leaving behind just sand.

The only exception was the big well in the main Gurukul. Word spread that this was a miracle occasioned by the holiness of the place. A water crisis followed and large crowds would come to take water from the Gurukul well.

I went to check on our house under construction. Several walls had completely collapsed, and a portion of the main hall too had fallen down. I was totally distressed, and had no idea what I would do if Pandit ji was not able to return that day. Fortunately Adhistata ji came shortly to inspect the Girls School and our house, and he insisted that there was no question of my staying there and I should move into the portion of his house which served as the girls wing. I had dinner with the girls and went off to sleep. At around midnight we were woken up by more tremors, although not as violent as before. We all rushed out and stayed awake the rest of the night. I went to the Girls School next morning and found Pandit ji there, who had managed to return early in the morning. We put a bed out in the open and spent the day there.

The main Gurukul building was largely unharmed. A Gogri man called Sukhdev used to work in the Gurukul kitchen and he delivered our food to us in the Girls School itself. I was just settling down for a snooze after lunch, when the earthquake struck again. The tiles came cluttering down the sloped roofs and we ran away as far as we could from the school building. Everyone was terrified with the recurring tremors, and we decided we would sleep outdoors despite the biting cold. A temporary shelter was created with straw and tarpaulin, and we slept under it, covered with blankets. Ugramohan slept at Adhishtata ji's house. Mercifully there were no further tremors.

Now I started worrying about Gogri. The newspapers carried horrific accounts of the havoc wreaked in Munger, which had been devastated by the quake. Muzzafarpur suffered the same fate. Ma. Babuji and Sabo would have been relatively safe in the diyara, but Bhai ji and Bhaiya used to spend a lot of their days in Munger and I was really worried about them. The whole of Bihar had been badly affected, and Gandhi ji toured the state accompanied by Nehru. I kept scanning the newspapers for mention of Bhaiya.

The earthquake had struck on fifteenth January, and within three days Adhishtata ji started supervising the reactivation of the well in the Girls School. The sand and mud was removed and fortunately clean water reappeared. The Gurukul took charge of similarly cleaning and reactivating many wells in the neighbouring area.

From the newspapers I gathered that the Congress had formed a State Relief Committee, and volunteers were fanning out for relief work. I guessed Bhaiya and Bhai ji would be fully involved with the relief effort. A week later a person came from Gogri with news that all family members were safe and that my two brothers were spearheading the relief work in that area.

The destruction caused by the earthquake pushed up the cost of constructing the house, and we decided to go for a tiled roof rather than a concrete one. We moved into our own house by year-end.

Chapter 16

Relief Work

Like everything else, Bhaiya approached the relief activity in a highly planned and organized manner. With food, clothing and medicines obtained from the State Committee, Bhaiya and his band of committed and disciplined volunteers plunged into the work, moving from one disaster zone to another, often leaving behind some volunteers while the rest of the group moved ahead. The government also helped a little. The local Congress workers took it upon themselves to ensure that the relief material reached the most needy, and Bhaiya's group was in the forefront of this effort. People spoke about his work for a long time. Helping the injured and displaced, removing dead bodies from under the debris and ensuring proper death rituals, distributing food, clothing, medicines--they worked day and night like men possessed. Where no one else was willing to venture, the Gogri Ashram team went readily and enthusiastically.

The earthquake created cracks and fissures in the diyara terrain, some so wide that grown men could be swallowed up in them. Ma and Sabo found themselves staring at one such fissure, and it is a miracle that they lived to talk about it. This is what happened. Ma and Sabo were out walking near the well when the well water suddenly rose like a fountain, and then disappeared to be replaced by sand. There was a loud rumbling noise and Ma thought aeroplanes were passing overhead. This was followed by violent tremors and she started feeling giddy and unsteady on her feet. She thought this was due to weakness following her ill-health in jail and lay down on the ground, while Sabo remained standing. Suddenly the earth split into two and a wide fissure appeared, with Ma on one side and little Sabo on the other. Shaking inwardly with fear, Ma nevertheless managed to keep an outer calm and told Sabo "Keep still and don't move, otherwise you will fall into the ditch". The little girl was terrified but remained stationary while Ma got to her feet and walked to the end of the fissure, made a u-turn and started walking towards her granddaughter. She reached her, immediately took her in her arms, and moved away from the opening in the ground, moments before there was another rumbling sound and the fissure closed up as quickly as it had appeared. This scene was a recurrent nightmare that haunted her for a long time.

Fortunately, the thatched hut survived intact and there were no cracks or fissures near it. The well took some time to reactivate, but those days the Ganga water was potable and they managed with water from the river.

After the relief work was over, a massive drive was undertaken across the state as per Gandhi ji's directive to rejuvenate the wells that had silted up as a result of the earthquake. This further enhanced the trust and confidence of the common man in the Congress, which came to be looked upon as a friend of the masses who could be relied upon in times both good and bad. In turn, the common man was ready to do whatever the Congress wanted them to do by way of collective action against the British.

In the midst of all this frenetic activity, Bhaiya also had a concrete well made in the diyara, since the Ashram there was now home to many volunteers and the old well was unable to meet their water requirements.

Chapter 17

BHAI JI GETS MARRIED

There was a big Vedic ritual, a *yagya*, organized in Ajmer. Pandit ji went to participate in it, and met Ramraksha Brahmachari there. He was actually Ramraksha Upadhyaya and not a real brahmchari (celibate), was married and had children too. He had studied in a Gurukul and as per the accepted practice continued calling himself Brahmachari even after leaving the Gurukul and getting married. He had become a Congressman and had gone to Champaran in response to Gandhiji's call during the Indigo Movement. He had stayed on after the Movement and worked among the farmers promoting education, hygiene and other aspects of social reform. He later established a Gandhi Ashram there.

He had heard of Bhaiya and was interested in exploring the possibility of his marriage to his younger sister Yashoda. He was looking for a Gandhian, social reformer and Congressman like himself. He was thrilled to learn that Pandit ji was married to Suresh Mishra's sister, and immediately started discussing the possible matrimonial alliance. He took down details of the family etc and soon landed up in the Shirnia Diyara Ashram.

Bhaiya politely told him that he had taken a vow not to get married till India attained independence, but suggested his younger brother Shiva Kant (Bhai ji).

Brahmachari ji's ancestral home was in Udantrai ka Bangra village of Chapra district. Bhaiya, Bhai ji and Pandit ji went there. Yashoda was a real beauty, the family backgrounds matched perfectly and the marriage was sealed.

Ramraksha Brahmachari ji's younger brother Ramdhari Upadhaya was in-charge of the Akbarpur Khadi Centre in Faizabad district of UP, and this Centre was part of a Gandhi Ashram. In preparation for the marriage, Yashoda went to the Akbarpur Ashram and lived there with her brother for some time to familiarize herself with Ashram life. Ramdhari ji was married to Bhagyavati, who had studied at the Girls School in Harpurjan!

Kanhaiyachak's well-known Congressman Suryanarayan Singh invited us for his daughter Chand's wedding. Pandit ji and I went to Kanhaiyachak, which was near Gogri, and were joined there by Ma, Bhaiya and Bhai ji. After the wedding, all of us went to the Diyara Ashram. We travelled by bullock cart to Dumaria Ghat for the river crossing, and walked on the hot sandy tracts of the diyara from the ghat on the other side to the Diyara Ashram. Ma said, "Shiva Kant's marriage is next month. Instead of going in this heat to Harpurjan and then coming back for the wedding, Kaushalya should stay back here with Sabo and Indu. Not only will you avoid travelling in this blistering heat with two young children, you can also help me with the marriage preparations."

So I stayed back with the children while Pandit ji returned to Harpurjan. A separate house was erected for the new couple. It was a thatched two-room hut with a wide veranda, but the mud walls were white-washed with lime, and colourful khadi curtains put on the doors and windows. It looked very beautiful and stood out in the wind-and-sand-swept Shirnia Diyara Ashram on the banks of the mighty Ganga River.

Bhai ji got married in May 1934. Babuji, Bhaiya and his Congress friends went for the wedding ceremony. This too was a "Swaraji" (nationalist) marriage, for both families were ardent followers of Gandhi ji and were totally immersed in the ongoing freedom struggle. All clothes exchanged between the bride and bridegroom were khadi garments. However Ma did give two silk saris along with the coloured khadi saris and some very basic gold jewellery. Babuji insisted that at least five tolas of jewellery must be given, because that is what was given to me.

When the marriage party returned, Ma and Sabo went from the diyara to the Jamalpur Dak Bungalow so that she could receive her daughter-in-law and escort her home. The bride arrived from Maheshkhunt Railway Station in a horse-driven buggy. Nathbihari, a close friend of Bhai ji's from Mansi who had studied at the National School in Gogri and had also gone to jail in the Satyagraha, was getting married the next day and so Bhai ji, Bhaiya and their friends went off for the wedding from the Dak Bungalow itself. Ma and Sabo travelled with the new bride to the diyara by bullock-cart and boat.

As per tradition, I received her into her new home by washing her feet and feeding her kheer-puri. After resting a bit, Yashoda told me to open the trunk that had come with her so that we could see the saris that had come from her mother for Ma and me. There was a lovely Assamese silk sari for me, and a finely woven khadi sari for Ma. The silk sari had been brought by her brother Rampreet Bhaiya who lived and worked in Assam, and the fine khadi sari had been chosen by her brother Ramdhari ji who was the Manager of a Khadi Centre. There was another trunk-full of household utensils, bedsheets and bedding. What caught our attention most were two intricately woven wicker baskets with lids, full of ornaments, cosmetics, and other items of daily use. Sabo particularly was fascinated by her new aunt and all the knick-knacks that had come with her, and refused to leave her side!!

Bhai ji had studied at the Sadakat Ashram in Patna for some time, and among his teachers was the renowned historian and revolutionary, Jaichand Vidyalankar. He was among those who had inspired the famous revolutionary Bhagat Singh. Bhai ji had been his favourite student, and shortly after his marriage came a letter from his former teacher inviting him to Delhi to help with a publishing house that Jaichand Vidyalankar was setting up.

Bhai ji travelled by himself to Delhi, promising that he would send for his wife Yashoda after making arrangements for their stay. Jaichand ji had taken up residence in Delhi's Bengali Market area. Bhai ji was very happy with the set-up and his work and, after finalizing a rented house, sent word that he would come home and take Ma and Yashoda to Delhi within a month.

Chapter 18

AFTER THE EARTHQUAKE, FLOODS

My Bhaiya, Suresh Mishra, had put heart and soul in the earthquake relief work. A large number of volunteers from Gogri Ashram spent day and night with Bhaiya, going from one afflicted area to another. Prominent among them were Brahmadev from Nayagaon, Saryu Sharma from Khajraitha, Jharkhandi Sharma from Bhadkhand, Kunjbihari from Kulharia, Tulsi Guruji and his wife from Baisa, Surendra Shastri, Raghunath and Jagpal, Dwarikadas from Parbatta, Ramavtar Das, Thakurdas, Ballabh and Mednikumar from Dumaria. These are just some of those whose names I remember, most were peasants and small farmers from villages in and around the Gogri area, so many of them that I just cannot remember their names and faces. These women and men were the core of the freedom struggle, unsung and unknown heroes who willingly gave up whatever few comforts they had in life to participate in satyagraha and brave police lathis ,bullets and jail. Homes and families were devastated but from 1921 to 1932 they were the backbone of the Movement.

Life was just about returning to some semblance of normality after the earthquake, when heavy rains and floods struck Bihar.

Almost all of North Bihar reeled under the fury of the swirling waters of its overflowing rivers. Once again Bhaiya and his band of volunteers plunged into relief work. The entire diyara area was submerged, wiping out the Ashram and all habitation near it. Ma and Bhabhi ji (Bhai ji's wife) had to take shelter in Nathbihari Sharma's house in Mansi.

Fields, homes, entire villages for miles around were inundated. The lucky few well-to-do folk who had relatives or friends, took shelter in their homes. But the vast majority of the afflicted villagers had no choice but to look for elevated dry patches of land and camp there. Some tied cots to the branches of trees and lived there, most did not have cots but clung on to the branches. They would swim across the flood waters to the surrounding towns in search of some means of livelihood and succour for their wet, hungry and often unwell family members. Many died of hunger and starvation, many died because they were forced to eat food not fit for human consumption, cholera and dysentery were rampant. It was again the State Congress Relief Committee that supplied food, clothing and medicines to Bhaiya and his co-volunteers.

The Gogri Ashram was still under government seizure, the Shirnia Diyara Ashram had been washed away. Babuji had bought a small plot of land to the west of the Gogri Ashram and Bhaiya constructed a small brick hut with tin roof on this plot of land, and used it both as a store for the relief material and a place to sleep in at night. Travel was possible only by boat, because the entire area was under several feet of water. I was later told that people were afraid to go near those afflicted by cholera, But Bhaiya and his friends tended to them, giving food, water and medication and thus managed to save many lives. Bhaiya was particularly good at treating cholera patients, but still could not save many of them. People were afraid even to cremate the dead cholera victims and it was left to the Ashram volunteers to do the cremation. It is no surprise then that they became famous as the "Brave Ashram Life-givers".

When the Congress had embarked on its campaign for the upliftment of Harijans, "magic lanterns" had been distributed. These were slide-projectors to show how hygiene could help eradicate many common diseases and ailments. Bhaiya had one of these projectors, which he now carried from village to village to spread the message of hygiene and disease control.

1934 will be remembered in Bihar as the year of the earthquake and floods.

Bhai ji got news in Delhi of the raging floods in north Bihar. Jaichand ji urged him to go back immediately and get his wife and mother to Delhi. Bhai ji reached Mansi and took Ma and Bhabhi back to Delhi. Ma had sent me back to Harpurjan before that.

Chapter 19

SATYAGRAHA PUT ON HOLD

In May 1934 we got information from Patna that Gandhi ji had put the Satyagraha on hold. The Movement had lost steam across the county anyway.

Angered by this decision, Jayprakash Narayan and Acharya Narendra Dev floated a new political outfit called the Congress Socialist Party. Bhaiya did not leave the Congress despite the fact that Jayprakash ji was a close friend of his. This new outfit did not fully separate from the Congress, it was more like a splinter protest group within the main Party.

Chapter 20

Bhai ji and Vidyabhusan ji in Delhi

Jaichand Vidyalankar ji had started a publication house and press in Delhi with the support of two people: his brother-in-law Professor Sudhakar and Bhai ji (Shiva Kant Mishra). The press was named "Sharda Mandir Press" after the Professor's daughter and was located in Daryaganj. Bhai ji got a monthly salary of rupees hundred which was more than adequate to pay for his rented house in Bengali Market and meet all other household expenses.

On her return from Delhi, Bhabhi ji told us that monthly expenses rarely exceeded forty rupees, such were the price levels in those days.

Bhabhi's brother Ramraksha Upadhyaya was married to Siwan resident Vidyabhushan Shukla's sister Radhika. Vidyabhushan ji studied at the Banaras Hindu University, where he completed his M.A with a first class.It was in Banaras that he came in contact with a revolutionary group, which included the later famous author Agyeya (Sachchidanand Hiranand Vatsyayan) and Chandrashekhar Azad. Plans were made for an armed uprising to attain Independence, and an outfit called the 'Hindustan Socialist Republican Army" was created. This was a pan-India organization with cells in various cities which worked underground in total secrecy. A bomb-making factory was set up in Delhi's Sitaram Bazaar. When they ran out of money to make bombs, they raided the premises of a rich businessman called Garodia. To his credit, because of his nationalist feelings, he instructed his Munim ji (financial controller) not to co-operate with the police in the subsequent police enquiry and identification of the suspected "terrorists". The Munim ji failed to recognize any of the young men presented in the Identification Parade.

Vidyabhushan ji was also involved in the famous Kakori Incident, which was master-minded by Chandrashekhar Azad. He was arrested in Banaras in 1932 and brought to a Police lock-up near Delhi's Chandni Chowk. The trial went on for two years. Bhai ji heard about Vidyabhushan ji when he started working in Delhi in 1934, and he started visiting Vidyabhushan ji. This alerted the Delhi Police. which started probing into Bhai ji's background. His khadi clothes and tall, hefty physique made him suspect in their eyes, and finally Shiva Kant Mishra was ordered by the Police to leave Delhi within twenty four hours, and he returned to Gogri.

Vidyabhushan ji was interned for eight years in a high security facility in Mirzagadh under very harsh conditions. Bhai ji was a big admirer of his and looked upon him more as a friend and mentor rather than a relative. Vidyabhushan ji got married to Shakuntala Bhargava, who had an MA degree (extremely rare for women in those days) and was an Honorary Magistrate in Mathura. She had met Vidyabhushan ji in Banaras Hindu University and they decided to get married. Vidyabhushan ji's secret life as an armed revolutionary ended in long years in jail, but Shakuntala ji was waiting for him when he was finally set free. This was a nine-year wait and the marriage became a legend in our family.I had a very informal and free relationship with Shakuntala ji,and I would call her my Bhabhi's Bhabhi's Bhabhi!! Her long wait and subsequent companionship gave her an honoured stature in our family as an "ideal woman and wife".

Chapter 21

Back again to the Girls School in Harpurjan

There were very few students left in the Girls School after the disastrous earthquake. Only Lakshmi, Gayatri and Shivkumari. The first two had come from Hathras, and Shivkumari had been a student right through in Harpurjan.

We had moved into our newly constructed house. Pandit ji spent his time outside teaching hours in pursuit of gardening and the Vedic science of music and song (sangeet sadhana).He was studying dhrupad, the classical rendition of mantras from the Sama Ved, and was very good at it.He also played the harmonium, tabla and the sitar.

To the south-east of the house he developed an orchard. After making a boundary wall, he had a well dug to provide water and planted seesham trees along the orchard perimeter. Then he bought many varieties of tree saplings from the Sonepur Fair and soon the orchard was alive with mango ,lychee, banana, guava, pear, amla, lemon, aadu, custard apple, phalsa and many other species of fruit trees and herbs. He personally spent a lot of time tending to his plants and this beautiful orchard became famous as "Pandit ji's Orchard". Pandit ji subsequently left Harpurjan after selling his house, but Adhishtata ji's younger son Narendra preserved the orchard with tender and loving care.I visited

Harpurjan after many years in 1995 and was received with a lot of love and respect by Narendra and his wife Kanti. They took me to see 'Pandit ji's Orchard' and a flood of memories coursed through my mind as I walked through it. The Gurukul has now become a government-recognized High School and Kanti teaches there. The couple carries forward Adhishtata ji's commitment to social reform, and Narendra is a doctor who serves society in his grandfather's mould and tradition.

Adhishtata ji presided over the marriage of the last three students of the Girls School. Gayatri got married to Vasudev Shastri who was completing his Snatak requirements at the Gurukul, while Lakshmi married an Arya Samaj preacher called Ranjit Singh. That just left Shivkumari. The school was closed down for lack of students and she started living in Adhishtata ji's house.

Now I immersed myself in household chores and the care of my two daughters.

I got a letter from Bhabhi ji that Bhai ji had returned from Delhi. I could not understand why this had suddenly happened when everything seemed to be moving smoothly in the Press in Delhi. All kinds of doubts and worries assailed me.

I got another letter from Bhaiya saying the government had relaxed its draconian measures to control the Satyagraha and had returned the Gogri Ashram to us, and it was once more attracting volunteers. Babuji had meanwhile repaired and extended the room Bhaiya had made on the plot of land adjacent to the Ashram, adding a kitchen and big veranda. Bhai ji, Bhabhi and Ma joined Babuji and moved into this house on their return from Delhi.

Ma was very unhappy about Bhaiya's vow not to get married until India attained independence, and periodically urged him to reconsider his decision. Singheshwar babu and Jaiprakash Narayan had left College with him, but they had subsequently completed their studies and had also got married. "Why is my son alone insistent on remaining a Yogi?" she wondered. But Bhaiya was adamant. "I am a member of the Gandhi Seva Sangh and have taken a solemn oath that till the country attains Independence I will remain fully committed to the freedom struggle. There is no saying when I will be arrested and put into jail, when I will have to face police lathis and bullets and whether I will be hanged."

Ma tried to reason with him. "I am doing work for the nation, am I not? Why don't you marry a girl who can join you in your work for the freedom of Mother India?"

His reply, "I am walking around with a coffin tied to my head. Why should I ruin some poor innocent girl's life?"

Bhaiya was now living in the Gogri Ashram, waiting anxiously for the outcome of the talks Gandhi ji was having with the British Government. Meanwhile the charkha-khadi activities of the Gogri Ashram continued unabated. The National School in the Ashram was also functioning, but with very few students. Surendra from Baisa village had gone to the Kashi Vidyapeeth for further studies after his release from jail. Bhai ji had also gone to the Vidyapeeth, but had come back without completing his studies and was now busy helping Bhaiya with the Ashram activities. Sachchidanand Jha and his brother Vedanand had been constant companions of Bhaiya in all his Satyagraha activities and had also gone to jail. They were our cousins.

Chapter 22

Bhai ji's first son

Bhabhi ji was glowing with radiance when she returned from Delhi. The air and water of Delhi suited her and in addition she was expecting her first child. She told us how much she loved the grapes in Delhi. Jaichand Ji's wife Sumitra Devi took good care of her, and Ma was there in any case.

I was summoned from Harpurjan to help Bhabhi through her pregnancy. I reached Gogri with Sabo and Indu. Bhai ji constructed a metre-and-a-half high raised platform in the front portion of the house, and this became the gents portion. Thus began Bhai ji's separate home away from the Ashram. Babuji had exchanged his Patharghat land for his elder brother Mircho Mishra's land in Shirnia diyara, and his son Jageshwar Mishra looked after the Patharghat land. My Aunt was not ostracized by the villagers and continued to live in Shirnia, from where she would often visit us in Gogri.

Babuji's Shirnia diyara lands were three miles from Shirnia village, and he kept adding land whenever he could save some money. Soon he had 75 bighas of land in Shirnia diyara. He used to personally supervise the farming operations and so now our economic situation was no longer perilous.

When Bhabhi gave birth to a son in November 1935, Ma and Babuji were very happy.

The father's sister puts kohl in the child's eyes on the sixth day, and although we did not perform the typical Maithil Brahmin rituals, we followed the Vedic way and did the Jat Karma rites before bathing the child and putting the kohl. For this act, as the Aunt I would traditionally be given some gift, generally money and clothes as per the parents' wishes. I was asked what gift I would like. I had heard in the Ashram that the Congress Convention was going to be held in Lucknow that year and I immediately said I would like to go to the Lucknow Convention. The family agreed readily.

On the eleventh day after birth the naming ceremony was held and the baby was named Chandrakant.

My bhabhi Yashoda had truly come into our family as the Goddess Lakshmi, for after her arrival for the first time a family home was built, with its own separate kitchen, and we lived together as a family. Till then we had all lived a communal life in the Ashram for many years.

Chapter 23

A Daughter of Deoria

Pandit ji received a letter from Shri Rameshwar, a rich Seth (merchant) from Deoria who had become an Arya Samaji. The contents of the letter were heart-wrenching. "Only you can resolve the complex problem I have. I have one daughter, who was just a baby when her mother died. In our large joint family, she could not be given the attention that she needed. Although her biological age is fifteen, Anardeyi's mental development is not even that of a seven-year old. My friends Yudhishthir Mimansak and Brahmadutt Jigyasu ji have both spoken very highly of the Girls School in Harpurjan. They say that students of that school are very cultured and well-educated. "It is my misfortune that the school has been closed down. I will be immensely grateful if your wife and you could accept my invitation to stay in my house for a few days, for I feel my daughter will benefit immensely by your being here".

Pandit ji consulted Adhishtata ji, and they came to the conclusion that given the purdah system, lack of education and blind belief in superstition that was prevalent in rich Seth families, this would be an excellent opportunity to spread the Arya Samaj views and practices that sought to address these malaises. Given our commitment to social reform, we should not hesitate to go wherever we were required. Seth ji had requested that we should stay in Deoria for at least a month.

My husband came to Gogri to take me to Deoria. Ma was not very happy about my going there, but she did not want to go against her son-in-law's wishes. So I left for Deoria with Sabo and Indu. Pandit ji stayed there for a couple of days to introduce me to the family and then returned to Harpurjan.

Two days before I reached, Anardeyi had disappeared from the house. Apparently, unknown to the Seth ji, her aunt used to beat her mercilessly every day and deny her proper food. This was an everyday affair, but that day the aunt's beating crossed all limits. Finding an apt moment, the girl slipped out of the house. Seth ji was alarmed to find her missing, and organized a massive search in all directions to find her. The aunt feigned innocence and said she had no idea what could have happened. Anardeyi was always in such mortal terror of her aunt that she had never mentioned a word of her maltreatment to her father or uncle. The aunt used to threaten her that if she ever talked about it to anyone ,she would kill her.

All wells in the neighbourhood were searched for the missing Anardeyi, and so too were the railway lines. It was feared that she may have taken her own life.

The next morning the neighbour's wife appeared with Anardeyi in tow. She said "Anardeyi is in a very bad state. She was sobbing copiously when she reached my house and could not speak out of fear. I kept her with me all night and perhaps it is my mistake that I did not inform you earlier that she was with me."

She showed the family members Anardeyi's back, arms and legs which were covered with welts, many of them oozing blood and pus. It was a horrifying sight and her Uncle was aghast to see her condition. It was obvious that this was the result of his wife's cruelty and he immediately declared "I can never forgive my wife for her bestial behaviour towards this poor, defenceless girl. From this day on my wife will not stay with the rest of the family."

When I reached Deoria, Anardeyi, her father and his brother had shifted to their own older house, having left the aunt in the new and better house. The Seth's brother and his wife had no children of their own. Anardeyi's elder sister was married and stayed with her husband. The only child or member of the next generation in the house was Anardeyi. Why her aunt was torturing her like this was beyond comprehension.

The next day, both Anardeyi's sister and the Seth ji's sister (bua), arrived and moved in with the other family members into the old house. Anardeyi's behaviour and speech was like that of a small child. Her hair was matted and full of lice, God knows when she had last had a bath, her clothes were threadbare and soiled. Constant beatings and malnutrition had reduced her to almost a skeleton. She would sit silently by herself, completely cowed down, and from time to time get up with a start and look fearfully in all directions. New clothes, soap, oil, comb and other essentials were bought. Her sister and bua bathed her lovingly, put on a new sari and did her hair. This by itself seemed to transform her personality. The love and care she experienced from her family members started restoring her self-confidence. She understood that there would no further beatings from the wicked aunt. Then she started opening up with me and told me how her aunt would beat her and lock her up in a room, give her just two dry rotis throughout the day and keep threatening her of far worse. I made sure she was in my sight the whole day, and personally fed her all meals. Within a month her health was restored. I used the Gurukul pedagogy to teach Anardeyi, and she started picking up some reading and writing. After early morning baths, the entire family would sit down together and perform havan. Evening time was for games and exercise. After two weeks Anardeyi's sister and bua returned to their respective homes.

One day we heard the rumour that the world was going to end, there was going to be an immense earthquake at night and all sinners would die. Panic spread like wildfire through the town. Seth ji had a huge garden outside the town, where there was a Gurukul for boys, presided over by an Acharya ji. Seth ji took all of us to the Gurukul for the night. When we woke up next morning, the world was as it normally was!! We returned home.

Anardeyi's "wicked" aunt came to see me one day. "I have been punished enough" she said. "I am living alone in the house and everyone looks at me as if I am a wicked witch. Please believe me, I don't know what demon possessed me that I would beat Anardeyi the way I did. I am truly sorry and full of shame and remorse, and beg that I be given one chance to prove that I have changed from deep inside.I swear I will never touch a hair on her head. Like you have transformed Anardeyi's life, please do me just this one favour and give me a chance to prove I have been transformed."

I had to return to Harpurjan and so I spoke to the Seth ji about allowing the Aunt back into the family. "I have to return, Anardeyi will find it difficult to live alone in the house without another woman. Please arrange for the Acharya ji to come every day from the Gurukul to teach Anardeyi. You should personally keep an eye on your daughter and her aunt every day to ensure that these horrors are not repeated."

Having made these arrangements, I returned to Harpurjan.

When I went to the Lucknow Congress Convention, I was delighted to see Anardeyi with her father, looking happy and beautiful. Another family at the Convention liked her so much that they proposed marriage. The marriage took place shortly and Anardeyi went off to her husband's home.

But, alas, happiness was not in her destiny. Within a month she was struck by a virulent attack of small-pox and died.

Chapter 24

The Lucknow Congress Convention

In 1936 the annual All India Congress Convention was held in Lucknow.

I had already requested Bhaiya and Bhai ji that I wanted to attend this Convention. A big group of us from the Harpurjan Gurukul departed for Lucknow. Chandrakant was very young, so Ma and Bhabhi ji did not come. My entire family, Adhishtata ji's wife and younger son Narendra, elder daughter Vidyavati and her husband Mangal Singh all reached Lucknow. One of the Gurukul Snataks, Vidyasagar, also came with his wife.

The Exhibition at the Convention was vast and impressive. Khadi Centres from across the country had stalls where they displayed a vast array of diverse khadi products. Bhabhi's younger brother Ramdhari Upadhyaya was the Chief of the UP Charkha Sangh. His wife Bhagyavati had been my student at the Girls School in Harpurjan and she treated me with a lot of respect and affection. She spent the whole day taking us around the exhibits and then invited us to dinner. I bought clothes for everyone in my family.

The next day was the Women's Convention, and it was a memorable day for me. This Convention was chaired by Vijaylakshmi Pandit and she gave a stirring speech. "A turning point is being reached in India's struggle for Independence, and I can clearly see that the nation will not be enslaved for long.

We have to be ready in every way for this final battle, you have to be ready to give up wealth and life. I need women who can devote themselves fully to this cause. I urge all such sisters to come forward and put their name and address in the register kept on the dais, so that we can call on you when the time comes."

At this point, another lady came onto the stage and started calling out the names of each State one by one. On the mention of their State, women would troop up to the dais and enter their name and address. When Bihar was announced, I literally ran to the dais, and wrote down both my Harpurjan and Gogri addresses. I was very happy that finally I would get the chance to go to jail. Till now it was Ma who went to jail each time, while I was given the responsibility of doing work outside. But this time it was only my name, not hers. If anyone went to jail, it would be me!! Such was my enthusiasm to work for my country's independence.

The other memorable event was the meeting with Mahatma Gandhi. Seth Jamnalal Bajaj had made the arrangements for Gandhi ji's stay, and it was through him that this meeting was organized. The entire floor of the room in which Gandhi ji was staying, was covered with mattresses on which white sheets had been spread. Gandhi ji was sitting on the floor, working on his charkha. I entered the room with my two daughters and greeted him with folded hands. Gandhi ji smiled and gestured for us to sit down. I reminded him of his visit to the Gogri Ashram where I had first met him as a young child. He remembered his Gogri visit. He kept spinning his charkha all the time till we got up, did Namaskar and took our leave.

This brought back memories of the song we used to sing in the Gogri Ashram as we spun the charkha:

"Do not let the yarn spun by the charkha break
Let the charkha keep spinning, O friends."*

---

* Tootay na charkhe ki taar
charkhava chalu rahe

Chapter 25

MA'S LAST JOURNEY

I returned from Lucknow smug in the belief that this time I would go to jail while Ma remained outside. Little did I know that Ma had made preparations for another journey without me.

The repeated terms in jail had considerably weakened Ma .When she came back after a six month spell in jail where she constantly suffered fevers, her fair and rosy complexion had turned sallow and there were wrinkles under her eyes. Still she did not rest and kept up her hectic touring schedule, going from village to village enrolling women volunteers for satyagraha.

The economic and physical hardships she had to endure on account of the Arya Samaj activities of Babuji, had broken her body. The loss of her elder daughter had always haunted her. The frequent jail terms of her two sons also took a mental toll, though she never mentioned it. Bhaiya's decision not to marry was another source of disappointment and sorrow. However the birth of her grandson Chandrakant had brought joy to her life, as had the fact that after Bhabhi came into our family, Bhai ji finally had his own home.

The Satyagraha Movement had been put on hold and Gandhi ji was in talks with the British for some kind of agreement. Bhaiya was not in favour of the proposed agreement but had not yet joined his friend Jaiprakash Narayan's splinter Socialist Congress Party.

He was very restless and could not stay put in the Gandhi Ashram, and kept moving around in the Gogri area. I don't think he even noticed that Ma's condition was deteriorating by the day. She could not eat properly and would develop a fever every evening. Dark patches started appearing on her face, and seeing this Bhai ji and Bhaiya pressed the alarm button and sent a message to me to come to Gogri with Adhishtata ji.

Ma had been cured of an earlier illness by Vaid Brijbihari Choubey, and this had made her a firm believer in the power of ayurvedic treatment. Adhistata ji prescribed some medication, but said her problem had become chronic and she should come to Harpurjan for extended treatment under his care.

Bhai ji, Bhabhi, the children and I moved to Harpurjan with Ma. Babuji stayed back to look after the farming, and Bhaiya was out touring somewhere. Bhai ji returned to Gogri after a few days, but Pandit ji really performed his duties as a son-in-law to the hilt, spending long hours in Ma's care.

Despite all care and experimentation with various potions and enemas, Ma's condition kept deteriorating. Ma finally said "Take me to Patna, to Vaid Brijbihari Choubey."

By then Bhaiya had reached Harpurjan, and we left for Patna with Ma. Choubey ji tried his treatment, but the deterioration continued unabated. Ma could not get out of bed, and then lost her speech. Bhaiya got her admitted to the Patna Medical College Hospital.

Sabo, Indu and Chandrakant were also with us in Patna. It was agreed that I would tend to Ma, while Bhabhi ji did the cooking. Sabo was now seven years old, and took care of Indu and Chandrakant who loved playing with her and following her wherever she went.

The Patna Medical College Hospital was something else those days. Starched and ironed white bedsheets, spotlessly clean floors, alert and smartly turned-out nurses who were extremely proficient in their work, and attentive doctors. Ma was admitted to the General Ward, where the beds were eight feet apart. No personal attendant could stay with the patients, visiting hours were strictly observed. Medicines, food, milk, fruits were all served on time by the nurses as per the patient's individual prescription. Seeing the current condition of the same hospital, it is impossible to even imagine that it could ever have been as good as it was in those days.

Bhaiya had rented a house for our stay just opposite the hospital. After making all arrangements, he declared "From now on Ma's care is my responsibility. Mark my words, my care and attention will restore her to sound health soon. I am just going for two days to the Gogri Ashram to attend to some urgent work there. I also have to arrange funds for the hospital treatment and our stay in Patna, since I came in a rush without any money."

Alas, Bhaiya never got the opportunity to care for Ma on his return. It seems she had been waiting just to see him. Tears were streaming down her eyes when he left her bed-side in the hospital to go to Gogri. She could not speak, I held her hand and stroked her hair. In a very short while she drifted into unconsciousness.

Next morning she opened her eyes and kept looking towards the ward doors, as if she was waiting for someone's arrival.

It was ten in the morning, the ward was humming with activity. The Matron was on her inspection round, ready to spot even the tiniest bit of dirt--and heaven help those responsible if she spotted any!

"The Head Doctor is coming" went the buzz round the ward, and everyone switched to full alert. Beds had been turned and early morning sponges given. Breakfast had been served to those who could eat, but Ma could only sip a few drops of water. The nurse said I should leave till the doctor had completed his round.

I begged her to let me stay since Ma was so unwell, but she insisted that I leave. However she said I could return when the doctor had left the ward.

When I returned, Ma's face was covered with a white sheet and a curtain drawn around her bed.

I was stunned and stood rooted to the ground, wordless. Was that my last meeting with Ma? What had she being trying to convey through her silent tears? She wanted to say something to Bhaiya, was that why she had kept looking expectantly at the door, the tears in her eyes the garland of her blessings to her children, especially her beloved Suresh?

I was lost in this whirl of thoughts, when a voice brought me back to reality. 'Kaushalya, what has happened?" Bhai ji was standing next to me.

"Ma has left us" I managed to say and then burst into uncontrollable tears. Seeing Bhai ji, seemed to have burst a dam somewhere inside me

I sat silently outside the ward, in a state of total shock. Bhai ji went home and returned with Bhabhi ji and the children.

Nandkishore, Ramesh and one other young man had arrived from Gogri the day before. They were joined by some friends of Bhai ji who he managed to send word to. Ma's body was taken straight from the hospital to the cremation ground on the banks of the Ganga.

It was not in Bhaiya's fate to perform his mother's death rites as the eldest son, it was Bhai ji who put the sacred flame in her mouth and lit the funeral pyre. Bhaiya could reach only the next day and join the havan ceremony.

Babuji, unaware of his wife's death, was still in Gogri.

With Ma's departure, it seemed that the thread which had bound the family together, had broken.

Life's journey had ended for the universal 'Mai ji' who had

fought relentlessly throughout her life against all odds. If she had died in Gogri Ashram, thousands would have thronged to pay homage to her, they would have rent the sky with cries of praise for her, flowers showered by her legion of admirers and devotees would have covered her dead body.

But as it happened, there was no prayer meeting in her memory, no procession was taken out in her honour, no stamps were brought out by the nation in remembrance of this brave and dauntless freedom fighter. She remained unknown, unrecognized and unheralded.

But memories of her were kept alive by family members and the faceless, impoverished masses she had devoted her life to.

The grief-stricken family went to Harpurjan, they could not live with her memories haunting them in every shadow, in every nook and corner of Gogri.

Bhai ji was disconsolate and restless in Harpurjan. The Arya Samaj would often send Pandit ji to Kathmandu. Bhaiya made a plan for the menfolk to go with Pandit ji to Kathmandu. Bose bhai came from Gogri and joined Bhaiya, Bhai ji and Nandkishore in Harpurjan and they went off to Kathmandu in a bullock-cart. It seems to have been a highly rejuvenating trip.

Now there was only one student left in the Girls School in Harpurjan-Shivkumari. We felt she and Bose bhai would make a good couple, and Adhishthata ji concurred with this assessment. The couple got married and my work with the School came to an end.

Activity levels in the Gurukul had also diminished considerably. The Acharya of the Vrindavan Gurukul, Jodh Singh ji (who was also known as Master ji), requested Pandit ji to come and teach in the Vrindavan Gurukul. The request was accepted and Pandit ji went off to Vrindavan. In 1937 my third daughter Nalini was born.

Bhabhi ji was expecting her second child and so I went back to Gogri to be with her.

In the meantime, Congress governments had been installed in several States, which included Bihar, where Shri Krishna Singh was appointed Prime Minister. In those days Chief Ministers of States were called Prime Ministers. Bhaiya was devoting more and more of his time now to the Kisan Sabha. It was announced that the annual Congress Convention would be held in Haripura, and Bhaiya started making preparations to attend it. Suddenly news came that the Congress cabinet of Ministers had resigned everywhere.

We asked Bhaiya about this sudden and unexpected twist of events, for we were hopeful that the formation of Congress Governments in various states was a pre-cursor to the total independence of the nation. He explained that during the election campaign for the Assembly seats, the Congress had promised the release of all political prisoners if it came to power. Prisoners serving life sentences in the penal colony jails of the Andaman Islands went on hunger strike against the horrific conditions they were subjected to. The British Government, which was in power in Delhi and controlled all major decisions, ignored their demands. This led to the resignation of the Congress ministries in Bihar and UP.

Bhaiya went to the Haripura Annual Congress Convention, which was presided over by Subhash Chandra Bose. Even as a College student, Bhaiya had been very impressed and influenced by the revolutionaries of Bengal and he now found himself resonating with Subhash Bose's views, and supported him. The British government meanwhile conceded to the State Congress ministries the authority and responsibility of dealing with the release of political prisoners. The resignations of the Congress ministries were withdrawn, and they resumed the good work they were doing for the upliftment of labourers and farmers.

The Tripura Congress Convention followed, and that too was presided over by Subhash Bose. There was severe disagreement between him and other senior Congress leaders. His supporters voiced their opposition openly, but the combined strength of Jawaharlal Nehru, Rajendra Prasad, Sardar Patel and others ensured a majority and victory for the anti-Subhash group. Subhash babu resigned in protest. Bhaiya had not gone for the Tripura Convention, but went to meet Subhash Bose in Calcutta. It was on his return from Calcutta that we got to know about all the goings-on in Tripura.

Subhash Chandra Bose's differences with the senior Congress leadership kept widening and ultimately he was expelled from the Party for a year.

Subhash babu had started organizing a new political outfit immediately after the Tripura Congress and called it the "Forward Bloc". He now focussed all his attention on this new party, which Bhaiya joined. He made an announcement to all his volunteers and supporters in the Gogri area that he had joined Netaji Subhash Chandra Bose's Forward Bloc. This announcement was made in a large meeting. The older Congress workers, who had been with Bhaiya from the beginning, were not inclined to leave the Congress, but the youth were inspired by Netaji and attracted to the new outfit floated by him. Many families saw the father remain with the Congress while son and mother joined the Forward Bloc. Many of those who joined the Forward Bloc said openly that they did not know Subhash babu, but knew and trusted Suresh Mishra who had been with them through every calamity that had struck this region-floods, earthquake, cholera...They said they would follow Bhaiya wherever and whenever he asked them to, and soon enough they got the opportunity to show their trust and support for him.

The Forward Bloc held its first Annual Convention in Ramgarh within the year. Bhaiya attended it along with a large contingent of his followers. Women came in large numbers for this Convention, ready to support fully Netaji's vision of attaining Independence through an armed revolution.

Chapter 26

Ramgarh Congress and the Forward Bloc

In 1940 the Congress held its annual Convention in Ramgarh, a small town in rural South Bihar. The town was in a picturesque location, nestling among hills and forests on the banks of the Damodar river. The Convention site was created by clearing a wooded patch, and setting up temporary thatch huts to house participants. Water was drawn from the river.

Bhabhi ji's elder brother Ramraksha Upadhyaya reached Ramgarh a month earlier, along with Bhabhi ji and Sabo. He was one of the main organizers and was given a brick hut without a roof. He had to construct a thatched roof to make it habitable.

The Forward Bloc chose to have its Annual Convention at the same time in Ramgarh. Subhash Chandra Bose came with a large contingent from Bengal, while prominent in the Bihar contingent were Swami Sahajanand Saraswati, Dhanraj Sharma and Suresh Chandra Mishra (Bhaiya). They called it a "Protest against the Agreement" convention, and large numbers of men and women followed Bhaiya to Ramgarh.

I was in Harpurjan at that time, and travelled to Ramgarh with Pandit ji, Nilu and Indu. We went straight to Ramraksha ji's house since Bhabhi ji and Bhai ji were there.

Bhaiya was staying in the Forward Bloc convention site. Coincidentally, Ramraksha ji's hut was located almost mid-way between the Congress and Forward Bloc sites, and the children would keep running from one site to the other.

Netaji took out a huge procession and Bhaiya was by his side throughout. We watched from our hut, and this was the first time that I was not supporting Bhaiya.

The next day there were torrential downpours. The Congress convention was to start at 6 pm and the rain had started around 4 pm. Very soon there was knee-deep water in the main shamiana and the current was so strong that people found it difficult to keep their balance. Rajendra Prasad spoke a few words to welcome the President of the Convention, Maulana Azad, and then the Maulana spoke a few sentences.The inaugural ceremony lasted just a few minutes. We were in one corner of the shamiana with all the children, and since we were all drenched to the skin in the heavy rain we hurriedly made our way back to the hut. Fortunately the roof was intact, but water had accumulated on the floor.

The next day Sabo came down with high fever. There were no decent medical facilities in Ramgarh and the Congress Convention was for two days. The Forward Bloc convention ended a day before the Congress's and Bhaiya came to meet us. He was very angry with me when he saw Sabo's condition, and berated me for being so negligent about her state of health. He made arrangements to rush her to the hospital in Hazaribagh. I followed the next day with Nilu, while Indu stayed back with Bhabhi ji.

Sabo was diagnosed with malaria, typhoid and kala-azar all at the same time, and after some tense and anxious moments in the first few days, started recovering slowly. It took two months of hospitalization for her to become well enough to be discharged, and we moved to Ranchi for her recuperation. The bracing and salubrious climate of Ranchi and Hazaribagh were famous for their regenerative effect, and a month in that environment ensured Sabo's return to normalcy. I too felt revitalized and re-energized.

Chapter 27

LIFE IN THE NATIONAL SCHOOL IN GOGRI

Nandkishore had come to the Gogri Ashram despite the strong objections of his sister and brother-in-law. He went to jail three times, and was at the receiving end of police lathis many many times. That was while still studying at the National School! He was from a very rich Rajput landowning family. Both his parents had died when he was very young, and his only uncle and aunt had also died soon thereafter. The family was from a place called Shahzadpur in Saharsa, through which flowed the Kosi, Bihar's "river of sorrow". The river used to bring floods every year, leading to epidemics of typhoid, malaria, cholera and kala-azar. These epidemics used to wipe out entire villages, and it was kala-azar that had taken the lives of his parents. Nandkishore and his orphaned first cousin Chandar both used to live with his sister in Basudevpur. Chandar was now married, but Nandkishore rebelled against the very idea of marriage at a young age and that too by accepting a dowry from the girl's parents.

Ramnandan Mishra was a well-known Congress functionary of Darbhanga. He had opened a Girls Vidyapeeth in Majhoul and Bose bhai's sister Malti used to study there. She used to speak very highly of her friend Chandrakala and recommended that Nandkishore marry her. Chandrakala's uncle was also a Congress man and had been to jail twice. He came to Gogri and was very impressed both by Nandkishore and the Ashram. The marriage took place and Chandrakala was received in Bhai ji's house.

Twenty women volunteers from the Gogri region had gone to the Ramgarh Congress, including Chandrakala, Malti and Surendra Shastri's wife Manorama, and many others from Kanhaiyachak. They all received volunteer training in a camp conducted in the Gogri Ashram by a trainer from Munger. I was in Harpurjan at that time.

Nandkishore bought a plot of land adjacent to Bhai ji's and made a house there for Chandrakala and himself. All the new houses were built on high plinths to be safe from the annual flood waters. The flood waters could not enter such high-plinth homes, but they would be surrounded by flood waters on all sides.

By this time the Ashram too had become of concrete construction and high plinth, and the National School had re-opened. It was able to attract good, trained teachers like Kanhaiyachak's Dhanushdhari and Vinay Singh. Seven to eight boys were in the hostel, among them Sundar Choudhry's son Valmiki. But Bhaiya shifted him to the Sadakat Ashram from where he went to jail with Rajendra babu. From that time onward he remained with Rajendra babu. When Rajendra babu became the first President of independent India, Valmiki Choudhry became his Private Secretary after Chakradhar babu. His wife Vrinda joined him in Delhi.

The Non-cooperation Movement had been called off. But I remembered clearly my signing up in response to Vijaylaksmi Pandit's call for full-time volunteers and I was waiting for her call. I sometimes wondered how I would manage to do it with three young children, and reasoned that they could always come to jail with me -- there was no shortage of enthusiasm and patriotic zeal in me!

Bhabhi ji's second son Satish was born in September 1938,followed by a third son Navin in November 1940.There were now six young children in the house and no shortage of fun, games and mischief. Babuji used to get along famously with his grandchildren. He used to come back home from the bazaar or the diyara with fruits for them-mango, banana, guava, orange etc. depending upon the season. On reaching home he would first take the children for a run and exercises in the Ashram maidan and then troop back home shouting slogans like 'Vandemataram' 'Victory to Mahatma Gandhi' and many other topical ones. After washing up they would have the fruits and then learn multiplication tables. Then it was time for storytelling. Babuji was a great story teller and held his young audience spell-bound with stories from his own life, in which Sati Mai and Arya Samaj adventures were repeated many times on popular demand. He also told them many tales from the Panchatantra.

The National School was running well. A Trust had been formed, and the school building and surrounding land were registered in its name. Bhaiya was no longer doing any Congress work.

Most of the school students were day scholars from the surrounding villages. However the hostel was functional and between students and teachers about fifteen to twenty people were resident in the school campus. There was still a dining hall and kitchen, but sources of revenue had dried up with the Khadi Centre having moved out. The enthusiasm and zeal of the Satyagraha days was missing, so were the old timers of the Ashram. The library had many books, but three had left an indelible imprint on my mind. These included 2 volumes of *British Rule in India* by Sundar Lal. They were thick tomes and banned by the government as subversive literature. The books described how the British came as traders and then used every trick in the trade, every deceit, lie and betrayal possible, to establish control over the entire country. The disgraceful manner in which the British behaved with the Nawabs of Murshidabad and Awadh, and Bahadur Shah Zafar the last Mughal Emperor, the atrocities committed on the Indian populace -- all were portrayed and described in graphic detail. The way in which the princely kingdoms were annexed, the cruelty and ruthlessness with which the 1857 Uprising was quelled, the number of people hanged and tortured -- reading all this made my blood boil with anger and frustration, and fired my revolutionary zeal.

The third book, or should I say booklet, was the issue of the magazine Chand on the subject of hanging. This was a detailed exposition of the various circumstances and ways in which Indians were hanged by the British.

"British Rule in India" was a very popular book among patriots and freedom fighters and became even more popular after it was banned. Secret underground copies of the book were circulating and if someone was really serious about reading it, copies could be obtained.

Bhaiya visited Deoghar and saw a school there which really impressed him, and he decided Sabo should study there and live in their hostel. She left for the Deoghar school in 1942, when she was 12 years old.

Sabo initially founded it difficult to adjust to that school and when she came home for the summer break she insisted that she would stay there only if I came and saw the facilities. School re-opened in the first week of July, but I could reach there only in the third week, taking Nilu with me. Indu was left behind with Bhabhi ji.

The Deoghar school was run by Protestant missionaries. The Principal was an English lady called Miss Ohms, and there was another English lady called Miss Tingley who helped the

Principal run the school. Both were missionaries. Miss Ohms was a very nice and empathetic lady and listened patiently to me. Sabo had done very well in her studies in her first term there, in fact had come first in the class and Miss Ohms was very fond of her. She was confident that if I stayed there for a few days, Sabo would settle down and start liking the school. She arranged for my stay in the Teachers Mess. It was now the first week of August.

Adhishthata ji had passed away, and Pandit ji went back to Harpurjan and tried very hard to revive the Gurukul. Unfortunately there were too many problems and the Gurukul had to be shut down leaving Pandit ji without a job and livelihood. He finally managed to get a job as "Cane Inspector" in the Sidhvalia Cane Mill. What a change it was from Vedic scholar to Cane Inspector, and Pandit ji just could not get used to it. He came to Deoghar and tried to get a position in the Gurukul there, but unfortunately there were no vacancies.

One of Sabo's class mates was Lila, whose mother was a Brahmin widow who taught in a Middle School to support herself and her daughter's education. I went with Lila to meet her mother. There I met Krena ji, who was Ugramohan's uncle and used to visit the Gogri Ashram frequently. He was a spirited Satyagrahi and had gone to jail in 1930. He too was teaching in that school, and suggested I apply for a teaching position there, he would try his best to help me. My daughters too could study in the same school.

I put in my application.

Krena ji would get up-to-date information on the national freedom movement from the Khadi Centre and would dutifully share all the news with me. Like me, he was very disappointed that he had not been able to participate in the "Individual Satyagraha Movement" of 1941. He told me.

"Sister, we did everything we could at the ground level, using all our initiative-you too, right? But I don't know what kind of programme Mahatma Gandhi created. We were experienced Congress campaigners, worked on the charkha initiative for years, did not believe in Untouchability. It is true we were not in leadership positions, which meant either a district level responsibility or membership of the Council. By these criteria we were not found qualified to offer 'Individual Satyagraha'! I am no longer sure that the path of non-violence will yield Independence. I am happy that Suresh babu has joined the Forward Bloc though the Congress has at least declared that we will not support the British in their War Effort. Sister, I am very keen to court arrest and go to jail shouting anti-British slogans. The British are cornered and surrounded by enemies on all sides, now is the time for a final push to get them out of our country."

Krena ji was mirroring the views of thousands of young men and women across the country. Subhash Chandra Bose had already parted ways with non-violence and had secretly slipped out of the country in 1941. There were all kinds of stories and speculations about his whereabouts but no one knew for sure what the facts actually were.

Chapter 28

THE '42 AUGUST REVOLUTION

Krena ji came to meet me on the morning of 9th August. "Sister, this time it is for real. Gandhi ji has given the call for us to rise. He has told the foreigners 'British, leave India' and has urged all Indians to 'Do or Die'! Total non-co-operation is the strategy from now on, no matter if we lose our lives doing so."

"On the night of 8th August, even as the Bombay session of the All India Congress Working Committee was finalizing its draft resolution to put it to vote, the British Police swooped in and arrested all the Members. Gandhi ji, Sarojini Naidu, Miraben and Mahadev Desai were taken and interned in the Aga Khan Palace on the outskirts of Poona. Nehru, Sardar Patel, Maulana Azad and others are in the Ahmadnagar Jail.'

'Oh my God" I blurted out. "I wonder where Bhaiya and Bhai ji are."

"I am sorry. Sister, I should have told you first that Suresh babu was arrested early this morning in Munger. I got this information on the phone from my nephew, who is a clerk in the Post Office. He has been taken to the Bhagalpur Jail."

"Any other news?"

"The government agencies have full information on Suresh babu's organization and its ability to harm the British Government. They are worried that the movement may take a violent turn.

But jailing our leaders has only increased the enthusiasm and determination of the youth to launch the final assault. We have to bring the government machinery to a grinding halt."

"What does that mean?"

"Uproot railway lines to disrupt rail movement, cut telephone and telegraph lines to disrupt communication channels, put obstacles in every possible way to disrupt the functioning of the administration, refrain from going to work-this is the meaning of 'Do or Die', for the police is bound to open fire and throw thousands into jail. Ordinary people will be mercilessly beaten to spread fear among the protestors, limbs broken...the government will retaliate brutally. But we will not be afraid, we will keep moving forward"

"But has Gandhi ji asked the Congress Party to do all this?" I asked.

"The government never gave him the chance to make any announcement, all the leaders were herded off to jail in the darkness of night."

"So what will happen now?"

"What will happen now? Gandhi ji's signal is clear-- 'British, leave India'. If the British decide to leave on the basis of the non-violent protests till now, well and good. Otherwise total non-cooperation. The form this will take will be left to local leaders based on their assessment of the situation in their respective territories. It is up to those common men who rise to the occasion and step into the shoes of the arrested leaders, to provide direction and instructions to the rank and file. This war will be fought by Indians of every social strata, of every caste and religion, this is no longer a war to be waged only by the members of the Congress Party. I will finalize my 9 point programme and start distributing pamphlets in town today. Inquilab Zindabad! British leave India! Do or Die!!!"

Overtaken by passion and enthusiasm, Krena ji stood up and, raising his hand with clenched fists, starting shouting these slogans.

By evening the streets of Deoghar were full of protestors and the air rent with their patriotic sloganeering.

"British, leave India.

Stooges of the British--shame on you, shame on you.

Inquilab Zindabad.

Victory to Mother India.

Sons of Mother India—do or die.

My brave lions--do or die".

A large crowd ,with flags in hand and shouting slogans, reached the City Jail, broke open the locks on the Main Gate and freed all the prisoners. Telegraph wires were cut. This procession marched to the neighbouring town of Jasidih and burnt down the Railway Station and Post Office.

News spread like wild fire throughout the country that Gandhi, Nehru, Patel and other senior leaders had been thrown into jail, but a second new line of leadership had stepped up and taken on the responsibility of bringing the government machinery to a grinding halt and the British Government to its knees. It was left to local leaders to interpret things as they deemed fit, and to act on it. A few government officials were killed, but only a very few. Mostly it was government property that was destroyed.

The very next day Krena ji landed up at the Mission School at the head of a large, excited procession. They stood in front of the locked Main Gate and started shouting:

"British, leave India

British, leave India.

Inquilab Zindabad".

On hearing the slogans, I rushed to the Main Gate. Seeing me, Krena ji motioned to the crowd to quieten down and came up to me. "I see that the old woman has gone inside to hide in fear"

"Which old woman?" I asked nervously, frightened by the sight of this menacing mob.

"Oh, the old British woman who runs this school, who else? She will have to leave this country. We will tie her up, burn the building down and destroy this school forever"

I took the excited Krena ji aside and tried to reason with him. "You must understand, Krena ji, that Gandhi ji has repeatedly said he has nothing personally against any Britisher, in fact he does not even look at their government with hatred and abhorrence. He is on very cordial terms with the Viceroy. I am sure you have not forgotten the Chauri Chaura incident -- at the first sign of violence, Gandhi ji called off the entire Movement across the country.

"This old lady has done no harm to the country. Quite the contrary, she is helping educate the young girls of this country, all her students are Indian. If you have the slightest respect and regard for me, I implore you not to touch the school and its two British missionary ladies."

He promised me, and took an oath, that they would not harm the school or its inmates and would not picket it. But processions passed by the school every day, shouting slogans. The minute we heard the slogans, I would rush to the Gate and stand there with Sabo, Indu, and Lila while the rest of the school residents rushed indoors to hide. I had told Krena ji that the mob would be able to enter the school only over our dead bodies.

The government hit back strongly and all hell broke loose, with indiscriminate arrests by the police and truckloads of British "Tommies" spreading fear and havoc in the town and surrounding areas.

One of the school teachers was from Munger and knew Bhaiya and our family. He told Sabo "Suresh babu was arrested on the 9th itself, but his younger brother has been shot dead."

I told myself I should not believe every rumour that I hear, for rumours there were plenty. I decided to go to the Khadi Store, for that was the place where I would get authentic news about the Movement. The Khadi Stores were the de facto nerve centres of the freedom struggle, where revolutionaries came secretly to hide at night and where vital information passed from one person to another. I reached the Deoghar Khadi Store with Sabo and Nilu.

The people there were totally surprised and shocked to see us. How could we have made it across town wearing khadi clothes? The Store employees had sent their families back to their villages. After five days of unbelievable work which succeeded in bringing the government administrative machinery to a halt, Krena ji had been arrested. As long as he was around, he was the undisputed leader of the large group of volunteers engaged in anti-government activities. But now the town was crawling with "Tommies", British soldiers sent specially to quell the "insurrection". They were brutal and cruel, beating and killing indiscriminately. Truckloads of demonstrators would be herded into trucks and thrown into the jungle after being beaten mercilessly-many died as a result of these beatings, many were maimed for life.

The safest place for us was the Mission School, they told us.

I told the Manager the "news" from Munger about Bhaiya being arrested and Bhai ji being shot dead. "If Suresh babu is in jail, he is safe there. These days many false rumours are being spread, please don't believe them without authenticating them."

I told him I wanted to return to Gogri. "All rail movement is stopped and buses are off the road.I myself want to get back to my village. We have planned to try going on foot after a week, when things simmer down a bit and will let you know. But I suggest you return immediately to the Mission School, before the Tommies get here."

No sooner had he said this then a young boy came running in, panting for breath "The Tommies are here."

We panicked. The only way out would have been from the back side of the house, but there was no door at the back. If we tried scaling the wall, the soldiers would see us. The Store would be surrounded from all sides very soon-what could we do? The Manager acted decisively, took us to the traditional Indian latrine at the rear of the complex, used a long bamboo stick to push the excreta receptacle out of the trap-door which opened outward on the rear wall, and told us to exit through the latrine interior! Fortunately the latrine opening was wide enough for us to pass through, and we managed to slip out. We had no time to check how much of the muck and filth had stuck to our clothes and body, we just ran for our life and honour for neither was safe if the Tommies saw us.

Fortunately Sabo knew the way back, but to our horror we saw a road-barrier manned by soldiers just a short distance from the school. We hid under a tree for some time and then, to our good fortune, saw a solitary rickshaw moving along the road. Initially the rickshaw-puller was not willing to go past the road barrier, but somehow we managed to convince him. As we reached the barrier, the soldiers levelled their rifles at us and demanded to know what we were doing out on the road at this time instead of being at home. Sabo replied instantly "We are students and a teacher from the Mission School and are on our way back there".

We were let through! The Mission School and its residents were supposed to be total supporters of the British, who could be trusted fully. It was only when we were inside the school premises that we heaved a sigh of relief and could breathe normally again.

The next two days were tense and time hung heavy on our hands. I had run out of money too, since I had come prepared for a short stay of two or three days only, when the August Revolution suddenly broke out and turned my plans upside down. I felt trapped and imprisoned, even though I was not in jail.I just could not think of how to get out of there.

A few days later I saw two young men with bicycles standing under a tree outside the school compound. I went to the main gate and overheard them telling the school chowkidar "There is a girl in the hostel here called Savitry Sharma. We have come from her house." I went closer and saw it was Mahendra and Jageshwar!!

"How come you are here? Where are you coming from? How is Bhai ji?" I asked.

"Bhai ji, Bhabhi and the children are in Maheshpur, and have sent us to fetch you."

"Have you come all the way from Maheshpur by cycle?"

'Yes, there is no other reliable means of transportation nowadays. But we will get you back, no matter what."

"I was thinking of going back to Gogri on foot. Now that you are here, let us somehow leave at the earliest possible."

Early next morning Mahendra arrived with a horse -- carriage, and it was decided we would go to Bonsi in that carriage. From there we might be able to find some other means of transportation to Munger. Bonsi is a small town mid-way between Deoghar and Bhagalpur. As we reached the outskirts of Deoghar, we saw a bus about to leave for Bonsi and we quickly boarded it after Mahendra had loaded the two bicycles on the roof of the bus. Sabo had left all her belongings behind in the hostel and we just had a small bag with clothes in it for a few days for the three of us. We also had a tumbler to drink water from. We had been warned that we might get arrested for wearing khadi clothes. Fortunately Mahendra and Jageshwar were wearing shirt and trousers, and no one could even guess they were Ashram people-I could hardly recognize them myself in this attire.

Looking at the two young men in these foreign clothes, it suddenly hit me how different things were in August 1942 compared to earlier Satyagraha movements. Earlier we used to openly carry the national flag in processions, shouting patriotic slogans and waiting for the police to come and arrest us. Now we were in hiding, avoiding the police, me included. It felt strange, but reflecting on the turn of events in the past few weeks, I figured this was the right way to go.

We reached Bonsi around noon, only to discover that the Bhagalpur bus was about to leave. We somehow managed to get in and reached Bhagalpur after nightfall. We had a good night's sleep in a Dharamshala after a hearty meal of puri and vegetables that Jageshwar got from the market. Next morning we discovered that the only way to get to Bariarpur was by horse-carriage. With great difficulty we managed to find one that was willing to take us there. The two girls and I sat in the carriage, while the two young men followed on their bicycles. The horse looked listless, perhaps it was hungry. Mahendra gave the carriage driver some money to buy food for the horse, and it was only after it had been fed and watered that the horse started moving at the normal pace we expected. We had only some *sattu* mixed in water for breakfast.

I overheard the two talking as we moved, and was a little concerned that they were discussing death. I immediately thought someone had died. But on asking them, they replied that they were just having a general discussion, given the severity of the government reprisal and the uncertainty of everything around. As committed Ashram satyagrahis, their freedom and lives were always in danger, they were not even sure that they would make it to Maheshpur or get arrested on the way.

"Who all have been arrested?" I asked.

"I know about Bihar -- Shri babu, Anugraha babu, Rajendra babu, Jaglal Choudhry, Mathura babu, Satyanarayan babu and many other senior leaders are behind bars. The Patna students were amazing, they reached in a huge procession to fly the Tri-colour atop the Secretariat. Eight or nine were killed, about fifty seriously injured, but they put the Tri-colour where they had intended to! The jails are overflowing, the Bankipur jail became so overcrowded that they had to transfer prisoners elsewhere. At 3 pm lorries came to transport the prisoners, and one lorry came out of the jail gate. There was a huge crowd waiting outside, they attacked the lorry and freed the young men inside. Armed police had to be called to disperse the crowd before the other lorries could leave with their load of prisoners. This revolution is the revolution of the common man. The fearlessness being displayed by the masses is unbelievable, I cannot even begin to describe it appropriately."

"After escorting you to Maheshpur we are off to join the revolution. Our blood boils on hearing about all that is going on."

Mahendra and Upendra were cousin brothers from Pipla village, and had studied in the Gogri National School. Mahendra had recently wed Bose bhai's cousin sister Malti. This was an inter-caste marriage since Malti was a Rajput and Mahendra a Bhumihar. The Ashram welcomed such marriages and saw them as promoters of social reform. Malti was with Bhabhi ji in Maheshpur, and hearing Mahendra talk this way I could not help wondering what Malti would do if something were to happen to Mahendra.

It started raining heavily, accompanied by thunder and lightning -- it seemed as if the sky was being split open. The two young men had to get off their cycles and trudge through the sludge and mud in the pouring rain, dragging their bicyles behind them. We had hoped to reach Maheshpur by dark, but that was now impossible. Rain water had flooded the surrounding countryside, earth and sky had become one and everywhere we looked there was only a sheet of water. The carriage driver said he would not be able to continue after dark, his horse would refuse to go further and suggested we spend the night in the village we were approaching, and release him.

Jageshwar stepped up to me and whispered, "Elder Sister, no one will be willing to shelter you at night because of the khadi clothes you are wearing. God knows what village this is, staying at night in an unknown place is fraught with danger."

As he said this, we saw a villager walking on the road. Mahendra spoke to him in the local dialect, "O brother, what village is this?"

"Kalyanpur," he replied, as he strode past us towards the village.

"This is Sakaldeep's village", said Jageshwar, and we all heaved a sigh of relief.

Sakaldeep and Jageshwar were classmates in the Gogri School, and the former had even stayed for some days in Bhai ji's house. But relief and hope gave way to doubt and anxiety in my mind, for when problems come they come all at once from all quarters. Would Sakaldeep's family take the risk of putting us up for the night? Mahendra had asked Jageshwar to go into the village and locate Sakaldeep's house, while we took shelter from the torrential rain under a tree outside the village. The carriage driver had by now lost his patience, took his fare money and started on his return journey.

Jageshwar returned soon and with him came Sakaldeep's father with a storm-lantern and a big bamboo staff in his hands. The road was submerged in the rain water , so Nilu was put on Mahendra's shoulder and I held Sabo by her hand as we made our way to the village. Once we turned into the village from the road, the water became waist-deep and it was with great difficulty that we reached Sakaldeep's house. We were received warmly and with great respect by the family members. It seemed as if they were fully aware of the problems that had befallen Bhaiya, Bhai ji and the entire family.

They first gave us dry clothes for we were drenched to the skin and our cloth bag could not keep our change of clothes dry. I reluctantly agreed to wear the mill-made sari that was offered to me, while the girls changed into frocks. Our clothes were wrung out and put to dry, and we had just sat down to eat when one of the neighbours arrived. Seeing me she blurted out "Isn't she the one whose child...." before another woman standing next to her tried to shush her by gesturing furiously to stop. But the woman continued." Something happened to the child, poor thing."

'Oh my God, something has happened to Indu,"I said and got up at once. The family members tried to reassure me that nothing had happened, but I could not believe them and was troubled the whole night by all sorts of horrible thoughts.

Sakaldeep arrived late at night.

It was bright and clear next morning. Our clothes had dried, but the harsh August sunshine made it difficult for us to step out of the house. However, Mahendra had manged to arrange a horse-carriage and we set out from the village after lunch.

We took the road to Bariarpur, but it was almost sunset by the time we reached. The carriage driver refused to go any further, and we had to halt for the night in a Dharamshala. I had been crying almost continuously since Kalyanpur, and kept entreating Mahendra and Jageshwar to tell me the full facts and not withhold any information.It is much easier to handle a situation after you know the facts, rather than being in the dark and imagining all kinds of things.

We sat on a straw mat in the veranda of the Dharamshala. Mahendra spoke. "Elder Sister (*behen* ji), I am finding it difficult to prevent myself anymore from telling you all the facts, so I will tell you everything. Bhai ji has fractured his ankle but is safe in Maheshpur with Bhabhi ji and the children. Here is the flow of events.

Suresh babu was arrested in Munger on the 9th itself. Bhai ji was out on flood relief work, moving around in a boat in the Gogri region. There was a cholera epidemic raging, he was distributing medicines, clothes and food from village to village. A young man informed him on the boat itself that there was a "shoot at sight" warrant against him and that he should immediately go into hiding. Kashi Jha, Jageshwar and Satish (a youngster from Jamalpur) were with him. They decided to quickly bathe and then moor the boat in a safe place, from where they could go into hiding. Bhai ji dived into the water for a quick swim."

"But he is a very good and powerful swimmer", I chimed in.

"Yes, that he is, but who can prevent that which is destined to happen? As he dived into the river, the edge of his pyjama got stuck in the boat rim, so that while his head and body were in the water his foot remained stuck on the boat. The boys tried to pull him out of the water, but his head remained submerged and he kept ingesting water -- his ankle had been fractured and the pain had made him unconscious. The boatman showed presence of mind and used his long bamboo oar to lift the head out of the water and then they were able to pull him onto the boat. With his long experience of handling such accidents on the river, the boatman (*mallah*) then pumped the water out of Bhai ji's bloated abdomen, and Bhai ji slowly regained consciousness. But the pain was excruciating. The Jamalpur Hospital was nearby, but it was right next to the Police Station so there was no question of taking him there."

Jageshwar continued. "Groaning in pain, Bhai ji urged us to leave him and run otherwise we too would be shot along with him, for the police would surely be there soon. I flatly told him that there was no way Kashi and I would leave him and run to save our own lives. As soon as the boat reached the river bank, Satish ran home and returned with freshly cooked food, much like Hanuman bringing the *sanjivani* herb for the grievously injured Laxman. Bhai ji now said that we should immediately take the boat mid-stream and make for Khagaria where we should somehow locate Dr. Bidubhushan Bose, who was a friend and a nationalist.

It was dark by the time the boat reached Khagaria. We hastily assembled a make-shift stretcher and took Bhai ji to the good doctor's house. He immediately took him in, attended to the injury and put his ankle in a plaster cast. We sent Jageshwar to inform Bhabhi ji in Gogri about the turn of events and to re-assure her that Bhai ji was safe.

The next day it became common knowledge in Khagaria that Shiva Kant Mishra was hiding in Dr Bose's house. The police got this news and started for Dr Bose's residence-cum-clinic. But fortunately the more the authorities cracked down on the revolution, the larger became the number of supporters and sympathizers. One such person came running to Dr Bose and told him that that the police was on its way. As luck would have it, a seriously ill woman patient had just arrived at the clinic in a curtained palanquin. At the doctor's instructions, the palanquin bearers came into the inner courtyard and while the nurse took her in, Bhai ji was put into the palanquin and covered fully with a sheet.It was in this covered palanquin that he reached Maheshpur by boat, across the swollen Ganga."

"Isn't Maheshpur the village where the brothers Ramkisun and Ramgulam, close friends and followers of Bhaiya, live?' I asked.

'Yes," replied Mahendra. "They are Bhumihar Brahmins and prosperous farmers, and have really looked after Bhai ji with great care and affection. Kashi Jha has been with Bhai ji continuously, and the plaster has been removed a few days ago."

"You have said nothing about Bhabhi ji and the children. How did they manage to reach Maheshpur?"

"I am just coming to that", Mahendra said. In Shirnia fights, fuelled by old enmities coming down generations, are commonplace among extended families. This time they murdered Tejnath Mishra and Shivanand Mishra. 'Shivanand' was mistaken for 'Shiva Kant' and word spread throughout the region that Shiva Kant Mishra had been killed. I am a little surprised though that this news reached you even in Deoghar. The families of the two murdered men fled to the Gogri Ashram for refuge because their homes were vandalized and then burnt down. They camped in the school building since the school had been closed down due to the anti-government Movement. Some also stayed in Nandkishore's house.

"There was a cholera epidemic raging all around, a surreal atmosphere of fear and hopelessness prevailed. The women who had fled Shirnia, kept crying incessantly.

"A woman came from Bhojua village and told Bhabhi ji that Shiva Kant babu had been shot dead, there were eye-witnesses who reported seeing him fall into the river after being shot. His corpse floated a long way down the river.

"Bhabhi ji listened without saying a word. Jageshwar had come from Khagaria that morning with a letter and all the news about what had actually happened, and Bhabhi ji knew the actual facts.

"One of your aunts from Shirnia overhead the Bhojua woman and burst into tears, beating her chest and lamenting the untimely death of her nephew. Bhabhi ji told her to be brave and not cry.

"Chandrakant was seeing all this and became very afraid. Satish and Navin also started crying. That night Chandrakant came down with cholera. Curfew had been imposed but Babuji managed to send someone to the hospital to fetch a doctor. The doctor flatly refused saying he did not want to lose his government job by going to the Ashram since everyone knew there was a 'shoot at sight' warrant against Shiva Kant ji.

"Bose bhai happened to be in the Ashram, he ran and somehow managed to bring a private doctor. By now it was early morning, and the doctor had just started the intravenous drip when Chandrakant breathed his last. Bhabhi ji was disconsolate with grief, her condition was pitiable to watch. Your babu ji, Bose bhai and a few other Ashram inmates took the body for cremation on the banks of the Ganga. Many saw Mohit Sharma cry for the first time in their lives. He kept on repeating "You were born to give me the sacred fire on my death, but I am going to do that for you -- what cruel twist of Fate is this? You died for lack of any medical attention, a needless sacrifice to the Freedom Struggle -- how many people will be able to understand that?" When the distraught old man returned home after cremating his grandson, he found his second grandson Satish down with diarrhoea and vomiting. Bose bhai and Malti were nursing him, Bhabhi ji was in a state of shock and unable to do anything. That night Kashi Jha arrived from Maheshpur and told them that Bhai ji had asked all of them, including Babuji, to join him in Maheshpur. Fortunately, Satish's condition improved and they were able to leave for Maheshpur the next day."

Both Mahendra and Jageshwar broke down as they narrated this sad flow of events. Sabo, Nilu and I were in any case sobbing our hearts out. Somehow that awful night passed and we left by boat the next morning since all roads were submerged in the flood waters. We reached a clump of four trees, and alighted from the boat there. After the boat had departed, Mahendra told us that Bhai ji was hiding in the thatch structure they could see some distance away. They did not want the boatman to see that house.

It was good that they had left their cycles behind in Kalyanpur, because we had to wade through waist deep water and strong currents. Nilu was perched on Mahendra's shoulders, the water came up to Sabo's chest. Clutching her hand, we slowly made our way through the water. It took us about forty -five minutes to finally reach close to a big thatched barn perched atop a small mound. "'Where are you taking us, Mahendra?" I said. "This place is meant for cattle to stay in, how can human beings live here?"

Jageshwar answered, "Elder Sister, when Bhai ji was staying in Ramkisun's house, one day the village was surrounded by the 'military', someone had informed them that Shiva Kant babu was hiding in the village. The soldiers said they would burn the whole village down unless Shiva Kant Mishra was handed over immediately to them. The villagers feigned complete ignorance of someone called Shiva Kant Mishra. They conducted a house-to-house search but could not find Bhai ji. Frustrated in their attempt, the soldiers went away but not before threatening dire consequences if they later discovered that Shiva Kant Mishra had in fact been harboured by the villagers. After that it was decided that it was far too risky for Bhai ji to continue in the village and he was shifted to this remote and godforsaken haystack for his own safety once his fracture had healed a bit.

We reached the barn. It had mud walls and cattle were tethered in front. Several rooms were full of hay. Three small children were standing in the veranda, watching us wade through the flood waters that surrounded the structure on all sides as far as the eyes could see--Indu, Satish and Navin, fear and anxiety writ large on their young faces.

All of us cried for a long time, including Bhabhi, and this was a cathartic experience which dissolved some of the pain of Chandrakant's death.

This barn belonged to the local landlord, Isuri babu. I salute the courage of those amazing folk who, though surrounded by police and Army personnel and repeated threats from them not to harbour any fugitives, took the grave risk of giving shelter to Bhai ji till his fracture healed sufficiently for him to be moved to the haystack, and that too for his safety and not their own. By end August the anti-government activities had simmered down, most of the prominent participants and leaders were in jail, and yet some determined and committed freedom fighters kept on disrupting government functioning.

After escorting us safely to Maheshpur, Mahendra and Jageshwar went off and started sabotage activities in Munger and Bhagalpur districts with a small band of violent revolutionaries. Mahendra rarely visited his wife Malti, who was always in a state of worry and anxiety about her revolutionary husband's safety. She was our constant companion in those difficult and dark days.

Fear of the police made us stay in the haystack most of the time, we rarely ventured out. Isuri babu's herdsmen would draw potable water every morning and evening, and we had to make do with that. There was flood water all round, and the mud floors were wet and oozing, our feet used to slip and sink into the ooze when we walked. We had kept our wooden beds in the front veranda, each of the bed legs balanced on two bricks. The rooms were not fit for sleeping in. We also had to be very careful before lighting the cooking fires, for fear of the smoke giving away our whereabouts to the police and its informers. It was therefore agreed that the herdsmen would burn straw every morning and evening, and under cover of that smoke we would hurriedly light our own fire for cooking meals. There was one more fugitive from the police hiding with us, a person called Girdhar babu against whom also there was a shoot-at-sight warrant.

We would pack *parathas* and vegetables for Bhai ji and Girdhar babu every morning, and they would leave with the herdsman and the cattle for the day, wearing soiled clothes and a red '*gamcha*' on the head to look like one of them. They would stay in the jungle the whole day, and sometimes Mahendra, Jageshwar and their band would come to meet them, share the food we had packed and discuss matters. Differences started surfacing between Girdhar babu and Bhai ji on one side and the violent revolutionaries on the other.

Mahendra insisted that Gandhi ji's articles in the *Harijan* journal allowed room for uprooting railway lines, cutting telegraph wires, burning railway stations and Post Offices and disrupting other government work by force, and so they were doing precisely that.

Bhai ji tried to explain Gandhi ji's insistence that all protest should be non-violent in nature, and even disruption of rail movement and the functioning of Post Offices should be done without any violence and loss of life by giving due notice to the authorities, thus ensuring that innocent people were not harassed and arrested.

In due course, Mahendra and his band shifted their sphere of operation to a different region, and for some time did not make any contact with either Bhai ji or Malti.

The villagers of Maheshpur had told Bhai ji that if the police or army was seen approaching, someone would climb atop a brick kiln on the village outskirts and wave a red cloth. This would be the signal for Bhai ji and Girdhar babu to immediately go into hiding.

It was the job of the children to keep a strict watch on the brick kiln for the red flag whenever Bhai ji and Girdhar babu were at 'home' in the haystack. This vigil was not necessary when they were out in the forest with the herdsmen.

Early one morning Satish, Navin and Nilu started shouting "Red cloth, red cloth, red cloth". Girdhar babu and Bhai ji rushed out with the herdsman and their cattle, wading through waist-deep water. They stayed the whole day without food and water, they had not even had breakfast. They returned home at dusk, thirsty and hungry and bone-tired. Bhai ji had constant nagging pain in his injury, but today it had flared up.

A villager came to see us late at night. He told us that army soldiers had come looking for Shiva Kant Mishra and had conducted house-to-house searches in the village the whole day. They had surrounded the village since morning and had just left. They had even pointed to the haystack and asked what it was, and were told it was a haystack where cattle were kept and was used by the herdsmen.

Bhai ji decided that it was time to leave Maheshpur at the earliest possible. He had been drenched in the rain, developed fever and his injured ankle was throbbing with pain. Kashi Jha arrived late at night. Babuji had sent him to the *diyara* to sell some maize and get money from the sale, which task he had accomplished with his usual efficiency and effectiveness. The brothers Ramkisun and Ramgulam came at 10 pm with some puris and vegetables. We all had a hearty meal, and also put aside food for the next day. Ramkisun told Bhai ji and Girdhar babu to leave before dawn the next morning. Kashi Jha and a few other men somehow managed to make a stretcher for Bhai ji and helped him cross the flood waters.

Before leaving Bhai ji told Babuji that we should all try to get to Harpurjan somehow, he would join us there.

Within three days Jageshwar came and took Malti with him to a secret and undisclosed location where Mahendra and his band were camped.

The day after Malti's departure, Ramgulam came to tell us that the police was now on the look-out for the entire family. A few days earlier a small plane had crash-landed near Mansi and the two British airmen in it had been killed by the local herdsmen. The rumour spread that the killing had been done by members of Suresh babu's family. He himself was in jail but his brother Shiva Kant Mishra had a lot of fire-arms in his possession, and even the women members of the family were experts in the use of these fire-arms!!

When the first plane did not return to base, a second one was sent to trace its whereabouts. These aircraft were used to inspect the Barauni-Assam railway line because it was a vital link for supply of men and materials to the war front of the British Army in Assam. There was an important railway bridge near Mansi which was a critical bottleneck in that route, and needed to be kept under constant surveillance.

The second plane must have spotted the debris of the first one and its pilot landed the small aircraft. Some locals were crossing the river by boat, and seeing the white men they fell on them and killed them. This brought the number of Britishers killed on that spot to five. The rumour spread that this was all the handiwork of the Gogri Ashram folk, Suresh babu had a device that could destroy even aircraft. This rumour was further garnished and exaggerated and spread all over the Gogri region.

"They must be attributing these amazing powers to the magic lantern" I surmised.

Ramgulam said that may be so, but in any case the police was now on the lookout for the entire family and would reach Maheshpur any moment. God knows how they had got information that a woman and a young man had left this village a little while ago. We guessed that someone must have spotted Malti and Jageshwar leaving and had informed the police.

Ramkisun said he had information that select trains had resumed service, and promised us that somehow they would ensure that we reached Harpurjan via Chapra. This was their responsibility and they would fulfil it.

Ramgulam also informed us that Jaglal Choudhry's son was gunned down by Tommies in his own house and Jaglal and his daughter thrown into jail. "There is a death warrant on Bhai ji, there is no saying how the police will treat you if they find you."

All our lives we will bless these two brothers, and never forget how they put their own lives at risk to help us. They had nursed Bhai ji day and night when he was incapacitated with the fractured ankle. Their courage and the support of Isuri babu and the villagers was a manifestation of the way the common man rose up against the British in the August Revolution across India. What was surprising was the speed with which a second line of leadership sprang up from nowhere and led the revolution right from the next day after the top leaders had been arrested on 8th August. Ramkisun said it was the common peasant who risked life and limb carrying information and instructions from one village to the next.

We departed immediately, leaving behind our meagre belongings in Ramkisun's house. The girls were dressed in mill-made cotton frocks, the boys in trousers and singlets. There was no visible display of khadi for that would have attracted unwanted attention. We dipped our oldest saris in muddy water, and with our heads covered looked like the typical peasant women of that area. We kept an earthenware pitcher of water, a glass and some snacks that Ramkisun had got for us in a satchel, that was all we carried as we walked from Maheshpur to Bariarpur. Babuji had left earlier with the Jamalpur Satish to get information on the train schedules and make any other arrangements if possible. Ramgulam, Bhabhiji, Sabo, Satish, Navin, Indu, Nilu and I trudged along and by the time we reached Bariarpur railway station Bhabhi ji's feet were covered with blisters because, unlike me, she was not used to walking such large distances.

The platform was overflowing with people because no train had arrived from either direction for the past four days, and no food or water was available. Babuji had managed to create some space and was waiting for us in one corner of the platform.

We were fortunate that the Patna bound train arrived that day itself, but boarding it was a Herculean task and we were literally pushed in through the windows by the coolies like pieces of luggage. Somehow we reached Patna.

Finding a place to stay in Patna was not going to be easy. We had the address of Bhaiya's friend and compatriot Ganeshprasad Sahi, who was a practising lawyer in the High Court and had a house in the Kadam Kuan locality. But since so many of us could not reasonably just land up at his house, it was agreed that Babuji and Satish would spend the night in a *dharamshala*. Ramgulam would accompany us to Ganesh babu's house and then stay elsewhere. We reached our destination in two rickshaws, unsure what kind of reception awaited us for we were fugitives running from the law. The minute she saw us in our bedraggled state, Sahi ji's wife burst into tears, embraced Bhabhi ji and me, and took us inside. When she heard all the details, she clutched Bhabhi ji and both cried for a long time. One of her own sons, who was Chandrakant's age, had died of typhoid a month ago and she could understand a mother's sorrow at the loss of her child. We all bathed, had a hearty meal and slept soundly. After a long time we were savouring the joy of good home-cooked food and a comfortable bed.

We resumed our journey next morning, Babuji and Satish had already left for Gogri.

We boarded the steamer dressed as we were when we had left the barn in Maheshpur, and on crossing the swollen Ganga we took the narrow gauge train to Sonepur, and from Sonepur to Chapra. In Chapra we learnt that the train service to Masrakh had been disrupted because railway lines had been uprooted and stations burnt down. The Chapra station and its surroundings were crawling with security personnel.

We left the station hurriedly. Adhishthta ji's elder daughter lived in Chapra where her husband ran the Vani Mandir Press.

We went to her house and were greeted warmly, fed dinner and given comfortable beds to sleep in. Ramgulam meanwhile went to the town and arranged for a horse-carriage to take us to Masrakh. We left at the crack of dawn and halting at several places en route, finally reached Harpurjan.

Chapter 29

Harpurjan Again

On reaching home, we found the house locked and were told Pandit ji had gone to Sidhwalia. Rajendrapal's cows were tethered on the veranda. Indu went running to his house to tell him of our arrival, and Adhishthata ji's wife Munnikiya came quickly with two servants in tow. The cows were removed and the verandah cleaned up while she took the children home with her. She sent back two cots with bedding, bathed the children, fed them and organized food for the adults. Her warmth and affection overwhelmed us, and her care-filled behaviour came as a huge pillar of support for us in these difficult times when we had been shunned by many who were supposed to be close to us. We got hope that we might be able to stay safely here, and managed to persuade Ramgulam to return to Maheshpur.

We started the process of settling down, though it was difficult to do so with the house locked up. I summoned Mahangu bahu with her husband Mahungu, and sent a letter with Mahangu to Pandit ji's elder brother Ramprasad Tiwari in Teliya. I wrote that we had somehow reached Harpurjan, hiding from and avoiding the police, only to find the house locked and no sign of Pandit ji.I requested him to send rations and cooking utensils back with Mahangu and somehow get word to Pandit ji that he must return immediately to Harpurjan.

We were still awaiting Mahangu's return from Teliya when Pandit ji arrived on his cycle. The children rushed to him and greeted him by touching his feet. He was horrified to see us in such a bedraggled and forlorn condition. "Where is Chandu, I don't see him here?" he said. Bhabhi ji started crying, and so did I. Pandit ji understood that Chandrakant was no more. We always wondered whether Chandrakant would have survived if there had been no death warrant and Bhai ji was with us, if Bhaiya was not in jail and if the government had not created the conditions where doctors were afraid to come to the Ashram.

The children were scared by the deserted look of this huge, rambling house, and got even more anxious seeing us cry. Pandit ji spoke gently to Bhabhi, telling her that she must be strong and now focus on looking after Satish and Navin.

It was growing dark, and Mahungu bahu had by now swept the rooms clean, washed all the utensils, got the kitchen operational, filled water for drinking and bathing. We bathed and changed into clean clothes. Mahungu was now back from Teliya with a full and ample supply of rations sent by my sister-in-law. Dinner was cooked by me. The lantern was lit, Pandit ji got some more bedding from Adhishthata ji's house and we started life once again in our own home in Harpurjan.

I decided I must first ensure proper food for all. Satish and Navin were down with dysentery and I sent Nilu to get some curd from Munnikiya. She returned with a lot of it, and without waiting for sugar, the children hungrily ate the curd with the flat rice that had come from Teliya. These were the same children who made every effort to avoid drinking milk in normal times in Gogri! Children understand and adapt to situations very fast, they demonstrated that time and again in the haystack in Maheshpur, where they would eat whatever was available without any fuss. They never complained about anything in those fear-filled days in Maheshpur, quietly and obediently doing whatever they were told to do.

Bhai ji reached a week later and narrated the saga of his escape from Maheshpur.

He boarded the train in Bariarpur along with Girdhar babu. God knows how the police got scent of their journey to Patna, for as soon as the train left the station they heard their fellow passengers talking about the police and Army personnel who were conducting a thorough search on every train for two fugitive Congress workers who were on the run. Though they were disguised as ordinary peasants, they decided it was too dangerous to continue the journey, and slipped off the train at the first stop, which was a small flag station. They reached Patna by changing trains every few stops and spent the night at Ganeshprasad Sahi's house where they were relieved to get news about us.

They separated in Patna and went off in different directions. Bhai ji crossed the Ganga by boat and reached Dighwara by bullock cart and spent the night at the home of an acquaintance. He left the next morning on foot but found a bullock cart in Chapra which agreed to take him to Harpurjan. They spent the night in the bullock cart itself, parked under a tree. His ankle was in a bad shape when he reached Harpurjan.

However, a few days of rest and care worked wonders for his ankle.

Slowly Harpurjan starting becoming a focal point for revolutionaries on the run from the police. They would halt here for a few days and then move on. The in-laws of Tarakeshwari Sinha (who later became a Cabinet Minister in Delhi after Independence) had a farm in Gopalpur. Her elder brother-in-law was also on the run from the law. He was a good friend of Bhai ji's and the two would alternately hide in Gopalpur and Harpurjan. As the days progressed, we started getting news about other people too, both relatives and friends. Bhai ji would cycle to his in-laws place in Bangra, to his sister-in-law in Madhopur, to Chapra, Siwan and other neighbouring towns and villages. Bhabhi ji's elder brother Ramraksha ji had been arrested in early August. Ramvinod Singh of Malkhachak was a well-known Congress personality in Bihar and played a prominent role in every phase of the freedom struggle. His younger brother Satyanarayan Singh was another active revolutionary, and both brothers landed up in jail.

Ramvinod babu had two daughters, Sharda and Saras, who deserve to have their courageous exploits written in letters of gold. They would start walking with the national flag held aloft in their hands, and crowds would start joining them. If two young women could dare to march, how could the young men lag behind? The marchers would uproot railway lines, burn stations, cut telegraph wires and bring the government machinery to a halt. These two sisters created havoc for the government in the entire region. After evading the police dragnet for many days, they were finally arrested by the Inspector General of Police of Bihar, an Englishman called Tynbrook. Both were given life imprisonment and incarcerated in Bhagalpur Jail. When the revolution petered down, many political prisoners were released and the two sisters were among them. They occupied pride of place in the galaxy of revolutionaries in Bihar and are both still alive, living domesticated family lives. What a shame that the government of Independent India gave no recognition whatsoever to these two brave daughters of Mother India!

Bhabhi ji's other brother, Ramjas Upadhyaya, was never arrested. He came one evening to Harpurjan, spent five minutes with us and then left for an undisclosed destination. A young man accosted him in Rajapatti Station and entered into a long conversation with him, making him increasingly suspicious that he was a police informer out to betray his presence and get him arrested. Fugitives on the run had to be alert and look at everyone as a potential Mukhbir (informer) -- fortunately, as it transpired, nothing untoward happened that day at the Rajapatti Railway Station.

It was now 1943.Bhai ji went to Madhopur one day, and decided to cycle back to Harpurjan with his brother-in-law Suraj Mishra. I don't know why they chose to return via Siwan, but it was there that a member of the CID spotted him and Bhai ji was immediately arrested along with Suraj Mishra. He was first taken to Chapra Jail and then transferred to the Patna Camp Jail.

Bhaiya was first in Bhagalpur Jail, but was then transferred to Hazaribagh Jail as an 'A' class prisoner. 'A' class political prisoners got extra amenities and several prominent Bihar politicians, including Jaiprakash Narayan, were in Hazaribagh Jail. Some were high-security prisoners who had been given indefinite jail sentences. Both Bhaiya and Bhai ji were high security prisoners. When he was released, Bhaiya gave us a detailed and vivid description of jail life.

Chapter 30

Jail

The Hazaribagh Jail housed 'A' class prisoners. Shri babu, Anugraha babu, Acharya Badrinath Verma, Satyanarayan Singh from Samastipur, Jagjivan Ram, Chakradhar Sharan, the famous revolutionary Batukeshwar Dutt (who had been a part of Bhagat Singh's group and had served time in the infamous penal colony in the Andaman Islands), Yadugopal Mukherji, Ramvinod Singh and his brother Satyanarayan Singh, Ramraksha Upadhyaya, Sardar Harihar Singh and others were all in Hazaribagh Jail at that time. An 'A' class jail was also created in Motihari and other Bihar leaders lodged there including Mahesh babu, Birchand Patel, Rajeshwar Patel, Jaglal Choudhry, Prajapati Mishra, Rameshwar Singh, Deepnarayan Singh, Binda babu, etc.

Bidyanand Dubey (who was to later marry my eldest daughter Sabo) was also there. This jail was soon transformed into a Women's Jail and all earlier inmates transferred to Hazaribagh.

Unlike 'B' and 'C' class prisoners, 'A' class prisoners could move freely from one ward to another during the day and had access to books and newspapers. But the books were censored by the jail authorities, as were all the letters, periodicals and newspapers. "Objectionable" matter in letters coming in or going out were inked over. The government spent 75 rupees per month per prisoner on food, clothing, soap, oil and other essentials. There were separate small messes where convicts cooked food for the 'A' class inmates. These were convicts serving long sentences in jail who had learnt how to cook well and food was mostly decent. Each 'A' class prisoner was also assigned a helper, another ordinary convict, who used to wash their clothes, clean their cells, get food from the mess and wash the eating utensils after meals.

Each political prisoner had a cell in which he was locked in at 6 pm. This cell had no window, but a door with iron bars which was padlocked. A lit lantern was put in the cell because there was no electricity. A wooden bed with a cotton mattress, sheet, pillow and a mosquito net. A wooden commode was kept in one corner. Dinner would be served at 6 pm in the cell. The cell door would be opened at 6 am next morning. Political prisoners did not have to wear jail clothes.

They would read and write, play chess, cards, carrom, etc. In the late afternoon some would play volley ball or badminton in the small courtyard attached to each ward.

Some people used this time to learn the Gita by heart, recite the *Ramcharitmanas* regularly and commit to memory many verses from it. Discussion groups were formed, senior leaders asked to speak on different subjects. Regular hand-written bulletins were produced, and several people even wrote books. This is how people coped with their indefinite incarceration.

Jaiprakash Narayan escaped from Hazaribagh Jail, and this led to vastly tightened security measures. His fellow-escapee Ramnandan Mishra was recaptured quickly and brought back to jail. He was severely tortured, put in shackles and kept in a separate cell.

Bhaiya said 'A' class prisoners had it very easy compared to the 'C' class, who were all kept in a large hall, with cement slabs for a bed and just a blanket in addition. Food was terrible. However, compared to 1930 conditions were vastly better for political prisoners in 1942.But no one knew how long they would remain in jail.

Bhaiya devised a new method for teaching Sabo. Every week he would send her a thin note-book with questions in it, and she had the week to answer and return the filled up note-book to him. Arithmetic, algebra, geometry were covered, essays had to be written in Hindi and English, translation done and even grammar!! Along the lines of Nehru's *Letters From A Father To His Daughter*, he would cover history, write about famous people who whose life and writings had influenced him, and cover other topics of interest and relevance. Sabo worked hard and diligently to send in her answers. Unfortunately these note-books did not come back with him when Bhaiya was finally released from jail in 1945. We all felt this was a real pity, for those books were a treasure-house of facts and views.

Bhaiya had been jailed before 1942 also, and he had used that time to try and mould himself into an ideal non-violent satyagrahi. He not only read whatever books he could get hold of, he also initiated dialogue and discussion on topics of relevance and importance to the Movement.

In 1933 he had fallen ill in jail, and there was little hope of his surviving after he remained unconscious for many days. This led to his establishing a good rapport with the jail doctor and taking personal care if any fellow-prisoner fell ill.

Nandkishore, Ugramohan and Bhai ji often accompanied Bhaiya to jail, and they too would describe life inside a jail.

It is very difficult for a young, energetic man who was 20 or 21 years old, to adjust to jail life. The will and spirit gets broken, constant anxiety and fear play havoc with the nervous system. Bhaiya must have experienced all these emotions but learnt not only how to survive but in fact grow into a stronger and better person by using jail time in a creative and constructive way.

All his political companions and followers who went with him to Bhagalpur Jail and the Patna Camp Jail would attest to the fact that Bhaiya not only had the ability to inspire people to follow him to jail, but that once inside he also made every effort to make their stay easier and more palatable.

Gandhi ji always said that in jail it was essential to keep yourself constructively engaged and be active mentally and physically throughout the day, to ensure the level of mental and physical well-being required to bear the rigours of imprisonment. Bhaiya followed this advice religiously and with iron discipline.

Before 1929 political prisoners were kept and treated like convicted 'C' class prisoners. When the numbers of political prisoners suddenly swelled in the aftermath of the Salt Satyagraha, the political prisoners were separated from the ordinary convicts, though they continued to be housed in similar facilities. Large halls with 16 to 18 cement platforms which acted as beds, with one end raised to act as a pillow. Woollen blankets were given to act as both bed-sheet as well as to cover the body against the cold in winter, and the same woollen blankets were used as bed-sheets in the summer also. So many bodies crammed into each hall made the summer heat unbearable, creating conditions that are difficult to imagine for someone who has not actually lived through this hell.

Four or five such halls made up one jail ward. Political prisoners tended to be well educated and cultured, so the wardens and the jailors would normally behave better with them than with ordinary prisoners. But they were not allowed to move from ward to another. Each ward had a small courtyard, hardly big enough to accommodate a volley-ball court. If Bhaiya could manage to get the Jailor to provide a ball or material for badminton, he would insist his fellow-inmates played in the evening to keep themselves active and fit. Otherwise they could always play kabaddi or *kho-kho* which did not require any accessories.

There were many students in jail too. Bhaiya tried to ensure that they were allowed to continue their studies inside the jail. Bhai ji took up the responsibility of teaching one such student called Bhagwat Jha Azad, who was to later become a senior Cabinet Minister at the Centre after Independence.

The Jailor would turn to Bhaiya to resolve issues if any of the political prisoners created commotion or unrest in protest against the jail conditions. Slogans of Inquilab Zindabad or going on hunger strike were the common expressions of protest. Sometimes the pressure of being cooped up in a confined space led to fights and scuffles amongst the prisoners themselves. Bhaiya was adept at resolving such situations with wisdom and maturity.

It was difficult to improve the quality of the jail food, but political prisoners were allowed to get ghee and snacks from home to supplement the terrible jail food. When Bhaiya learnt in 1942 that Bhai ji and several Gogri Ashram residents were kept as 'C' class prisoners in the Patna Camp Jail, he managed to get himself transferred there as a 'C' class prisoner so that he could keep them company. Moving from the relative comforts of 'A' class in Hazaribagh to 'C' class in Patna Central was a big sacrifice, but Bhaiya insisted that it was his duty to be with his fellow freedom-fighters and his younger brother.

Chapter 31

Commentary on the Sama Veda in Lahore

Pandit ji did not like his work at the Sidhwalia Mill at all. His friend Brahmadutt Jigyasu, who used to publish the booklet *Vedvani*, sent him a letter saying that a Trust in Lahore wanted someone to translate the Sama Veda into Hindi and also give a commentary on it. He himself was busy with some other work, and felt there was no one else who could do this work as well as Pandit ji, and entreated him to go to Lahore on this assignment. The Trust would make all arrangements for board and lodging and also give him a decent remuneration. This offer came as a boon to Pandit ji who was very unhappy with his current job and wanted to leave the mill as soon as possible. He left for Lahore in mid-1943.

Babu ji was managing the farming in Gogri and would regularly send money for us in Harpurjan. I would manage the day-to-day expenses from Pandit ji's salary, which he would dutifully hand over to me every month.

Vaidyanath Shastri was also sent to Lahore to assist Pandit ji, who had plunged headlong into his new work with vigour and enthusiasm. Vidyanidhi, whose studies had been disrupted in the '42 Movement, joined him and was followed shortly by his brother Nagarjeet. Both brothers completed their Shastri studies from Lahore.

Pandit ji completed the assignment given to him by the Trust to their full satisfaction and returned home in mid-1945. The partition of India meant that his work was not published. Much later, to his horror, he discovered that his translation and commentary on the Sama Veda had been published but under someone else's name. He was very upset but could do nothing about it, so decided to do another translation of the Sama Veda with much more extensive commentary, based on further deep research and study. In fact he spent the last ten years of his life on this massive project, but unfortunately died before it could be published. The handwritten documents were with me when he left on his last journey to the burning ghat. But I have leapt many years into the future and must return to the train of my narrative.

Pandit ji had left for Lahore and Bhai ji was in jail. We called Ugramohan to live with us in Harpurjan, and he came from Gogri with two cows and one servant, and also money sent by Babuji. In the meantime, Mahendra's wife Malti had given birth to a baby girl. She was constantly on the run, going from one place to another with her revolutionary husband Mahendra, who firmly believed that he was furthering the cause of Independence through his armed violence. It was at this time that Jaiprakash Narayan, Ramnandan Mishra and others made their daring escape from Hazaribagh Jail and the freedom struggle entered its next phase. Ram Manohar Lohia was part of Jaiprakash ji's band. He had set up a radio station in the jungles of the Nepal Terai and was broadcasting insurrectionary messages from there throughout the country. Other small revolutionary groups sprang up and started amassing weaponry of all kind. Mahendra was the leader of one such band of violent revolutionaries, young men fired by patriotic zeal and fervour. They made a significant impact on the fight for freedom.

Mahendra sent Malti to Harpurjan in March 1943. That same year my son Anil was born in June, and Bhabhi ji's son Sunil in November. The older children's studies really suffered since there was no school there. Sabo had returned to the Mission School in January of the same year. We organized a Pandit ji for the children's studies. Ultimately, Indu and Nilu also went to Deoghar and both completed their Matric from there.

Chapter 32

Mahendra is Arrested

Malti had been staying in Harpurjan for some time now. She was unhappy being away from her husband and always appeared depressed. We tried our best to lift up her mood, but she continued to pine for Mahendra. It was March 1944 and Holi was two days away. Later that week, their daughter Manju would celebrate her birthday.

Those days each village had one or two police informers (*mukhbirs*) who would continually feed information to the police on the village goings-on. In addition, there was the village security guard (chowkidar), also on government payrolls. We had seen one person hanging around our house for the past few days. The next day two palmists came and everyone wanted their palms read, since this provided some diversion from the monotony of daily life. People surrounded the palmists, eager to know what the future had in store for them. Malti was sitting quietly on one side with little Manju in her lap. One of the palmists requested to see Manju's feet and then said "This girl is staying far away from her father. A bird flies in every night from the north and licks her feet. That is because her father's life is in danger. Why don't you call him? I would like to see his palm also."

Malti blurted out, "He is not here at the moment." Ugramohan took Manju in his arms and walked away. Without taking any money, the two palmists left soon thereafter.

"These were certainly people from the Police CID. Malti should leave this place immediately," said Ugramohan.

But Malti could not do that. The next evening a horse-carriage drew up, and out stepped Mahendra and his cousin brother Upendra. There were two servants walking behind the carriage, who were actually revolutionaries in disguise, Ramesh and Karia.

Seeing them, Ugramohan rushed up and said, "Mahendra, you must leave right away in this same carriage. If you stay here, you will be arrested."

Malti intervened and begged her husband to stay on for just two days so that they could spend Holi together. There was much crying and drama, and finally Mahendra agreed to stay for two days. Holi was celebrated with gusto, and the family stayed up till late at night exchanging news and gossip. Finally everyone went off to sleep. Upendra, Ugramohan and Mahendra's two comrades slept in the front room, the cowherd Sahadiya in the veranda. Anil, Nilu and I were in the room across the veranda, while Bhabhi ji and her three sons Satish, Navin and Sunil were in the room adjacent to ours. The rooms had very large windows and we used to keep the beds near them to catch the breeze. Mahendra and Malti were in the room in the interior of the house.

I was rudely awakened by Ugramohan shouting "take out the spears" (probably thinking thieves were trying to enter the house), to which a distant voice responded "Raise your rifles!"

I was now wide awake, and as my gaze shifted to the window I saw the silhouette of a man with raised rifle. Bhabhi ji too woke up and saw a similar sight at her window --a policeman with raised rifle. She whispered, "O sister-in-law!" I slid off my bed and crawled silently to her room through the open door between the adjacent rooms, and the two of us managed to sit upright in a corner, waiting for events to unfold.

There was a knocking on my door. It was Ugramohan, saying, "Sister, open the front door."

I did so and immediately several rifle-carrying policemen rushed in, led by the Masrakh police-in-charge (Daroga), who we knew. After carefully searching our two rooms, the policemen opened the back door which led to the rear veranda. On one end of the veranda was the room Mahendra and Malti were in. They rained rifle butts on the door and as soon as Mahendra opened it, he was seized by three policemen. One of them asked,

"What is your name?"

"Harish," Mahendra replied.

"There is no point in telling us lies. We have come here with definite information that you are the much-wanted terrorist Mahendra Choudhry."

Mahendra knew the game was up. "Yes, I am Mahendra," he said. Four policemen held Mahendra, and one each held Ugramohan, Upendra, Ramesh and Karia. The house was surrounded by armed policemen on all sides, and every yard there was a policeman with raised rifle. Clearly they were taking no chances. They had stopped their trucks 3 miles away and had come to the house on foot in the darkness of night, to make sure Mahendra did not escape their dragnet this time.

One man was despatched to get the trucks while our rooms were subjected to a thorough search. Everything was turned upside down and inside out. When they opened the almirahs, they were surprised to see only books--a large number of them.

"Whose books are these?" they asked.

Ugramohan replied, "They belong to my brother-in-law Pandit Ramavtar Sharma, who is a well-known and highly respected Vedic scholar."

"Where is he?"

"In Lahore, translating and writing a commentary on the *Sama Veda*."

The police went through each book and saw only Sanskrit tomes: the Vedas, Upanishads, Puranas. They were surprised that there were no firearms, for they had been informed that Mahendra Choudhry and his associates were here with heavy firearms, and they would not surrender without fierce resistance. They would not only fire bullets but also hurl bombs. But the reality had been completely different.

The Daroga announced, "We also arrest Shrimati Kaushalya Devi on charges of harbouring Mahendra Choudhry in her house".

The police trucks came and we were made to sit inside one. I went in with little Anil in my arms. They had also seized Sahadiya, and Bhabhi ji protested "Why are you taking him away? He is only a household help. If you take him, how will I manage all these little children on my own? We also have a problem of thieves in these parts. Whose responsibility will it be if I am robbed?" The Daroga was a decent man. The village chowkidar of Harpurjan also spoke up. "This man is only a cow-herd, and has been here for a long time." Sahadiya was set free and the chowkidar was instructed to guard the house against thieves.

It was dawn by the time the police trucks finally left. After a short halt in Masrakh, we were taken to Chapra. The men were locked up in the Police Station, while a cot was put under a tree for me. Anil had an upset stomach and fever, and was crying with hunger. I too was famished. The Police Officer there, Chandramohan Jha, knew Bhaiya and Bhai ji well and behaved with great empathy towards me.

Food and water was arranged for me. I could not hear what was being discussed inside the Police Station, but after some time a person came out and asked me if someone would be willing to sign surety for me and bail me out. I replied that in these circumstances no one would come forward to sign surety for me, so they might as well send me to jail. The man went back inside for another round of confabulation and then returned with a sheet of paper. "We do not want to put you in jail or keep you in the police lock-up. Please sign this document, we will release you on self-surety. However, a case will be filed against you and you will have to appear for all hearings."

I signed the document and was free to go home.

It was evening by now, and I stood with Anil in my arms, confused and perplexed about where I could go at this hour. Anil was burning with fever. Who would be willing to give shelter to a person from a well-known anti-British Satyagrahi family in whose house armed terrorists had been found and arrested? Should I spend the night on the Railway Station platform? But the thought of spending the night alone in the open platform with a little child who had high fever was too daunting. I suddenly remembered that a friend of Pandit ji's, whose daughter had studied in Harpurjan, lived in Chapra. I took a rickshaw from the police station and reached his house.

As soon as the wife, who had often met me in Harpurjan, saw me she became hysterical. "How come you are here at this time? We have just received news that a large contingent of policemen had gone to Harpurjan and the entire family was arrested and brought here in a truck. They especially mentioned that you had been arrested. God knows what crimes you people have committed that the police is after you."

"It is true that I was picked up by the police, but I have been released on bail. I just need shelter for the night, my son is down with fever, we will leave tomorrow morning."

"Oh no, we don't want to get involved with people like you. Please proceed to the station in this rickshaw, I am sure you will be able to find a train to take you home."

I realized that it would not be appropriate to try and find any other household that would be willing to put me up for the night, since it would put people to inconvenience and possible harassment by the police. I told the rickshaw to take me back to the police station.

The police were shocked to see me back. When I explained the situation, Chandramohan Jha respectfully took me to his own home, gave us dinner and arranged for a doctor friend to examine Anil and give him medication. He found out the time of the next train to Masrakh and deputed a policeman to take us to the station. The same policeman escorted us all the way home to Harpurjan.

Bhabhi ji was unable to believe her eyes when she saw us. "I had assumed that you would be sent to jail. I was wondering how to manage the four children and this large house on my own."

"I myself am amazed at what happened. To think they granted me bail on the basis of a self-surety, with the bail amount still not known to me!!How and why this happened is beyond my comprehension."

Those were really difficult times. Fortunately Babuji was at home looking after the farming and family lands. In 1940 Bhaiya had bought land in Bhelwa diyara in an auction. Singheshwar babu, Jaiprakash Narayan and Bhaiya had left College together to join the Satyagraha Movement, but Singheshwar babu returned to his studies after some time , completed graduation and joined the Provincial Civil Service. He was the "Receiver" of the Banaili princely estate in 1940 and knowing the financial distress our family was going through, advised Bhaiya to tell Babuji to buy this land which was being sold at a throw-away price. The money was somehow raised and 200 bighas of land were bought on the banks of the Ganga. Babuji manged this tract of land, along with the Shirnia diyara land, with the help of share-croppers and kept the family finances going, regularly sending me money in Harpurjan.

Sabo and Indu were both in the Deoghar Mission School hostel. Pandit ji also used to send money home to me. But there was total uncertainty regarding the jail terms of both Bhaiya and Bhai ji, for they were both in jail 'indefinitely' with no idea of when they would be released.

Adhishthata ji had died in 1938. He had been a tower of strength and support when he was alive. However his family continued to always be very kind and supportive.

Upendra was a member of the Communist Party. He arranged for two trunk-loads of books to be delivered to me through a comrade. These books included novels by Prem Chand, Yashpal, Rahul Sankrityayana and the full collection of Sharat Chandra Chatterjee's novels, and we spent many hours reading these amazing books whenever we got time from our household chores.

Ugramohan was released after three months because no case could be built against him. He would often read aloud to us from these books after lunch.

Chapter 33

Meeting in Jail

We had not met Bhaiya and Bhai ji in a long time and so made a plan to go and visit them in jail. Bhabhi could not join us because Navin was unwell, so Ugramohan, Anil and I went to the Patna Camp Jail to meet them.

I stayed with Tarakeshwari Sinha's father in Patna, while Ugramohan stayed in the Gandhi Hotel. Uchit, the owner of this hotel, was a nationalist who used to study in the Gogri Ashram School and had been to jail several times. In 1940 he had started the hotel in Patna's Muradpur locality. It was more of a lodge than a hotel, and had also been a hiding place for fugitives in the 1942 Movement.

We went to the Jail the day after we reached Patna. We were admitted via the Main Gate and taken to a nearby room where we were asked to sit and wait. Both the brothers arrived shortly and we sat on chairs around a table. There was a jail person standing there all the time and so we confined our conversation to family affairs. Bhaiya said, "I can understand that Yashoda and you are alone with the children. You are both very brave, look after the children with your usual positive and fearless spirit."

"By when are you likely to be released?"

"We are incarcerated indefinitely, you know that. You have to learn to be self-dependent. Just ensure that the children's education continues and does not ever suffer."

Bhai ji said, "The Bengal famine and the War must have pushed up prices of all essentials and so you must be finding it difficult to manage."

'No, the farming is good and we get sufficient money every month, and so are comfortable."

Bhaiya remarked, "If we get Independence this time it will be good, otherwise there may be a long wait."

"We are ready to suffer any hardship for the good of the country. Ashram life has taught us to live frugally and austerely and we are teaching our children to imbibe these values. We are making every effort to give them a good education. Sabo and Indu are both in Deoghar."

I could not tell him much about Mahendra. Bhaiya later told me that my letter had been censored before it reached him, the entire section describing Mahendra's arrest had been inked out. I mentioned the name 'Malti' but Bhai ji quickly signalled that I should speak no further about her. The jail official had perked up on hearing this name and had moved closer to us. I mentioned that Mahendra had engaged a lawyer called Bisnath Parsad to fight his case.

We carried on the conversation for a short while in a desultory manner and soon it was time to leave.

I am a strong and courageous person, but the thought that the children might have to grow up with Bhaiya and Bhai ji still languishing behind bars, saddened me and my spirits drooped. My patience and enthusiasm were beginning to wane.

Chapter 34

Mahendra's Hanging

We were worried that a good lawyer may not be ready to take up Mahendra's case. We were looking for a lawyer who was a nationalist and patriot who would handle the case as a political offence involving armed revolutionaries, and was not a serious criminal matter.

Malti had had very little contact with her in-laws and the rest of Mahendra's family. But with both Mahendra and Upendra in jail facing serious charges of murder, the family rallied behind her to offer whatever help was required. A renowned Patna lawyer agreed to take up the defence against these charges.

Several small armed revolutionary groups had emerged in the '42 Movement. They would uproot railway lines, cut telegraph wires, capture or burn down railway stations, Post Offices and police stations. Escaping the police dragnet and finding opportunities for creating more disturbances kept them fully occupied. Mahendra's armed group had some rifles and pistols but needed more weapons. A plan was formulated. Chandrachud was a big landlord near the town of Beguserai. Mahendra decided they would loot his ill-earned wealth to finance his group's needs, and reached his home one dark night with six members of his group. They had hoped they would be able to frighten him and extract the money, but Chandrachud had a small private army waiting for them and a regular firefight ensued. Both sides took casualties in the pitch darkness.

It was Malti and Mahendra who gave us the details of this incident. One of Chandrachud's people died and he himself was injured in the eye. A water-tight criminal case was made and Mahendra found himself legally trapped.

The Lower Court sentenced both Mahendra and Upendra to death. Upendra was Mahendra's first cousin and a member of the Communist Party, and had actually opposed the '42 Movement. He had merely accompanied Mahendra to visit Malti in Harpurjan. But because he was arrested in Mahendra's company he was sentenced to death.

I was acquitted by the Lower Court, but while this certainly gave us financial relief from fighting a long drawn-out legal case, we were deeply saddened by the death sentence passed on these two young men.

My acquittal gave me no joy. Malti stayed with us. We tried every means to comfort her, hoping that the nation would get Independence before the death sentence could be carried out and he would escape the gallows. Malti too nursed this hope and dreamt that her husband would be alive and be hailed as a brave freedom fighter once India became free.

Mahendra and Upendra's appeal against the death penalty was filed in the High Court.

In mid-1945 a large number of political prisoners were released and Bhai ji was one of them. One of the conditions under which Bhai ji was released was that he would have to stay within the geographical limits of Chapra district.

Rajendra babu and all members of the Congress Working Committee were released on the 15th of June. Bhai ji told us that under the terms of the agreement with Lord Wavell it was expected that a National Government would be sworn in. He also wanted to approach Rajendra babu for his help in saving Mahendra from the hangman's noose, but with the restriction of not being able to travel outside Chapra district, Bhai ji had to send a letter. Rajendra babu was fully aware that many revolutionaries were being charged and convicted under wrong sections of the penal Act. Many were hanged in this way, a fact he wrote about in his autobiography. But he was unable to do anything for Mahendra.

As I have mentioned before, Upendra was a member of the Communist Party which had opposed the '42 Movement on the grounds that the British were opposing the Nazi and fascist forces and hence should be supported in the War effort. The Movement was in effect supporting the fascists. The lawyer was able to prove in Court that being a member of the Communist Party he had not participated in the Movement at all and so there was no question of his being involved in killing or maiming anyone. This was correct, he had in fact opposed the '42 activities and had only come to Harpurjan to visit Malti when he was arrested. The High Court acquitted Upendra but affirmed the death sentence for Mahendra.

Bhaiya also was released in July of 1945. He tried his best for Mahendra, speaking to Gandhi ji to try and get him a 'King's Pardon". But all efforts came to naught and Mahendra was hanged in July 1946 in Bhagalpur Jail, where he had been kept imprisoned all this while.

Till now we used to hear stories and be moved by how the Gadar Party's Kartar Singh or the violent revolutionaries Bhagat Singh – Rajguru – Sukhdev - Khudiram Bose went singing to the gallows. Such stories of the heartless and draconian actions of the British only strengthened our resolve to throw them out of our country. But for one of our own younger brother-like member of the Gandhi Ashram to be hanged was a heart-wrenching experience. A letter had come from Mahendra a week before his execution.

At that time Nandkishore and Chandrakala were in Harpurjan and the letter was addressed to Chandrakala.In it he had written that he was going happily to the gallows for his country, but was worried about his daughter Manju and wife Malti, for whom he had not been able to leave behind any means of livelihood. If Chandrakala and her husband could take the responsibility of looking after the two, he would be able to die in peace. Chandrakala replied immediately promising that she would take this responsibility.

Malti, Upendra and Ugramohan were in Bhagalpur on the day of the hanging. The dead body was handed over to them by the police for the final cremation rites, but on the strict condition that there would be no procession taken out and no slogan-shouting. They left for the cremation grounds in a truck. Malti tried to jump out of the truck in a bid to commit suicide, but Upendar and Ugramohan managed to prevent her from doing so.

A few days more and Mahendra could have been saved. The formation of an Interim Government shortly thereafter had saved many convicted prisoners from the gallows. Malti conducted herself with courage, fortitude and self-respect and did not ask anyone for help. After Independence she got a job as Welfare Officer in a colliery near Dhanbad, and lived there with her daughter in a house provided by the company. Upendra was always there to support her at the time of need.

Many years later when the Indian Government announced a pension scheme for Freedom Fighters, both Upendra and Malti were recipients of the scheme. Malti educated her daughter Manju, who later married into a very well-to-do and respectable family. Manju had three children, all of whom were good students and did well for themselves in life.

Chapter 35

Keeping Hope Alive

As "high-security" prisoners Bhaiya and Bhai ji were in jail indefinitely, Bhabhi ji and I were alone with the children in Harpurjan. Pandit ji was in Punjab, under lonely and difficult conditions, working on the translation of the Sama Veda to be able to earn some income to keep our household going. Ugramohan too was in jail. Those were really difficult and trying times, when everything seemed dark and bleak and there was no hope in sight.

How does one keep oneself going in such times and not sink into despair and hopelessness? Happy memories of the past and musings on a bright and happy future, living in the present with the children and the goings on in village life, seeing joy and happiness in the smallest of things, in the beauty of the flowers and trees, the wind and the sun, the clouds.....

From morning till lunch we were busy with household chores and the children. We really got time to ourselves only in the long afternoons. Time to read or listen to someone else read from a novel, newspaper or bulletin. The other enjoyable past-time was to imagine what the future would hold for us after Independence. Bhaiya and Bhai ji would be out of jail, that was the biggest thing. Then we would not have to live the way we were forced to right now. Bhaiya would definitely get an important position, a big house in which we could all live together in comfort and peace.

Good, wholesome food, nice clothes, a car which would take us swiftly from one place to another.

Whenever my feet ached, I would remember those days when I would get blisters on my feet from trudging bare feet from village to village, with no possibility of getting permission to stay at home to rest, not even from my mother. The minute I thought of Ma, tears would start pouring from my eyes. Even if we got Independence, I would never be able to see her again.

This is how we passed our days in Harpurjan.

Chapter 36

Return to Gogri

A month after Bhai ji's release from jail, Pandit ji returned from Lahore after completing his translation and commentary on the Sama Veda. He was having some dental problems and decided to get himself treated in Patna from an Arya Samaji dentist who had also been his student.

The flow of regular income which used to come from Lahore had stopped, and we were finding it difficult to manage both the expenses for Sabo and Indu's education in Deoghar as well as the regular household expenses. Vidyasagar came to visit us at this juncture with the news that Seth Rameshwarlal had opened a Girls Gurukul in Deoria and his wife was working there.I decided to apply for a postion in that Gurukul and sent in my application. Back came the reply saying they would be honoured if I could join them and requesting me to come at my earliest convenience.

Pandit ji dropped me in Deoria and went off to Patna for his treatment. Anil and Nilu were with me and I was able to find decent accommodation near the Girls Gurukul. I wrote to Bhaiya who was still in jail at that time and he replied that he was very happy to see that I was putting my education to good use, and was self-reliant. I slowly established my household while teaching Hindi and Sanskrit in the Gurukul. The monthly salary was fifty rupees, of which I sent twenty to Sabo and Indu. Sabo was already getting a scholarship, so this was more than adequate for the two girls. I could manage with the balance thirty rupees, but it was not easy.

What had happened earlier repeatedly with me, happened again this time — three months after I joined the Gurukul an epidemic of cholera and small-pox broke out in Deoria. People started dying in large numbers and many of the girls stopped coming to school. News would come in some day of this girl's death, and of so-and-so's parents' death the next day. The situation was dire, and in this overall scenario I developed symptoms of diarrhoea and vomiting one night. The next morning I sent the Seth ji a letter through Nilu, and he came immediately with a doctor. It took two days for me to recover, thanks to the prompt medical treatment.

I replied to Bhaiya's letter mentioning the outbreak of the epidemic in Deoria. Perhaps that was a mistake, because he replied immediately that I was taking too much of a risk staying here with my young children, he would never forgive me if anything happened to Nilu and Anil. I should pack my bags and leave immediately. He had written simultaneously to Bhai ji that he should ensure I left Deoria at once. Ugramohan landed up from Harpurjan and informed me that Bhai ji was unwell and had asked for me. I was ready to leave at once without my belongings, but Ugramohan suggested it would be better if I took my belongings with me.

All the way to Harpurjan I kept thinking of how I had never had a stable home right from childhood, had always been on the move from one place to another. I remembered a saying which the elders of Shirnia often repeated "The daughters of Shirnia never find happiness on all fronts". This was proving true for me!

After the closure of the Gurukul in Harpurjan, our regular work there had stopped. The various phases of the freedom movement saw me going back and forth from Gogri to Harpurjan many times .Now I was once more leaving a job and returning to Harpurjan. On reaching I found Bhai ji hale and hearty, the news of the illness was just a ruse to get me back in a hurry.

Two months after my return to Harpurjan, Bhai ji told me that Bhaiya had been released from jail but could not travel beyond the limits of Monghyr district. Since he was stuck in Chapra and would not be able to see him, I should go to Gogri which was a part of Monghyr district. Not only would I be with Bhaiya, I could also help oversee the farming.

We started the process of packing up the household belongings for shifting to Gogri. Bhai ji's elder brother-in-law Ramraksha Brahmachari ji had also been released, and his elder daughter Shanti was getting married into a family in Patna. We all went to Gogri, and it was decided that Bhabhi ji would go to Patna from there. A widow called Sahodra used to work for us in Harpurjan and when we were leaving she said, "Please take me along also". We agreed to take her along.

Mahibli was a Muslim girl whose house was close to Sahodra's and who used to come to our house to help out with certain chores. Her husband had left her when she was fifteen, and she insisted she would also come with us. We did not agree. We left with several bullock-cart loads of goods and belongings with Sahodra in the last bullock-cart. Mahibli was hiding in an orchard which was on our way, and seeing Sahodra, jumped in with her. Bhai ji was busy booking the luggage on the train to Gogri, while we tried to persuade Mahibli to return home. In the meantime her family members landed up armed with big lathis, and took her away.

The Gogri house was not in good shape. Those villagers who had left Shirnia in 1942 and come to take shelter in the Gogri Ashram, had established a new village to the north-west of the Ashram, on the other side of the Maheshkhunt Aguani Road and called it Shri Shirnia. When we reached Gogri in end-1945, this village was still not fully ready and several of the families were still in the Ashram. After our return, they slowly moved out to Shri Shirnia. Bhai ji's house was named "Chandra Bhavan"in honour of Chandrakant. But this name was used only for the formal postal address, everyone continued calling the house also as Ashram. Two months later Bhai ji also moved to Gogri.

We were all staying in Bhai ji's house. I was struck by a virulent attack of small-pox in the early winter and Bhai ji really tended to me with care and expertise and I recovered. He had picked up a good knowledge of medicines during his relief work. He was also very good at football, chess, carrom, cards, volleyball and badminton. He was very fond of reading, had read lots of English Literature classics while in jail and had a great collection of books. He was fascinated by new gadgets which came into the market and among many other things, had bought a sewing machine in 1941 which Bhabhi ji used extensively. While many of the household articles were destroyed in the chaos of 1942, his sewing machine survived intact!! He once returned from a trip to Calcutta with tea leaves and a tea-set. He also bought a gramophone and many records.

Bhabhi ji became famous in the region as "Bhabhi ji". A bicycle was bought for her and she would ride it wearing a churidar pyjama and salwar. It is my regret that I could never learn to ride a cycle! Next came a horse, a thorough-bred from the Sonepur Mela. We also kept 3 or 4 ordinary horses in the Bhelwa diayara, which were used for moving around the extensive landholding there, and for travelling from the Gogri Ashram to the diyara. These horses were a necessity for moving around during the monsoon and the post-monsoon days when the roads were in a really bad shape.

Bhaiya also kept two small boats in Bhelwa diyara. Both Bhabhi and Sabo started learning horse-riding when the horse came from Sonepur, and soon both were adept riders. The children went frequently to the diyara and learnt how to use the boat and to swim under Bhai ji's expert guidance.

Bhabhi ji and Sabo also learnt rifle shooting and the locals admiringly said they had become like the legendary Jhansi ki Rani.

Chandrakala and Nandkishore had moved back to their home in Shahzadpur after the Ramgarh Congress leaving behind their vacant house in Gogri. It was getting crowded in Bhai ji's house and I felt that if we had to stay in Gogri then we should buy Nandkishore's house. Pandit ji had to have all his teeth extracted in Patna, and had then moved to Jamshedpur to work with the Arya Samaj there. I wrote to him suggesting we sell the Harpurjan house and buy this house in Gogri. Pandit ji agreed immediately and started the process of finding a buyer for his house.

Sabo passed her Matric exams in 1946 with first rank in the entire Bhagalpur Commissionary and was given a Divisional Scholarship of twenty rupees a month for further studies. Bhaiya always paid a lot of attention to the children's studies and believed that the younger lot would emulate the path shown by the eldest.

This was correct. He had left his studies to plunge into the freedom struggle and Bhai ji and I followed him. He now felt the responsibility of ensuring that the next generation completed their education and obtained higher degrees, and it was his decision to send Sabo to the Mission School in Deoghar. Sabo subsequently got admission to the Women's College in Patna in July 1946.

We settled down in Gogri and focused on getting the economic situation of the family in better shape. The focus of political activity had shifted to Delhi by now where the leaders were in talks with the British Government for transfer of power and the formation of a National Government.

Bhaiya had joined the Forward Bloc at the time of the Ramgarh Congress and was in the Patna Camp Jail from August 1942 to July 1945. He spent a lot of this time studying and writing. He translated Karl Marx's "Das Kapital" into Hindi and in addition wrote two books: *The ABC of Indian Politics" and Two lessons from the Indian Freedom Struggle*. The latter two were published but the Karl Marx translation could not be, and its manuscript disappeared mysteriously. We do not have a single copy of the two books that were published.

Bhaiya had an exceptionally brilliant mind, but like Arjun's single-pointed focus while shooting his arrow at a target, he would pour his entire self into the work that he took up while showing total disregard for everything else. His differences with the Congress leadership had surfaced as early as 1937 when the Congress had formed the government in Bihar. Bhaiya started a Farmers Movement in Lagar village of Parbatta sub-division. Shri Krishna babu was the Prime Minister of Bihar and Bhaiya was supposed to have been his right-hand man during the Satyagraha Movement days. He started pointing out to him all the shortcomings that he perceived in the functioning of Shri Krishna babu's government. In a massive rally in Nayagaon to felicitate Shri Babu, of which Bhaiya was one of the main organizers, Bhaiya was the third speaker. While highlighting the problems of the farmers and peasants he said that the current government had not lived up to its expectations and promises. This created an alienation with Shri babu, even though Bhaiya continued to work for the Congress till the formation of the Forward Bloc.

In January 1941 Netaji Subhash Chandra Bose left India secretly. Bhaiya had met him in Calcutta before this, during Neta ji's illness, and had worked tirelessly at the grass-roots level to strengthen the Forward Bloc organizational structure and processes. Bhai ji and I never left the Congress. Subhash Bose went to Germany and Italy and made plans to raise an Army to fight the British and obtain freedom for India. He then went to Singapore and breathed new life and energy in the creation of the Azad Hind Force whose slogan was "Give me your blood, I will give you Freedom." An Azad Hind Government was announced and currency notes printed. Netaji's army reached till Kohima, but that was the time the Nazis started losing the Second World War and Netaji disappeared suddenly and mysteriously. Captives from the Azad Hind Force were imprisoned in Delhi's Red Fort. The names of Dhillon, Sahgal, Shahnawaz, Captain Laksmi and Sheelbhadrayaji were most mentioned.

Many marching songs of the Azad Hind Force captured the imagination of the Indian masses

"One step forward after another
Sing songs of happiness"
"May happiness and peace rain upon us
India's fortunes have woken up
Punjab, Sindh, Gujarat, Maratha
Dravid, Utkal, Banga"*

All the Azad Hind captives were released in April 1946.

Towards the end of 1946 Bhaiya told us about the annual convention of the All India Forward Bloc in Arrah. We all went, but as spectators. But Sabo, Satish and Navin were inspired to participate in the procession and shouted the Azad Hind slogans with gusto. The convention was successful, large crowds had gathered to see the brave soldiers of the Azad Hind Force and cries of 'Jai Hind" rent the air.

Dhanraj Sharma opened the Patna Forward Bloc office in the Machhuatoli area, and Bhaiya, Mathura Mishra, Triveni Kunwar and others would meet there regularly. They even brought out a bulletin called "Azad Hind".

---

*Kadam kadam badhaye ja
Khushi ke geet gaaye ja

Shubh sukh chayan ki barsa barse
Bharat bhagya hai jaga
Punjab, Sindh, Gujerat Maratha
Dravid Utkal Banga

Chapter 37

THE PLAGUE

We had just returned from Arrah when we heard that plague had been detected in Maliya village near the Jamalpur bazaar. Rats are the first victims of the plague. As soon as the rat dies, the virus leaves its body and attacks human beings. On seeing a dead rat people would immediately flee from their homes and stay out in the open fields or under tents, after having poured kerosene on the dead rat and burning it, hopefully along with the deadly germs. The government used to send fogging units which would spread a medicated smoke that was supposed to kill the plague germs. The plague resulted in high fever and enlargement of the glands in the armpits and groins, and very few infected people survived. Whole villages would be decimated. By 1946 people had figured out some ways of survival and the government also tried its best to help. Bhaiya and Bhai ji got busy organizing the fogging operations, we left our homes and pitched tents out in the open fields.

My Chachi (aunt) and her son Jago bhai lived in Shri Shirnia. Chachi's landholdings were in the Pathar Ghat diyara and she had gone there on an inspection visit. It was late by the time she set out on her return journey, the sun had set. She lost her bearings in the dark and stumbled on to the burning ghat situated on the banks of the Ganga. There were so many people dying of the plague, and the burning ghats were so busy, that the corpses were not being burnt fully. People would hurriedly light some kind of fire under the corpse and leave without waiting for the body to be burnt to ashes, there was so much fear of contracting the infection. It seems my Chachi picked up the plague infection there. The fever started that night, the swollen glands appeared the next day and she was gone on the third day. Jago bhai took her body to the burning grounds with the help of a few people and cremated her. That day Bhai ji was not in the Ashram, and was informed of Chachi's death the day after when he returned. He immediately forced all the Shri Shirnia residents to leave their homes and camp out in the open.

Kunti didi's son Manikant and Jago bhai used to stay with my Chachi. The villagers told Jago bhai to perform the *shraddha* ceremony for his dead mother. Jago bhai was an eccentric and an emotionally volatile person who had never married. He did not care about others' opinions. He was shattered by his mother's death and cried for days on end, piteously calling out for his mother in the darkness of night. With the residents staying in tents out in the fields, the distance between the Ashram and Shri Shirnia was effectively reduced a lot, and his wailing shook us to the core. Jago requested Manikant to get his mother Kunti didi from Badgaon so that she could supervise the *shraddha* ceremony. Kunti didi was a widow who lived with her younger son Shivkumar and two daughters Sondaiya and Chandrika and was barely able to eke out a living. On hearing of her mother's death, she came immediately with her family. But before she could reach, tragedy struck again.

Jago bhai had gone to the diyara, and the plague symptoms consumed him as he was walking back home a few days later. He was on fire with high fever and in acute pain, and collapsed before he could reach home. His dead body was found next morning under a tree, some distance from the village of Shri Shirnia. The villagers were afraid to touch his corpse and finally it was two or three elders who loaded his dead body onto a bullock cart and took it for cremation.

Kunti didi arrived that day. Manikant was given the role of "Uttari" in the *shraddha* ceremony that was now performed for both our Chachi and Jago, which meant that for ten days he had to observe a very simple diet and wear some specific kind of clothes and perform all manner of rituals in the typical Maithil Brahmin tradition.

Kunti didi was in a state of shock at having lost both her mother and brother almost together, and was a mute spectator to the *shraddha* goings on. She said nothing, but must have been deeply hurt by the fact that her relatives seemed to be more concerned about the ceremonial meals than about the death of her loved ones. They knew that Kunti didi had no money so they suggested she sell her land to finance the *shraddha* ceremonies and feast. These were the same people who, when they were residents of Shirnia before the floods forced them to flee, had excommunicated Babuji from the Maithil community. Babuji never participated in any of the rituals of these villagers. However, Shri Shirnia used to send invitations to us for major feasts. But they did not invite us on the death of my Chachi and Jago.

However Kunti didi came to meet us and confided in Bhai ji. He told her, "How does it matter to these people? They will see you sell your land, enjoy a lavish feast paid for by the sale, and then watch the spectacle of your poverty and destruction. I want that Jago bhai's share of the Pathar Ghat diyara land should go to you and your children. Don't get into this racket of lavish rituals, do the *shraddha* if you must for the sake of not being cast out of your community, but for God's sake do it simply without much fanfare . I will take care of the expense ."

Kunti didi accepted this advice.

No other rat died and there were no further plague deaths in Shri Shirnia.

With Bhai ji's help the land was transferred in Kunti didi's name. She settled down in Shri Shirnia, married her daughters to good grooms and in due course her grandson entered the Bihar Provincial Service. The wheel of fortune turned in favour of the family.

We were camped in tents in the fields, the government people had come to do fogging in the Ashram premises and Anil ran out to be with them. He developed high fever that afternoon and we were certain that it was the plague. Bhabhi ji shifted to Nandkishore's house with the other children, Ugramohan remained behind with me. Next day measles rashes broke out and I heaved a sigh of relief that it was not the plague. But that very day Ugramohan developed very high fever, and was racked by such pain all night that he would shriek in agony. I left Anil sleeping and went to Ugramohan's room to give him water and do whatever I could to ease his agony. As I returned to my room I was horrified to see a huge jackal standing next to the sleeping Anil. I froze in shock and fright, expecting to see the animal pick up my son and run off with him. There had been many such instances in the recent past in this area. Fortunately the animal turned and ran off as soon as he saw me, disappearing in the fields that surrounded us on all sides. The nearest human habitation was at least a mile away from the Ashram and the surrounding vegetation was home to plenty of small animals and reptiles.

Ugramohan was in bad shape. The doctor came the next day and after examining him declared that he was infected by a less virulent form of the plague which did not result in enlarged glands but was very painful. It took a week for Ugramohan to recover. I stayed on in the same house with Anil and continued to look after Ugramohan.

Chapter 38

FREEDOM

In 1945 Gandhi ji, Nehru, Rajendra Prasad, Sardar Patel and other senior leaders were all released from British jails. From that time onwards it was clear that the British would not be able to rule over a country which was capable of so much protest and anti-government agitation. Preparations started for the transfer of power.

Jinnah wanted a separate Pakistan while Gandhi ji was totally opposed to the partition of the country into two. He tried very hard to persuade Jinnah, even suggested that they wait for the British to leave and then work out a mutual agreement on partition. But Jinnah insisted that the partition should be done by the British before they leave.

On 16th August the Muslim League declared "Direct Action" which the common man interpreted as "We will fight to create Pakistan". Hindu-Muslim riots broke out in Calcutta.

Bhaiya had started living in Patna, and when he came to Gogri in September 1946 he told us "An Interim Government has been formed in Delhi."

The children asked him the meaning of an Interim Government. Was it not a Government of Indians? "It is our government all right, but not entirely. We need to prepare ourselves for the transition from an interim to a final government.

This interim government will run the affairs of the country,but Lord Mountbatten will continue as the Governor General while a Constituent Assembly prepares the Constitution of India. The Congress has formed governments in several states, but. in Bengal there is a Muslim League government. Jinnah wants a separate Pakistan, and the Muslim League is part of the Interim Government."

Bose bhai was also in Gogri that day, and he expressed his doubts about whether the British would really hand over power.

"They will have to go, the tide has turned completely against them. The 1942 movement, Azad Hind Force, the mutiny in the Navy — they have no choice but to leave."

"But Pakistan?"

'That is a real problem which Gandhi ji is trying to sort out, he wants a United India."

Nandkishore, Nathbihari, Bhuvaneshwar babu and many of the old-timers came to Gogri and keenly followed the developments from day to day. Would their long-cherished dream of a free and independent India be finally realized? Would the long years of struggle finally end in victory and would their beloved Tri-colour fly proudly atop the Red Fort in Delhi?

While Nehru, Patel and other leaders were parleying with the British on the formation of a new government, Gandhi ji was parked in a Harijan slum in Delhi, living in a small hut and holding evening prayers sitting on a small platform. National and international leaders and journalists would travel to this slum to meet him and understand his views. Mridula Sarabhai and Lady Cripps would also meet there.

"Perhaps Gandhi ji is trying to distance himself from the decision to partition the country" thought Bhaiya.

Gandhi ji travelled to riot-hit Calcutta and tried to calm down the enraged and murderous mobs. Bhaiya did not stay put in Gogri, he took a band of four people and went to Calcutta. Meanwhile news came of a terrible communal riot in Noakhali. Thousands of Hindus were massacred, large-scale forced conversions done to Islam, Hindu women kidnapped and untold atrocities perpetrated on them. Temples were burned and idols of Hindu Gods and Goddesses destroyed.

When this news reached Bihar, the reply given was "Blood will be avenged by blood".

Communal riots broke out in Bihar and Bhaiya rushed back. Phulwari Sharif, Bihar Sharif, Munger, Tarapur — violence exploded in many places, thousands were killed.

Gandhi ji sent a common Letter of Appeal to the people of Bihar. "This is not the Bihar of my dreams. If Muslims are killed like this in Bihar, will it not prove Jinnah's contention that the Congress is a party of Hindus? It was Bihar that hosted the very first Congress Convention. Will it now dig the grave of that very Congress? If the people of Bihar do not stop this violence, I will go on fast unto death."

Bhaiya held meetings and rallies urging people to stop this mindless violence, he took Gandhi's appeal to the towns and villages of Bihar.

One day Bose bhai came with the news that Nehru, Patel and others were in Bihar trying to restore peace and harmony. Nehru is said to have lost his temper finally and said "If Bihar does not heed our pleas then I will have it bombed."

Eid passed peacefully in Bihar and Calcutta. Gandhi ji declared "I will now go to Noakhali, I am needed there. "He reached Noakhali in a special train with his band of trusted followers. With him were Pyarelal ji, Dr. Sushila Nayyar, Sucheta Kripalani, Abha Gandhi, Manu Gandhi, Kanu Gandhi, Professor Nirmal Bose, Parsuram, Devchand Jha etc. They travelled through the ravaged villages on foot, striding fearlessly down bood-soaked alleys, urging communal harmony and an end to this mad slaughter.

Bhaiya decided he would work for communal harmony in Tarapur.I protested that it was far too dangerous for him to venture there, and he replied, "If Sushila Nayyar, a lone woman, can stay by herself in a village in Noakhali, if not only her but all members of Gandhi ji's entourage can fan out singly into the ravaged Noakhali countryside to restore peace and put an end to the senseless killings, if they can practice what they preach, how can I not go to Tarapur?"

Bhabhi ji countered, "But you have left the Congress years ago, so why do you have to follow in his foot-steps now?"

"Gandhi ji is the Father of the Nation. He thinks of the welfare of the entire nation. This calamity has befallen all of us, we have to stand up as one and fight against it. This is not the time to think of fractious politics."

Bhai ji went to Munger, he had several Muslim friends there. Bhaiya went to Tarapur, and from there to Phulwari Sharif, Patna and several other violence-hit zones.

On his return to Gogri from these visits, he would tell us what was going on in other parts of the country. "Look at Gandhi ji, at the age of 77 he is tramping through the Noakhali countryside on foot, subsisting on local fruits and vegetables and goat's milk. It is now March 1947, and he has been doing this since November 1946.

Gandhi ji left Noakhali in April 1947 and reached Patna, using it as his base to travel around in Bihar. In Patna he stayed with Shri Anugraha Narayan Singh, a Minister in the Bihar government, in his house next to the Patna Maidan on the banks of the Ganga. In one corner of the Maidan, near St Xavier's School, a platform was erected from where he conducted daily prayer meetings.

My elder daughter Savitry (Sabo) was studying in the Patna Women's College, and the two heroines of the '42 Satyagraha, Sharda and Saras, were also there. They sought permission from the Mother Superior to attend Gandhiji's evening prayer meetings, and on the request of some Congress functionaries, girls from the hostel lined up as a guard of honour all the way from his residence to the Prayer Assembly site, and then joined the meeting. This way they saw Gandhi ji every day for a month and got to know his thoughts and views.

Gandhi was the beloved and trusted leader of the common man and woman of India. Every evening he would be given bagfuls of cash, and women would take off the jewellery they were wearing and donate it to him for relief work.

Nehru ji requested Gandhi ji to come to Delhi in May. The formation of the new government was in its final stages, historic and far-reaching decisions were being taken, and his presence was essential. Gandhi ji left Bihar for Delhi, and was never able to come back.

Chapter 39

O, Walk Ye Alone

In the first week of July 1947 it was known that India would declare its Independence on 15th August with Jawaharlal Nehru as its first Prime Minister.

Ugramohan read aloud this news from the 'Aryavarta' and we found it difficult to believe that after so many obstacles, India was actually gaining freedom.

With the freedom struggle at an end, divisive forces reared their ugly heads. Communal riots seemed to go on and on, the nation was going to be split into two. That news reached us too, Pakistan was declared on 14th August, with Jinnah as its Governor General.

A voice inside me said, "Well, if peace and harmony is going to return, there might as well be two nations. When differences arise within a family, a division of property takes place, so let it be for the country".

The old Satyagrahis were really excited. Nandkishore said, "Ugramohan, come, let us go to Delhi and see for ourselves the signing-in ceremony of the new government. From this distance it all seems like a dream, we need to experience this historic moment in person."

"You are right, Nanda bhai. But I have no money for this journey. And, anyway, where will we stay in Delhi?"

"Leave all that to me. We leave on 12th August."

Some more people joined them, and after witnessing all the Independence Day happenings in Delhi, the Gogri group returned after 15 days.

A wave of joy swept through the country on the 15th of August 1947. The sky was ablaze with the national flag, the beloved Tri-colour, for which so many had made the supreme sacrifice. Sweets were distributed, lamps were lit, and firecrackers were burst. Celebratory processions were taken out, rallies held. The entire nation heard Nehru's midnight address on the radio. The grizzled old satyagrahis were visibly moved and could not control their emotions. Tears of happiness poured down our faces.

We were free!

But this euphoria was short-lived, for very soon disturbing news started coming in of renewed communal violence. Gandhi ji had anticipated this renewal of violence and had left Delhi for Calcutta on the 9th of August itself. He declared that it was not possible for him to stay on in Delhi and celebrate Independence. He spent the 15th of August in prayer and fasting.

The communal violence worsened. On 31st August Gandhi declared a fast unto death. People, both Hindus and Muslims, trusted this fearless fakir. Congress and Muslim League leaders went to him, telegrams came from Pakistan, all of them assured him that they would restore peace at all cost. Gandhi ji broke his fast after 73 hours, having saved Calcutta from a holocaust of terrible proportions.

Gandhi ji was getting news of the killings in Punjab, and wanted to go there.

Nandkishore said, "We heard that he would transit through the Delhi Railway Station and were among the thousands that thronged the platform in the hope of getting a glimpse of the Mahatma. We could only see him for a split second in the far distance. We also recognized Sardar Patel who had come to the station to entreat Gandhi ji to stay on in Delhi and not proceed further. He agreed and left for the Birla Bhavan.

We were part of the thousands who marched to Birla Bhavan shouting slogans in honour of the Mahatma.

Gandhi ji was aghast and deeply saddened to hear of the inhuman atrocities being committed on the riot -torn streets and by-lanes of Delhi.

Daily prayer meetings were held in the rear lawns of Birla Bhawan and we were regular participants. We were also part of his band of followers whenever he went out to the riot-afflicted areas.

We saw the refugees from Punjab take over and occupy any property left behind by the Muslims who had migrated to Pakistan, including shops. Any resistance was met by violence.

Gandhi ji spoke up in one of his prayer meetings. "I have heard that a fifty-seven mile long column of displaced refugees is winding its way from Western Punjab to India. I bow my head in shame today. 15 million homeless and displaced refugees are on the move. These are poor peasants who have no means of transportation. With their meagre possessions laden on bullock-carts, this sea of humanity is making its way on foot-old people, little children, sick men and women. The seriously ill and dying are left to breathe their last on the dusty roadsides. Cholera and small-pox have broken out.The column crawls along, leaving a trail of corpses in its wake. Hungry vultures circle overhead waiting for the weak and dying to drop off so that they can feast on them."

He broke down and started sobbing, it was only the refrain of his favourite hymn 'Vaishnav jan to tene kahiye...' that brought some succour to those of us who were witness to this sad spectacle.

Nehru ji had a Refugee Camp established on the outskirts of Delhi. Dr Sushila Nayyar, Rajkumari Amrit Kaur, Sucheta Kripalani, Lady Mountbatten and women from other respectable

Delhi families did relief work in the overcrowded Camp. They also collected funds and knit sweaters for the refugees.

Loudspeaker announcements were continuously made in the railway station requesting all refugees to proceed to the Camp and register their names and other details before settling down. They should move out only later from this Camp if they were able to make alternative arrangements for their stay.

But many refugees disregarded this instruction and disappeared into the bowels of the city to seek out friends and relatives. They would narrate in lurid detail the unspeakable atrocities committed on them during their flight from Pakistan. Many came penniless and with just the clothes they had on, many saw their entire families massacred mercilessly in the most barbarous manner in front of their eyes. Such stories further stoked inflamed passions, creating an inferno of anger shouting for revenge, all humanity died in these mobs that were out seeking blood.

It was perhaps natural that these dispossessed refugees took over the vacant Muslim houses and chased away those that tried to resist them. Delhi resounded with the cries and shrieks of the mob victims, the streets and gutters started choking up with rotting corpses.

In this scenario Mahatma Gandhi appealed to his Muslim brethren not to leave India, this was their country too. But who would listen to him in this hell-house where blood-lust had taken over and reason had disappeared?"

Sister, we went out in the city with Gandhi ji but had to come back because we could not stomach the scenes of carnage. The Mahatma kept on repeating that he did not want to live any longer, he felt all alone and friendless. If even a well-known and respected leader like Zakir Hussain could not dare to leave the Jamia Milia premises, then how could the life of ordinary Muslims be safe?

He has started looking distracted and distraught in the prayer meetings, and spends more and more time in prayer by himself."

I was really saddened to hear all this. What kind of pyrrhic victory was this Independence, with so much slaughter, mayhem and sorrow accompanying it?

Mahatma Gandhi announced a fast unto death from 13th January, 1948. This was his solution to make his voice reach the masses. "This is the divine message I have received, this is the only recourse left to me to try and restore peace and calm in this country."

Nehru, Sardar Patel, Maulana Azad and others came to Birla Bhawan. In addition to the government taking responsibility for the safety and security of Muslim lives and property, Gandhi ji laid down one more condition for breaking his fast. An amount of Rs 55 crore was to be transferred to Pakistan from the Treasury as part of the terms and conditions for Independence agreed with the British Government, and Gandhi ji wanted this transfer to be done immediately.

All conditions were agreed to and, in addition, Muslims who had left for Pakistan and wanted to come back, could do so and even reclaim the assets they had left behind. After these promises were made to him, Gandhi ji accepted a glass of orange juice from the hands of Maulana Azad. The Birla Bhawan premises reverberated with the sounds of the Vedic hymn

"From untruth to truth
From darkness to light
From death to immortality"*

Gandhi ji had become frail and extremely weak but the evening prayer sessions continued, and he kept on meeting

---

* Asato ma sadgamayah
Tamso ma jyotirgamayah
Mrityor ma amritam gamayah

members of the Press and answering their queries. In one of the evening prayers a young refugee threw a bomb. The intended target was Gandhi ji, but he survived this attempt without any injury and continued with his normal routine.

On the 30th of January, a young man came forward to touch Gandhi ji's feet when he was leaving the evening prayer session. As he stood up, he took out a revolver and riddled the Mahatma's chest with bullets. Gandhi ji collapsed, and his last words were "Hey Ram" before he slipped away into eternal sleep.

Chapter 40

After Independence

Bhaiya stayed on with the Forward Bloc for some time after Independence. When the Azad Hind Army captives were released from Delhi's Red Fort, they were greeted fondly and warmly by the masses.

Bhaiya liked challenges and had sent his life overcoming them. For some time after Independence, he found life empty and purposeless.

News had come of Netaji Subhash Chandra Bose's death. In Bihar a few devoted people carried forward the Forward Bloc organization and its activities, and efforts were made to enrol women members. Asha Sahai even came to Gogri while Manvati Tiwari, who had fought as a member of the legendary Rani Jhansi Regiment, addressed a meeting in Patna.

A Forward Bloc camp was held in Rajgriha and on Bhaiya's insistence I participated in it.But I was not interested in doing Party work and that angered him. Once I asked him to loan me some money and he retorted, "I have requested you so many times, but you refuse to listen to me. With what face can you ask me for money?" This was an example of his complete dedication and devotion to political work.

Bhaiya had rented an old villa in Patna's Lodipur locality. It was called "Yellow Mansion" (Pili Kothi) and had huge grounds in front and at the back, and we were told that it was originally the residence of some Nawab which had also functioned as a cinema hall in the past. Bhaiya re-christened it "Home of the Poor" (Garib Niwas).

All credit to Bhaiya for ensuring that the children of the next generation got a good education. He insisted that Satish, Navin and Anil be admitted into St Xavier's School, Patna (Indu and Nilu were already in the Mission School in Deoghar.) He told me to live in Patna and look after the children, this would be better and more economical than their staying in the school hostel. Sabo also shifted to Garib Niwas from the Women's College hostel. So once more I left Gogri, this time for Patna.

This arrangement continued for some time. In 1948 several artifacts connected with the Azad Hind Army and the Singapore--based Azad Hind Government were brought and stored in one of the Garib Niwas rooms. Prominent among them were parachutes of various colours and currency notes printed in Singapore.

The children's studies continued smoothly, Sabo got married in 1950 and went away to join her husband.

In 1951 Bhaiya reconnected with his old friend and fellow–Satyagrahi Jaiprakash Narayan, and they started meeting regularly. I saw Bhaiya looking relaxed and happy, and was delighted to see the smile back on his face after a long time. One day he said, "Kaushalya, Jaiprakash and his wife Prabhavati are coming across this evening, they will have dinner with us."

The couple came and for some time we all sat together and talked about family matters. After that Bhaiya and Jaiprakash ji sat and talked alone for several hours. They talked mostly about the Socialist Party. Both were convinced that after having been in the Interim Government for some time, the Congress leaders had tasted power and the benefits it could bring. They would win the elections, form a stable government and run the country with the help of the bureaucracy, which would also help to formulate and execute the development plans of the nation. They would slowly but surely lose touch with the grass-roots and the real voice of the people. The Socialist Party would have to sit in Opposition in Parliament and make sure the grass-root realities were voiced and acted upon.

Jaiprakash ji said, "Suresh, you have always worked among the masses, you will be able to do this work admirably. Join me, together we will infuse new life and vitality into the Socialist Party."

Bhaiya happily agreed and joined the Socialist Party.

The first Lok Sabha elections were held in 1952, and Bhaiya was the Socialist Party candidate from the Khagaria constituency. The Party also put up candidates for the four Vidhan Sabha seats in the Lok Sabha constituency.

While the Congress threw in a lot of resources, Bhaiya had just one old jeep he had bought second hand in 1947 at an Army disposal. Bhaiya of course knew the Khagaria constituency like the palm of his hand, he had spent years working among its masses first as a Congress man and later as part of the Forward Bloc. When Jaiprakash Narayan saw the vast resources the Congress had deployed, he quoted the following lines to boost the morale of his Party workers:

"Ravana had a chariot,
Ram (Raghuvir) had none."

Bhaiya won hands down and we were all very happy. I too campaigned actively for him, for which I was expelled from the Congress. I did not join any political party after that.

Bhaiya was respected as a hardworking, knowledgeable and committed Parliamentarian who worked for his constituents and the people of India and stood up for the causes he believed in.He used to study and prepare before raising questions on the floor of the House, and gave a very impressive maiden address. The lack of a formal College degree never stood in his way.

A short while later Jaiprakash ji joined Vinoba Bhave's "Bhoodan Movement" and took an oath to devote all his time to the Movement. Ram Manohar Lohia formed a separate Party and Bhaiya chose to join him. He was the lone MP wearing the Socialist Party's red cap in the Lok Sabha and was the leader of his Party in the House.

The 5-year tenure of the first Parliament was coming to an end. There was a reorganization of the States and a part of Bihar was sought to be made part of Bengal. Bhaiya went on fast against this proposal. The statement he made in Parliament before going on this fast is a shining illustration of his political understanding and sagacity. A lot of his predictions came true.

Bhaiya lost in the second Lok Sabha election.

In 1950 a Marwari in Purnea wanted to sell the large tract of sandy land he owned. Bhaiya's land in Bhelwa diyara was in constant danger of being swallowed up by the river in the regularly changing course of the Ganga, and he reasoned that the Purnea land would be a good insurance against that eventuality. He negotiated a bargain price of Rs. 35 per bigha and Bhaiya and Bhai ji jointly paid for several hundred bighas of land. I also paid for 45 bighas. The entire tract was bought in Babuji's name, who was still alive. He was happy with Bhaiya for what he had done, but always rued the fact that he did not get married.

In 1959 Shri Krishna Singh got Bhaiya back into the Congress. He won an Assembly seat to the Vidhan Sabha, where he served one full term, in the course of which Shri Krishna babu died.

In 1965 Bhaiya decided to retire from active politics and devote the rest of his life to developing his Purnea farm.

He developed the Purnea farm as a Model Farm, converting the arid sandy soil into a highly productive one where he grew field crops and vegetables. It was his nature to plunge with zeal, enthusiasm and single-minded focus into whatever task he took up. Shortly after he acquired the land, the Kosi River Canal was constructed and one stretch of it went through his land. Bhaiya used this water to create highly efficient irrigation systems throughout his vast acreage. Labour was difficult to find, so he got unemployed and poor youth from the Gogri area and settled them on his land, a Hindu settlement on one side and a Muslim settlement on the other. For his requirement of wood, he planted a mini-forest which was regenerated even as wood was taken away for use elsewhere on the farm. A tractor was brought in and the driver given 15 bighas of land to incentivise him to stay. Chemical fertilizers were initially used but soon the switch to organic was made under Bhaiya's guidance.

The organic manure was made from the dung of the more than 100 cows, bulls, buffaloes and goats on his farm. Production and productivity soared and the farm prospered.

When his legs started giving him trouble in old age, he created an ingenious contraption to move around his estate: a chair with large wheels pulled by a large billy goat!

Bhaiya did not know how to accumulate wealth, he reinvested or spent whatever income was generated. All kinds of innovative machines and contraptions were bought and experimented with. He would go to Delhi to buy rubber boots, rain coats and woollen clothing for the labourers on his farm from Delhi and serve them mid-day meals during the sowing and harvesting seasons.

The farm transformed the local economy and we got a regular supply of food grains in Gogri from the Purnea Farm. Bhai ji and I never asked any questions about our share in the Purnea farmlands. Much before the government enforced land ceilings,

Bhaiya had transferred the land in the name of all the children. In this way he tried to ensure the land remined with the family.

But it was not to be. Within two weeks of his death, the Communist Party (Marxist) organized for the land to be occupied by Santhal tribesman, two thousand huts springing up overnight all over the farm. A lot of efforts were made to get back the land, but it was all in vain, and we were left holding paper titles in the names of many family members with little chance of getting back possession of the encroached land. But it will always remain Bhaiya's legacy to the region, regardless of who occupies it.

His land in the Bhelwa diyara was also swallowed up by the Ganga and re-appeared some years later on the other side of the river, but it was not possible to gain control over it in the existing law and order situation of the diyara region. Bhai ji's land however survived the capricious nature of Mother Ganga.

Whatever Bhaiya achieved went back to the people, and I often thought that this was in a way philosophically aligned to the principles and values that ruled his life.

Bhaiya remained healthy almost till the end. His health suddenly took a downward dip in February 1993 but the news reached Bhai ji in Gogri only in March. Bhai ji rushed immediately to Purnea and brought him to back Gogri Ashram. I rushed from Delhi with Sabo, picking up Nilu from Patna on the way. Bhaiya had fever. He was talking a lot, but had completely lost his memory. He did not recognize any of us.

A confirmed atheist all his life, he would keep shouting "Let me go, let me go."

"Where?" Bhai ji would ask.

"To God" would be Bhaiya's reply.

All of us took turns tending to him. Sabo and Nilu would sponge him and change the bedsheets. I would feed him. Other Gogri people would sit around him all the time. Large groups from Shri Shirnia, especially women and children, would come and touch his feet with reverence and feel blessed by the touch. "He has become divine" the women would say.

Bhaiya could not sleep, would keep shouting all night. Till the end, his voice was strong and resonant.

On the 30th of March Bhai ji sat by his bedside, stroking his forehead gently and saying, "Brother o brother, look it's me, Shiva Kant. Kaushalya is also sitting by your side". He read aloud the Gita for some time, as was his wont every day. That day Bhaiya was particularly thirsty, and we had given him some pomegranate juice in the morning.

Suddenly he shouted, "Take me, take me, take me quickly."

"Take you where, Bhaiya?" asked Bhai ji.

"Gogri Ashram. I will stay only in the Ashram, and nowhere else," was the reply.

"But you are in the Ashram."

"Where is everybody? Hurry, hurry to the Ashram....." his voice trailed away and he stopped breathing.

We took Bhaiya's body to Aguani Ghat for the last rites. His body was draped in khadi and sixty to seventy people from Shri Shirnia, Ratan and Bhojua joined us as the truck bearing his mortal remains started its journey to the Ghat. By the time we wound our way to Jamalpur, a large number of people had joined us and we reached the cremation site to the accompaniment of loud cries of victory and homage to Bhaiya from the by-now large crowd accompanying the cortege.

A Vedic havan was performed for three days after the funeral and this too was attended by a large number of his friends and admirers, including many Arya Samajis.

It was not even 3 months since Bhaiya's death that Bhai ji had a heart-attack in Munger. Both Satish and Navin were working in Calcutta at that time, and Satish came to take him to Calcutta where a pace-maker was installed. But Bhai ji never really recovered after the operation. Satish-Kalpana, Navin-Padmaja, Shailesh-Nilambari (the youngest son and his wife), Veena-Kanhaiya (daughter and her husband) were there, and were soon joined by Shanti and Manish (son Sunil's widow and her son). Nilu's son Sanjay and his wife Shweta, who were also both working in Calcutta, also lent a helping hand when required. In addition Kalpana's family members and other Calcutta-based relatives were also very helpful. I arrived from Delhi with Sabo.

Before I arrived, Bhai ji went into a catatonic state where he could see but not be able to speak.

When news of his worsening condition reached Gogri, Nandkishore, Surendra Shastri, Bidhan, Tunni, Subodh, Avinash, Ajit -- all reached Calcutta. Nilu too arrived from Patna.

Bhai ji always liked to be surrounded by people. He left on his final journey to the electric crematorium surrounded by a large number of relatives and friends. Then we all left for Gogri. Indu, Munmun, Sharda-Mangal, Shanti, Kanti, Daddan and Karna were all there. We attained closure with a havan.

Within a short while, Ugramohan and Nandkishore also passed away. An era of amazing Brotherhood and Camaraderie passed into history and local legend.

Chapter 41

THE INHABITANTS OF GANDHI GRAM

As I massaged my aching feet, I ruminated on the long journey covered by them. I had never paid attention to them before, I would walk barefoot through mud and dust for upto twenty miles in a day. Fired with patriotic zeal, I hardly ever noticed the thorns and sharp stones that pricked the soles of my feet as I went about my task of spreading awareness in the villages of the Gogri region. It was only before I went to sleep that I would find time to pull out the thorns and then be on my way the next morning. Blisters would appear and burst as I walked mile after mile in the bowels of rural Bihar.

We were told that Gandhi ji walked on the burning sands of Gujarat barefoot and he was our beloved Leader who we all followed and tried to emulate. All Gogri Ashram residents went barefoot. I wore slippers for the first time only after marriage. And now I cannot walk without wearing shoes!!

All the old-timers went one by one.

Babuji, my dear father, died in 1956 on Vaishakhi Purnima at the age of 79. He had spent his entire life fighting against the evils of caste, untouchability and blind superstition. It was Mohit Mishra, my father, who laid the foundations of the life, principles and values that Bhaiya and Bhai ji lived. The course of my life too was moulded by the principled lives of my parents.

It was a matter of regret for Bhaiya all his life that he was not present when either of his parents died.

In our generation, the first to go was my beloved Bhabhi ji Yashoda Devi. She had lived continuously in Gogri since 1946. The old house had been augmented by an open living space in front of the house, and the courtyard was surrounded by a high wall. A bathing space was also created with a hand-operated tube well to provide water. This was in addition to the well outside. Bhabhi ji had an orchard planted to the north of the well with guava, pomegranate, banana, lime and coconut trees while *kachnar* and *amla* was planted to the west.

Son Shailesh was born in 1946 and daughter Veena in 1949.

Bhabhi ji kept up the family tradition of supervising the household affairs while her husband was busy with the freedom struggle, politics and other social engagements. It was she who kept the farming going with the help of a Manager and security guards. She slowly acquired 15 bighas of land near the house and added a deep bore-well. Wheat and maize were the main crops in this land, the Bhelwa diyara land gave wheat and, depending on the whims of the flood waters, maize also some years. The diyara land was superb for growing vegetables with *parval*, *karela*, *phoot*, *kakdi* and water melon in summer and potatoes, onion, cauliflower and tomatoes in plenty in winter.

Bhabhi ji acquired further land adjoining the main Maheshkhunt Jamalpur road and made it into a large orchard with *sheesham* trees all along the perimeter embankment and Maldah mango, lychee, phalsa and jamun trees inside. A well was dug in this orchard for irrigation purposes, and a platform constructed for seating. These are all still there.

Her third son, Sunil, came back to live in Gogri and took up the family farming operations after completing his MA and

Law studies, while the other brothers took up jobs elsewhere. The government introduced many schemes to promote agriculture, and Sunil took up farming seriously and in a scientific way. He made vast improvements and Bhaiya and Bhai ji were very happy and satisfied with him.

Bhai ji never left the Congress. He was everyone's Bhai ji in the Gogri region, and he never turned away anyone who came for help. Whether it was to settle family disputes, finalize a marriage or advise on an illness that was persisting, Bhai ji was there. His long experience in relief work during floods, earthquakes and epidemics had given him vast knowledge of healing, and he used to keep a medicine kit that came in handy on many occasions. He was particularly famous for healing snake bites and I have seen many victims brought to him unconscious and walk away hours later after he tended to them.

When Bhaiya decided to retire from politics, the Congress invited Bhai ji to stand for the Assembly elections. Bhai ji accepted and won the election.

Everything was going smoothly. Sunil got married to the daughter of Dr Ramashankar Pandey, a well-known Hindi scholar in Jamshedpur. They had a son who was named Manish.

Sunil made a very decent earning from the harvest that year, and Satish, Navin and Shailesh were all doing well in their various jobs. Sunil decided to buy a petrol-pump as close as possible to the main National Highway that passed by close to the Maheshkhunt Railway Station. In addition to the Jeep, Sunil purchased a motor-cycle. Bhaiya had purchased a 1901 Ford, that had now become a showpiece parked outside the front gate.

Sunil got ready to go to Patna on his motor-cycle. It was perhaps some kind of premonition that made Shanti tell him that he should go in the Jeep, Patna was too far away to make the trip by motor-cycle.

"No, it is too expensive to take the Jeep, Gopi da is also coming with me and I will not be alone on the motor-cycle."

A short distance from Patna, in a place called Kumhrar, the motor-cycle collided with a truck. Sunil sustained a fracture in his leg, and Gopi got away with minor bruises. Sunil was brought to Patna and operated upon in a local nursing home. Satish, Bhai ji, Bhabhi ji and Shanti all rushed to Patna to be with him. They were all by his side when he suddenly complained of pain in his chest and died in moments, while the doctors watched helplessly. Later it was found that a blood clot had travelled to his heart and caused a heart failure.

Bhabhi ji was unable to cope with this loss, it broke her completely. The situation was further complicated by her existing diabetic condition. She was already troubled by Satish's decision to resign from the Indian Police Service (IPS) just a couple of years after he had competed for, and joined, this prestigious All-India service, and his declaring that he would never get married.

Satish had topped the IPS exams and after doing brilliantly in the training and probationary period, was posted to the West Bengal cadre. His first assignment was in Jalpaiguri, a centre of Naxalite activity and located next to Naxalbari. The State Government was engaged in ruthlessly stamping out the Naxalite movement. Satish was a principled and sensitive human being and was horrified by what the police was being ordered to do. Unable to stomach the atrocities he was being told to perpetrate, he started talking of putting in his papers and leaving the IPS. Everyone advised him to reconsider, get himself transferred to another State. Bhaiya too tried to persuade him, but to no avail.

He started lecturing in the TNB College in Bhagalpur, and many years later married Kalpana Dasgupta, the younger sister of a close College friend. She was appointed Chief Librarian of the National Library in Calcutta and Satish started teaching in

Surendranath (erstwhile Rippon) College in Calcutta.

One tragedy followed another. Bhabhi ji stopped taking care of herself. In 1978 she was taken to Delhi and admitted to the All India Institute of Medical Sciences. She was in coma for one month and then passed away.

Shanti handled the family misfortunes with courage and patience. She shifted base back to Jamshedpur and started teaching in a Tata school. Manish completed his BA (Honours) from the prestigious St Stephen's College and is now studying Law. All the brothers contributed financially to support his studies and gave a lot of love and affection to both Shanti and Manish.

After buying Nandkishore's house, Pandit ji decided to settle down in Gogri and started teaching Sanskrit and Hindi in the National High School located in the Gogri Ashram. He also supervised the farming in my Bhelwa and Shirnia diyara lands. In addition, he now had time to pursue his inherent scholarly interests and started by translating the "Brihat havan mantras" into Hindi, which was published by the Ramlal Kapur Trust.

He spent the last five to six years of his life working once again on the translation of, and commentary on, the Sama Veda. His deep anguish that his Lahore work had been published under someone else's name, had been festering inside him and now he expiated all those ancient ghosts by doing further research and re-visiting this project. He often said that he was staying alive just to complete this work. In his final years he found walking very painful and could not manage more than eight to ten steps at a time.

The seminal work was completed, 1800 pages of beautifully handwritten sheets carefully wrapped in khadi.

He passed away peacefully after two days of fever. Unfortunately, none of my children were in Gogri at the time of their father's sudden death. Due to the poor telephone and telegraph connections in Gogri, Anil could reach only two days later. Pandit ji's elder brother's grandson happened to be visiting, and it was he who gave the sacred flame to Pandit ji's dead body.

Pandit ji was a committed Arya Samaji. His last rites were held as per pure Vedic tradition. Anil, Nilu and Indu were there for the havan, Sabo and Vidyanand were in Africa.

Bhabhi ji's new house was built to the west of the Ashram building, and was built around the original single room. Bhaiya had a narrow road constructed, connecting the Ashram to the main Maheshkhunt-Jamalpur Road. Nandkishore's house, which I bought, was on the other side of the narrow road from Bhabhi's house, to the south. To the east of my house, sixty yards away,Nunu bhai's three sons Basant, Vijay and Tunkesh (Tunni) built their joint house. When Bedanand Jha left Shirnia,on Bhai ji's advice I gave him a portion of my land to settle on, between Nunu bhai's children's house and mine. This complex of the Gandhi Ashram and four houses was formally called "Gandhi Gram" as the postal address, but everyone knew it as "Ashram".

I have earlier described in detail Gandhi ji and Kasturba's visit and overnight stay in the Ashram. The cottage in which they stayed was to the west of the well, in a straight line south of the current High School building.

The Gandhi Ashram was converted into the National High School, Gogri. Before that happened, Bhaiya had planned to make an Assembly Hall on the site where that cottage was, and the foundation and plinth were laid. Then the Government took over and created the High School and all plans for the Hall had to be shelved. Consequently the foundation is still waiting for the building to come up!

We used to think that in memory of the old days a Gandhi Cottage and Prayer Hall would have been a befitting tribute to the Mahatma and the countless ordinary men and women who selflessly sacrificed all they had for the country's freedom, without giving a thought to what they would get in return either in material terms or in terms of fame and remembrance. People of later generations could visit this site and have discussions and debates. But that was not to be.

Shri Shirnia was built at some distance from the Jahnvi river, but now the flood embankments have been made and the area is no longer prey to the devastating annual floods of old times. All houses in the village are now concrete structures and the younger generation lives and works in the cities. Many of the girls are lawyers, engineers and doctors, several have migrated overseas. Gifts brought by returning sons and grandsons are welcomed, the question of purifying these "impure foreign objects" by cow-dung is no longer raised. Who filled water from the well and who drank it, is no longer an issue.

But some traditions have lived on. The Kali sacrificial site still exists outside the village. Every year images of Kali are made and worshipped, 'hukka pati' is still played and people jump over the fire with loud cries in praise of Sati Mai. Durga Puja is still celebrated with pomp and show and thousands still make the pilgrimage on foot to Deoghar, carrying the holy waters of the Ganga.

Babuji had fled from Shirnia, and ironically Shirnia came to him to re-settle as Shri Shirnia. The economic progress after Independence had a profound impact on social structures, practices and mores. The purdah system all but disappeared as girls came out of their homes to study and become professionals, inter-caste love marriages became more and more common.

The dusty roads we traversed on foot are now metalled, where buses, cars, tractors and motor-cycles ply frequently, while rickshaws are common-place. Bullock-carts are now used only to transport food grains and other merchandise.

Agricultural practices have become scientific, the Green Revolution has transformed the lives of farmers and peasants.

Many of the diseases which regularly claimed countless lives can now be prevented or cured. Cholera and plague took away Chandrakant, my Kaki and her son Jago. Ma possibly died of kala azar (black fever or Dumdum fever), the doctors in the family tell me now. These diseases have been practically wiped out. Malaria and smallpox were great killers and there was no cure for typhoid. These epidemics used to rage after the rains and floods, and I am so happy that is not so now.

The age of Gandhi ji and Nehru is over. When Kasturba died, I had felt that I had once again lost my mother. When Kamala Nehru died, Bhabhi ji and I cried thinking of how sad Nehru ji must be at losing his wife at such a young age.

How much we felt as one with all those who fought along with us for India's freedom! Every Gandhi Ashram resident was like a family member, we lived and ate together. Our needs and wants were few, but I think we were much happier than today's generation with all its material riches.

I am amazed to see the rise of the consumer society with its crazy proliferation of goods and services, and the ever increasing needs and expectations of people. I often feel awed and uncomfortable seeing so much materialism in people's lives and homes.

I see an endless mad race of milling humanity everywhere I look. In the trains, streets, markets, villages, roads...people, people everywhere. There is no respect for elders any more, I am often shoved and pushed by young people surging to move ahead, not at all mindful or apologetic of treading on my toes. Many times have I narrowly escaped falling down in railway stations because of being pushed around and elbowed. I wonder where these surging masses will live, where they will get food from, what they will do for a livelihood......

I hear they are celebrating the fiftieth anniversary of India's Independence this year. Indira Gandhi did well, gave many the means of earning a livelihood. However, I have personally known thousands of people who gave up their studies to take part in the struggle for Independence. and could get no jobs afterwards. They somehow survived, unsupported and anonymous. When the government announced a pension scheme for Freedom Fighters, it included those who had managed to evade the police and stay out of jail. I applied for it but my paperwork was found incomplete and I was declared ineligible for getting the pension!!!

I remember all those people I have talked about, many of whose names I am unable to remember now after so many years. My memory is full of people who will never be mentioned in any history book and were never recognized and honoured by the nation – the unknown people of the villages and hamlets of deep rural India who kept alive the flames of the freedom struggle with their selfless, brave and relentless sacrifice, who fed the fire of freedom with their own lives. The nation would never have attained Independence without these unsung heroes, but the irony is that they will remain forever unknown.

I pay homage to them:

"The World acclaims our beloved Tri-colour,
Let our flag be held high.
May its glory never diminish
Even if we lose our lives."*

❑❑❑

---

* Vajayi vishwa tiranga pyara
Jhanda uncha rahe hamara
Iski shaan na jaane paaye
Chahay jaan bhalay hee jaaye